BREAKING HISTORY

VANISHED!

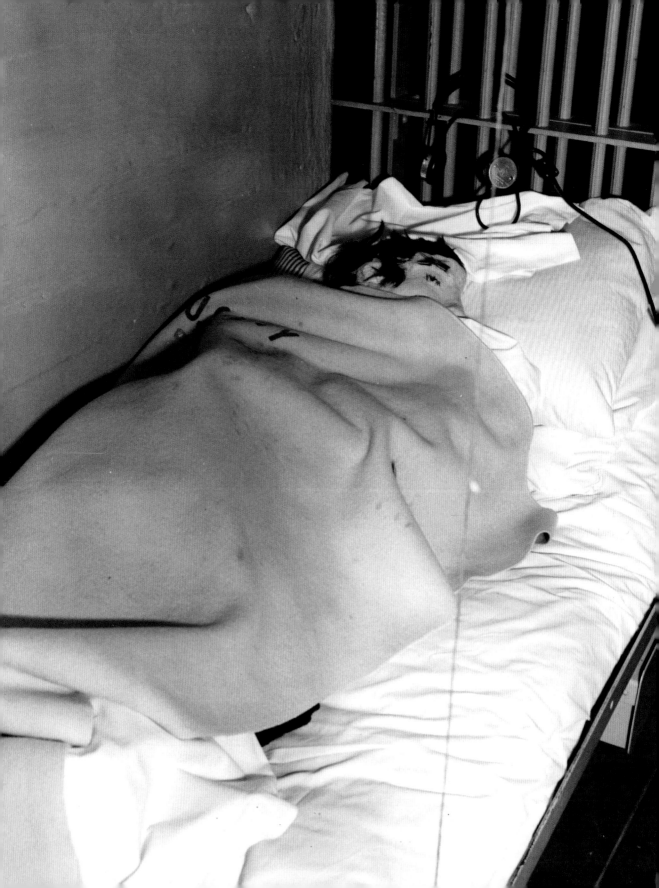

VANISHED!

AMELIA EARHART • JIMMY HOFFA • AMBROSE BIERCE • ALCATRAZ ESCAPEES • FLIGHT 19 • D.B. COOPER

AMERICA'S MOST MYSTERIOUS KIDNAPPINGS, CASTAWAYS, and the FOREVER LOST

SARAH PRUITT

Guilford, Connecticut

An imprint of Globe Pequot

Distributed by NATIONAL BOOK NETWORK

Copyright © 2018 A&E Television Networks, LLC.

British Library Cataloguing in Publication Information available

Library of Congress Cataloging-in-Publication Data available

ISBN 978-1-4930-3060-6 (hardcover)
ISBN 978-1-4930-3061-3 (e-book)

∞™ The paper used in this publication meets the minimum requirements of American National Standard for Information Sciences—Permanence of Paper for Printed Library Materials, ANSI/NISO Z39.48-1992.

Printed in the United States of America

To my parents,
who taught me to
love history.

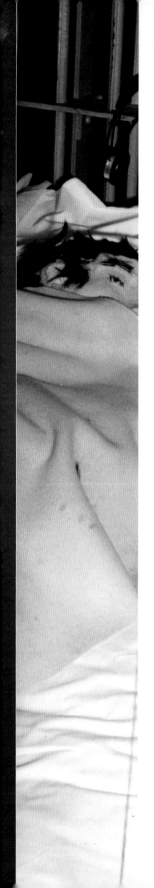

CONTENTS

INTRODUCTION

SOME MYSTERIES HAVE THE POWER TO SHAPE HISTORY. TAKE the case of Amelia Earhart, whose every move was tracked by newspapers around the country and the world, even after her twin-engine Electra vanished somewhere over the Pacific. The search continues even today. Or Jimmy Hoffa, the powerful union boss who disappeared from a parking lot in the Detroit area in 1975, and whose body has never been found.

There's the mother of all maritime mysteries: the case of the *Mary Celeste*, a brigantine found drifting in the Atlantic empty of its captain, his wife and young daughter, and all seven crew members. There's the missingest man in New York, Judge Joseph Force Crater, and the only unsolved skyjacking in US history, carried out by that most famous airborne outlaw, D. B. Cooper.

Going even further back, the history of English settlement in the United States began with a disappearance. Roughly one hundred men and women—and at least one child, the famous Virginia Dare—attempting to form a permanent colony on the eastern coast of North America in the late sixteenth century, vanished from their camp on Roanoke Island, leaving few clues to their fate.

Through newspaper headlines, photographs, and other images, *Vanished!* traces the origins of these and other confounding disappearances; the immediate reaction by the press and public at the time; the efforts made to solve these mysteries (some even ongoing today); the leading theories; and the lasting impact these mysteries have left on our society. ■

PART I

HAMM

DEPARTMENT OF

BUREAU OF AIR C

THE BIG THREE AMELIA EARHART, THE *MARY CELESTE*, AND JIMMY HOFFA

Amelia Earhart in 1935, two years before her mysterious disappearance. NBC photo

Earhart with her husband and publicist, George Putnam, in 1931. International News Photos

AMELIA EARHART 1937

HOURS AFTER HEARING A FINAL, ANXIOUS MESsage from Amelia Earhart at 8:43 a.m. local time on July 2, 1937, the US Coast Guard cutter *Itasca* began a frantic search for the celebrated aviator in the waters off Howland Island. The *Itasca*'s crew had been standing by to guide Earhart to a landing on the tiny, uninhabited coral atoll, where she planned to refuel for the last leg of her daring flight around the globe. Instead, the world watched as the Coast Guard and US Navy combed the vast Pacific for any sign of Earhart, her navigator, Fred Noonan, or her silver Lockheed Electra plane.

In 1932, Amelia Earhart winged her way into the international spotlight when she became the first woman (and only the second person) to fly solo over the Atlantic Ocean. In the midst of the Great Depression, she inspired girls and women to aim for the skies. She was also a best-selling author, fashion icon, and a personal friend of First Lady Eleanor Roosevelt. In the mid-1930s, Earhart and her husband and chief promoter, George Putnam, began seriously planning to fulfill her dream of flying around the globe near its midpoint, a journey of close to 30,000 miles. Before taking off from Lae, New Guinea, on her way to Howland Island—2,556 miles away—that July morning, Earhart had completed 22,000 miles of the journey, over forty days and more than twenty stops.

IN OTHER NEWS

Japan and Russia faced off over the Amur River (between China and Russia's eastern border) after the Japanese invasion of China that began the second Sino-Japanese War.

Conflict between the American Federation of Labor (AFL) and its rival offshoot, the Congress of Industrial Organizations (CIO) raged in the US House of Representatives, with fistfights threatening to break out between CIO supporters and opponents.

Don Budge reestablished American tennis dominance by winning Wimbledon singles (and doubles) championships.

Some 26,000 Boy Scouts from all parts of the world held a jamboree in Washington, DC.

CHRONOLOGY

July 24, 1897	Amelia Earhart was born in Atchison, Kansas.
1915	She graduated from high school in Chicago.
1917–18	Earhart worked as a nurse in a Canadian military hospital during World War I.
1921	She began taking flying lessons in California.
1923	Earhart became only the sixteenth woman in the world to earn a pilot's license from the Fédération Aéronautique Internationale.
1928	She became the first woman to fly across the Atlantic Ocean (as a passenger).
1932	She flew solo across the Atlantic Ocean.
1935	Earhart became the first person to fly solo across the Pacific Ocean from California to Hawaii, and the first person to fly solo from Los Angeles to Mexico City.
March 1937	She failed in her first attempt to circumnavigate the globe when her plane crashed during takeoff in Hawaii.
May 21, 1937	Earhart took off from Oakland, California, on the first leg of her second around-the-world attempt.

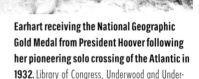

Earhart receiving the National Geographic Gold Medal from President Hoover following her pioneering solo crossing of the Atlantic in 1932. Library of Congress, Underwood and Underwood photographers

WHAT DID WE KNOW?

SOON AFTER TAKING HER FIRST AIRPLANE RIDE, Amelia Earhart enrolled in flying lessons. Six months later, she bought her first plane, and used it to set an unofficial women's altitude record (14,000 feet) in 1922. After briefly returning to school to study medicine, Earhart found a job as a social worker in a Boston settlement house for new immigrants. In 1928, a year after Charles Lindbergh flew nonstop across the Atlantic, a promotional team including book publisher George Putnam recruited Earhart to attempt the same trip (as a passenger). When the plane landed in Wales in June 1928, she became an international celebrity, and wrote a best-selling book about her experience.

With Putnam as her publicist—and later, her husband—Earhart set out to capture more flying records and expand opportunities for female pilots. On May 20, 1932, she flew solo two thousand miles across the Atlantic. President Herbert Hoover presented Earhart with the National Geographic Society's Gold Medal, and she became the first woman to win the Distinguished Flying Cross. In 1935, she joined the faculty of Purdue University as an aeronautics adviser and women's career counselor. With a new twin-engine Lockheed Electra 10-E, purchased in 1936, Earhart prepared to become the first woman to fly around the world. In March 1937, she got as far as Hawaii before crashing during takeoff there. That May, with the highly regarded navigator Fred Noonan at her side, Earhart tried again.

Fliers Quit Phoenix Hunt for Miss Earhart; Chance of Saving Her Held One in Million

By The Associated Press.

HONOLULU, July 11.—Aviators from the battleship Colorado to-night abandoned hope of finding Amelia Earhart and her navigator, Frederick J. Noonan, in ...ea after four ...islands from ...lanes.

...n H. Friedell ...atively ended ...r the Phoenix ...island group ...a rendezvous ...Drayton, Lamp- ...bout 350 miles ...d Islands, how- ...aboard the air- ...ington prepared ...effort.

...pproximate direc- ...Islands but with ...ination undeter- ...ton's 1,299 officers ...rated their imme- ...detailed plans for ...00,000-square mile ...the Equatorial Pa- ...ip has sixty-two

...r a chance in a mil- ...ue," said naval of- ...the search. ...d the main possibil- ...was that Miss Ear- ...girdling plane had ...e water and was still ...which case it could be

sighted from the Lexington's fleet.

The Lexington's armada wa...pected to begin the search to...row afternoon or Tuesday, prol...first scouting west and sou...Howland Island and extendir...search to the Gilbert Island...ward which the equatorial cu...in that area run.

Searchers said, however...there was only an outside...that the lost plane had d...as far short of Howland Is...goal, as the Gilbert Isla...miles east of Howland.

Until the Colorado's f...fessed that they had lost...Phoenix group had bee...as the most likely place...Miss Earhart, missing s...

The Colorado still wa...to send out her plane...and it was said they...a final flight Monday.

The planes searched...whole Phoenix area, b...ing to bolster hopes f...fliers' safety. One...flying over Sydney...group, reported s...scooped in the sand...of Polynesian wo...aviators, however...no sign of life and...the possibility tha...the sand could h...lost plane.

NAVY ENDS SEARCH FOR MISS EARHART

Flier and Her Navigator Are Dead, Officials Believe— Warships Are Recalled

VAST HUNT SET A RECORD

Aviator Was First Woman to Fly Atlantic—Only One to Cross 2 Oceans by Plane

By The Associated Press.

HONOLULU, July 18.—The United States Navy gave Amelia Earhart up for dead at sunset today, when it announced an end to the vast South Pacific hunt for the aviator and ordered the return of the giant aircraft carrier Lexington to her base at San Diego, Calif.

The carrier, which had sent her searching planes roaring vainly across Equatorial skies for nearly a week, was ordered to proceed directly to San Diego.

Three destroyers, also in the hunt for Miss Earhart and her navigator, Frederick J. Noonan, will return to the Pacific Coast via Pearl Harbor, Hawaii, where they will refuel.

The world-famous flier and Noonan vanished on July 2 on a 2,570-mile flight from Lae, New Guinea, to Howland Island, a tiny isl: two feet above the sea.

The naval authorities directing a search that had encompassed more than 250,000 square miles in every direction from Howland Island said they believed they had exhausted every possible hope of finding the missing pair alive.

Flier Greatest of Her Sex

The end of the search for Amelia Earhart and her colleague, Frederick J. Noonan, who vanished into the empty wastes of the south Pacific July 2 on an around-the-world flight, marks the conclusion of the greatest mass rescue effort ever undertaken for a lost plane. The rescue expedition finally included more than 3,000 men, 10 ships, 102 American fighting planes and an undisclosed number of Japanese Navy aircraft.

The attempt of Miss Earhart and her navigator to encircle the world at middle latitudes, never heretofore attempted by air, was to have been her last major flight. It was said

CALLS OF DISTRESS

For days after she disappeared, people all over the Pacific, and as far away as Florida, claimed to hear Earhart's voice on their shortwave radios. Some were clearly hoaxes, but others were more difficult to dismiss.

Take, for example, instances in Honolulu, Hawaii, and Melbourne, Australia.

The US Navy Radio at Wailupe, Honolulu, heard a jumbled Morse code message on July 5, including Earhart's call sign—KHAQQ—and the message "281 north Howland... won't hold with us much longer—above water—shut off."

Around the same time, an amateur radio operator in Melbourne reported hearing a "strange" code, also including the letters KHAQQ.

Earhart and the Lockheed Electra she and Fred Noonan piloted into history. NASA on the Commons

ARHART AND NOONAN TOOK OFF FROM LAE, NEW Guinea, around 10:00 a.m. local time on July 2, 1937. After crossing the International Date Line, they expected to land on Howland Island about twenty hours later, on the morning of the same date. The coast guard cutter *Itasca*, awaiting their arrival, had intermittent radio contact with the plane after its departure from New Guinea. But by 8:00 a.m., when they should have reached the island, Earhart's increasingly anxious transmissions revealed that she and Noonan hadn't spotted land and were running low on fuel. As the *Itasca*'s crew frantically sent more radio signals and Morse code, it appeared more and more likely that the famed aviator was lost. At 8:43 a.m., Earhart reported that they were on line "157" (southeast) and "337" (northwest), and running on line north and south; she failed to say in which of these directions she was heading. The *Itasca* waited, but heard only static after that point.

That afternoon, an all-out search began, as the *Itasca* steamed at full speed to comb the waters north and west of Howland Island, based on the position Earhart had given in that last transmission. On July 7, the US Navy battleship *Colorado* arrived, expanding the search southeast of the island; two other destroyers would soon join the search. Planes from the giant aircraft carrier *Lexington*, based in San Diego, took to the skies over the South Pacific for nearly a week. On July 18, the Navy abandoned the massive search operation, having failed to locate a single trace of Earhart, Noonan, or the plane, despite searching more than 250,000 square miles in every direction from Howland Island.

Earhart at the controls.
Library of Congress, Acme Newspictures

THE EARHART PROJECT

In 1988, the International Group for Historic Aircraft Recovery (TIGHAR) launched The Earhart Project, which aims to conclusively solve the mystery of Amelia Earhart's disappearance.

Since then, The Earhart Project has mounted more than ten expeditions to the South Pacific, starting in 1989 and continuing to the present day.

The organization and its executive director, Richard Gillespie, believe Earhart made an emergency landing on the uninhabited Pacific atoll of Gardner Island, which is now Nikumaroro, part of the Republic of Kiribati.

Nikumaroro is located some 350 nautical miles from Howland Island, along the "157–337" line Earhart said she was flying in her last transmission.

G EORGE PUTNAM CONTINUED TO FINANCE HIS OWN search for Earhart and Noonan until October 1937. On January 4, 1939, Amelia Earhart was declared legally dead by a Superior Court in Los Angeles. But despite the official conclusion to the case, many people—ranging from serious historians to amateur aficionados—refused to give up searching for clues about Earhart's fate.

In the fall of 1940, British colonial authorities recovered a partial human skeleton from what appeared to be the remnants of a castaway's camp on Gardner Island, an uninhabited Pacific atoll south of Howland. A British medical official examined the human remains and concluded they likely belonged to a Polynesian male; the bones themselves have since disappeared.

A new theory about Earhart's fate arose in the early 1960s, after a California woman who grew up on the Pacific island of Saipan claimed that Earhart was the "American lady pilot" she'd seen taken into custody there by the Japanese in July 1937. A CBS News team subsequently headed to Saipan and recovered what they said was the generator from Earhart's plane. The theory also drew strength from the account of US Army sergeant Thomas E. Devine, who claimed that soon after he'd arrived in recently liberated Saipan in 1944, he met US Marines guarding a closed hangar they said contained Earhart's Electra.

DEVELOPING STORY

TOP THEORIES

1 **After crash-landing in the Pacific, the plane sank, and Earhart and Noonan drowned.**
The official theory is also the simplest: Unable to find Howland Island and running out of fuel, Earhart was forced to crash-land the Electra in the 18,000-foot-deep waters of the Pacific. The plane sank, and neither she nor Noonan were ever seen alive again.

2 **They landed on Gardner Island and died as castaways.**
The theory favored by TIGHAR is that Earhart landed the plane safely on Gardner Island (now Nikumaroro) and died there before she could be rescued. US Navy planes flying over Gardner Island on July 9, 1937, saw no sign of Earhart, Noonan, or the plane, but did report "signs of recent habitation"—on an atoll that, aside from a brief stint in 1892, had been uninhabited since prehistoric times.

3 **The Japanese captured Earhart and Noonan as prisoners.**
A third major theory about Earhart's fate argues that the famous aviator and her navigator were taken prisoner, imprisoned, and eventually executed as spies by the Japanese. According to the most mainstream variation of this theory, Earhart and Noonan turned northwest after failing to reach Howland, and landed 760 miles away in the Japanese-held Marshall Islands, probably Mili Atoll; from there, they were taken to Saipan, where they met their fate. This version of the story is taken as fact in the Marshalls, where they even issued a stamp depicting Earhart's crash-landing there in 1987.

HAMMOND·Y

DEPARTMENT OF COMMERCE

BUREAU OF AIR COMMERCE

FRINGE THEORIES

Earhart was in fact a spy, and her around-the-world flight was a cover-up for her real mission: to fly over and observe Japanese fortifications in the Pacific. (No evidence supports this theory.)

After being taken prisoner by the Japanese, Earhart was repatriated to the United States at the end of World War II, and lived into her late seventies as the New Jersey housewife Irene Bolam. But numerous experts who investigated Bolam, who died in 1982, determined she was not the missing aviator.

Mike Campbell, author of *Amelia Earhart: The Truth at Last*, assembled testimony from US servicemen and Pacific Islanders that an American man and woman landed in the Marshall Islands in 1937 and were taken to Saipan, though not all the accounts are credible, and some contradict each other. Campbell also maintained that the US government knew Earhart and Noonan were on Saipan but didn't want to risk a clash with Japan, so kept it secret—and let them be executed.

Library of Congress, Harris and Ewing Photographers

EARHART'S FINAL RESTING PLACE?

Meanwhile, investigators for the HISTORY ® special Amelia Earhart: Finding the Lost Evidence have searched for clues into whether Earhart may have been taken captive and died in Japanese custody on Saipan.

THE ASSOCIATED PRESS CALLED THE SEARCH FOR Earhart in 1937 "the greatest organized effort ever undertaken in behalf of a lost flier." Officially, the case was closed for good in January 1939, when a Superior Court in Los Angeles declared Earhart legally dead.

But the search for answers continues. In 2002, the deep-sea exploration company Nauticos used sonar to comb the waters off Howland Island for Earhart's lost Electra, scanning 630 miles of ocean floor. Another expedition in 2006 covered even more territory—without success.

In 2012, seventy-five years after Earhart vanished, TIGHAR's Ric Gillespie told the *Washington Post* that he thought he'd solved "the last great American mystery of the 20th century." By that time, his group had assembled a cache of evidence—including a cosmetic jar identical in shape to a popular anti-freckle cream—over nine previous trips to Nikumaroro.

In the years since, TIGHAR has only intensified its efforts to probe the mystery of Earhart's final days.

UNSOLVED OR CASE CLOSED?

AMONG THE EVENTS IN AMERICAN HISTORY THAT have spawned the most conspiracy theories, Earhart's disappearance is right up there with the assassination of John F. Kennedy. Aside from the enduring interest in her disappearance, Earhart's brief, brilliant life—her courage, her independence, and her desire to blaze a trail for women in a male-dominated field—left an impact.

During the trying times of the Great Depression, Earhart expanded the public's view of what was possible, especially for women. She served as the first president of the Ninety-Nines, an organization of female pilots that today includes at least five thousand members in thirty countries. She also became the first female vice president of the National Aeronautic Association, which authorized official records and races. As the aviation editor at *Cosmopolitan* magazine, a lecturer on aviation and women's issues, and a career counselor at Purdue, she worked to inspire girls and women to follow their dreams and ignore the limits society placed upon them.

Before embarking on her historic attempt to circumnavigate the globe, Amelia Earhart wrote a letter to her husband, George Putnam, in case the risky flight proved to be her last. "Please know I am quite aware of the hazards. I want to do it because I want to do it. Women must try to do things as men have tried. When they fail, their failure must be but a challenge to others." ■

Raymonde de Laroche. Smithsonian Air and Space Museum via Wikimedia Commons

LASTING IMPACT

Bessie Coleman. Smithsonian Air and Space Museum via Wikimedia Commons

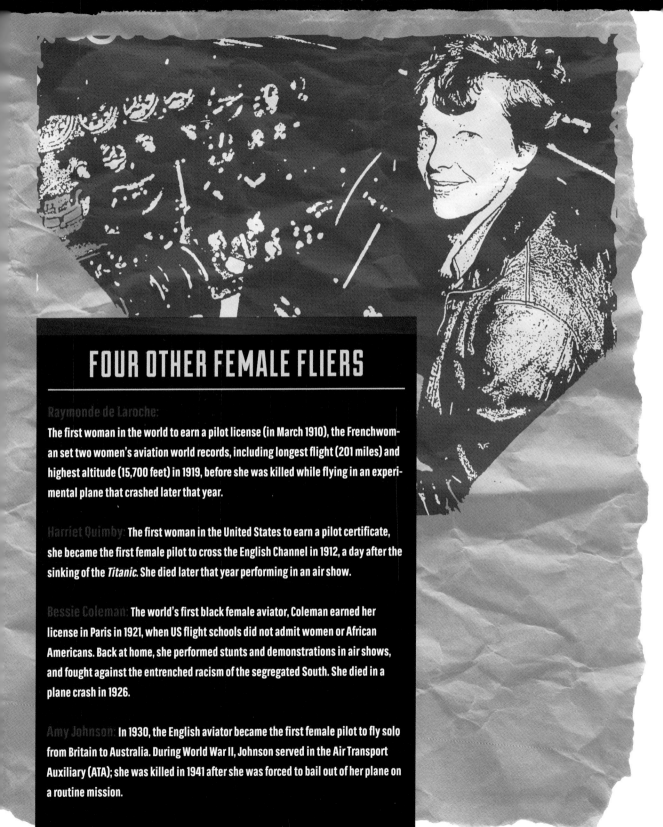

FOUR OTHER FEMALE FLIERS

Raymonde de Laroche:
The first woman in the world to earn a pilot license (in March 1910), the Frenchwoman set two women's aviation world records, including longest flight (201 miles) and highest altitude (15,700 feet) in 1919, before she was killed while flying in an experimental plane that crashed later that year.

Harriet Quimby: The first woman in the United States to earn a pilot certificate, she became the first female pilot to cross the English Channel in 1912, a day after the sinking of the *Titanic*. She died later that year performing in an air show.

Bessie Coleman: The world's first black female aviator, Coleman earned her license in Paris in 1921, when US flight schools did not admit women or African Americans. Back at home, she performed stunts and demonstrations in air shows, and fought against the entrenched racism of the segregated South. She died in a plane crash in 1926.

Amy Johnson: In 1930, the English aviator became the first female pilot to fly solo from Britain to Australia. During World War II, Johnson served in the Air Transport Auxiliary (ATA); she was killed in 1941 after she was forced to bail out of her plane on a routine mission.

A Brig's Officers Believed to Have Been Murdered at Sea.

From the Boston Post. Feb. 24.

It is now believed that the fine brig Mary Celeste, of about 236 tons, commanded by Capt. Benjamin Briggs, of Marion, Mass., was seized by pirates in the latter part of November, and that, after murdering the Captain, his wife, child, and officers, the vessel was abandoned near the Western Islands, where the miscreants are supposed to have landed. The brig left New-York on the 17th of November for Genoa, with a cargo of alcohol, and is said to have had a crew consisting mostly of foreigners. The theory now is, that some of the men probably obtained access to the cargo, and were thus stimulated to the desperate deed.

The Mary Celeste was fallen in with by the British brig Dei Gratia, Capt. Morehouse, who left New-York about the middle of November. The hull of the Celeste was found in good condition, and safely towed into Gibraltar, where she has since remained. The confusion in which many things were found on board, (including ladies' apparel, &c.,) led, with other circumstances, to suspicion of wrong and outrage, which has by no means died out. One of the latest letters from Gibraltar received in Boston says: The Vice-Admiralty Court sat yesterday, and will sit again to-morrow. The cargo of the brig has been claimed, and to-morrow the vessel will be claimed.

The general opinion is that there has been foul play on board, as spots of blood on the blade of a sword, in the cabin, and on the rails, with marks on the wood indicate force or violence

THE HEADLINES

A painting of the *Amazon*, later rechristened as the *Mary Celeste*. Unknown, possibly Honore de Pellegrin

THE *MARY CELESTE* 1872

ALTHOUGH THE NOTORIOUS BERMUDA TRIANGLE has claimed many a lost ship over the years, the greatest mystery in the history of maritime travel remains the disappearance not of a ship, but of its crew.

On December 5, 1872, Captain David Morehouse and the sailors of the British brigantine *Dei Gratia* spotted a ship drifting in the Atlantic Ocean waters some four hundred miles east of the Azores. Morehouse was astonished to find it was a vessel he knew. The *Mary Celeste* had departed from New York Harbor nearly a month earlier—eight days before the *Dei Gratia*, in fact—and should have already arrived at its destination, Genoa, Italy. Instead, the ship was abandoned, apparently undamaged, with six months' worth of food and water remaining in the hold.

A subsequent investigation found no evidence of foul play, and granted salvage payment to the *Dei Gratia*. The court paid only a fraction of the amount for which the ship and cargo had been insured, suggesting it was not entirely convinced of the salvagers' claims. With that, the vanished *Mary Celeste* entered the ranks of great mysteries—one that some are still trying to solve to this day.

IN OTHER NEWS

Two days before the *Mary Celeste* set sail from New York, President Ulysses S. Grant was reelected.

After the election, US deputy marshals would arrest suffragette leader Susan B. Anthony for illegally voting in Rochester, New York.

On November 9–10, 1872, a great fire ripped through the city of Boston, killing fourteen people, destroying more than seven hundred buildings, and causing more than $70 million worth of damage.

Land surveyor Clarence King exposed the Great Diamond Hoax, in which two Kentucky grifters managed to convince a number of prominent California financiers to invest in a worthless diamond mine in Colorado.

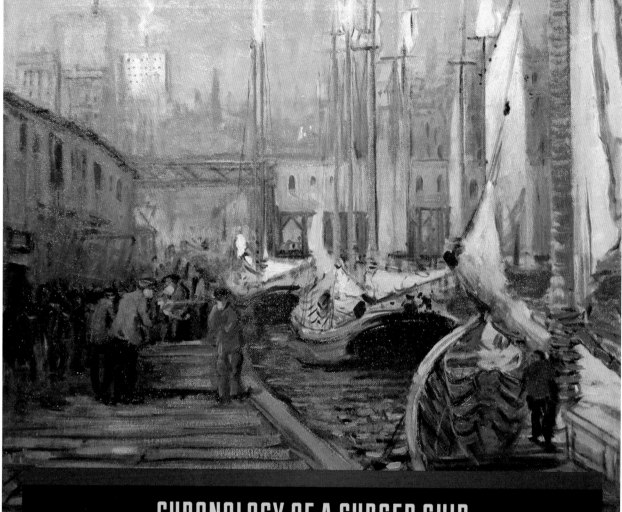

CHRONOLOGY OF A CURSED SHIP

May 1861   Joshua Dewis Shipyard at Spencer's Island, Nova Scotia, launches its first ship, the *Amazon*, into the Bay of Fundy.

June 1861   On its maiden voyage to Five Islands (Nova Scotia), the *Amazon*'s captain and part-owner, Robert McClellan, suddenly fell ill with pneumonia; the ship returned to Spencer's Island, where McClellan died.

Later 1861   Under new captain John Nutting Parker, the *Amazon* accidentally rammed and sank another brig in the English Channel en route to London.

1867   After several uneventful years working trade routes to the West Indies, England, and the Mediterranean, the *Amazon* was driven ashore in a storm at Cape Breton Island and badly damaged.

1868   The New York firm of merchant Richard Haines purchased the wreck for $1,750 and registered it under a new name, the *Mary Celeste*.

1869   Struggling financially, Haines lost the ship to broker James Winchester.

1871   The *Mary Celeste* underwent a major refit, with a second deck installed and planking replaced, and Winchester took on several new partners, including Benjamin Briggs.

WHAT DID WE KNOW?

LAUNCHED FROM THE SHORES OF SPENCER'S ISLAND, Nova Scotia, in 1861, the *Mary Celeste* had originally been christened the *Amazon*. A series of mishaps followed—including the sudden illness and death of its first captain, a collision with another vessel in the English Channel, and a wreck during a storm in the East Indies. In 1868, the wrecked brig was sold, repaired, and renamed.

Early in 1872, the ship's owner took on some new investors, including thirty-seven-year-old Benjamin Spooner Brooks, the son of a respected sea captain and an experienced naval commander in his own right. Named as the master for the ship's maiden voyage to Genoa, Italy, Brooks arrived in New York in October 1872 to supervise the loading and preparation. A devout Christian who abstained from alcohol, Briggs brought his wife, Sarah, and their two-year-old daughter, Sophia, along with him. (Their seven-year-old son stayed behind in Massachusetts with Briggs's mother.)

On November 7, the 282-ton *Mary Celeste* set sail from New York. In addition to Briggs and his wife and daughter, seven crew members were aboard, including the first and second mates, a cook/steward, and four sailors.

THE EVIDENCE

THE MISSING

Benjamin Spooner Briggs,
Captain

Sarah Elizabeth Briggs,
Captain's wife

Sophia Matilda Briggs,
Captain's two-year-old daughter

Albert Richardson, first mate.
A veteran of the American Civil War from Maine, he was handpicked by Briggs for the voyage (he had served with the captain before). A month before the ship sailed, Richardson had married owner James Winchester's niece, Fannie.

Andrew Gilling, second mate.
Just twenty-five years old, Gilling was born in New York to immigrant parents from Denmark.

Edward William Head, cook and steward. At twenty-three, Head was the youngest man on board, and also a newlywed, having just returned from his honeymoon when the ship sailed.

Volkert Lorenzen , Boz Lorenzen, Arian Martens, Gottlieb Goodschaad. The four German sailors who rounded out the crew all hailed from the small North Sea archipelago of the Frisian Islands. The Lorenzens were brothers.

THE LAST ENTRY IN THE SHIP'S LOG, DATED NOVEMber 25, 1872, at 5:00 a.m., recorded that the *Mary Celeste* was within sight of the Azores island of Santa Maria. On December 5, the *Dei Gratia* encountered the brig drifting erratically some 590 miles west of Gibraltar, between the Azores and Portugal (500 miles from the location noted in the log). After calling out with a megaphone and receiving no response, Captain Morehouse sent his first mate, Oliver Deveau, and two other men to board the ship and investigate.

On the ship's quarterdeck, the sailors found the wheel had not been lashed, which was standard procedure if a ship were going to be abandoned in an emergency. The binnacle (a case used to store navigational instruments) had been knocked over, and the compass inside had been smashed. Belowdecks, they found the captain's quarters seemingly in place, but couldn't find the chronometer, sextant, navigation book, or ship's register. The crewmen's belongings were similarly still in their quarters.

The sailors discovered several feet of water in the hold, but otherwise the ship's cargo (including more than 1,700 bottles of crude alcohol intended for Italian wineries) looked to be in order. The only things missing from the *Mary Celeste*, it seemed, was the ship's only lifeboat—plus the captain, his family, and the entire crew.

THE ADVOCATE GENERAL

In his capacity as advocate general for the Queen in her office of the Admiralty in Gibraltar, Frederick Solly-Flood acted as the prosecutor on the board of inquiry that investigated the case of the *Mary Celeste*.

Without Solly-Flood's stubborn pursuit of one conspiracy theory after another, despite a lack of evidence to support them, the case might never have become so widely known.

Though Solly-Flood won the support of US Treasury Secretary William A. Richard, another powerful American—Horatio Sprague, US consul to Gibraltar—was more skeptical, even hiring his own expert to examine the "ghost ship" at one point.

At least one good thing came of Solly-Flood's relentless prosecution of the case: As part of his investigation, the attorney general transcribed the recovered ship's log starting five days from its end. The original log was later lost, and Solly-Flood's transcription remains the only known record of the voyage.

Gibraltar at about the time of the *Mary Celeste* inquiry. Library of Congress, attributed to Alfred Guesdon

AFTER PUMPING THE WATER OUT OF THE HOLD, SEVeral crewmen sailed the *Mary Celeste* in tandem with the *Dei Gratia* to Gibraltar, where they reported the discovery to the authorities and claimed salvage rights. A British viceadmiralty court immediately launched an investigation. Frederick Solly-Flood, Gibraltar's attorney general, suspected something fishy was going on from the start, and assumed initially that Briggs and Morehouse had conspired together to defraud the insurance companies. But when a rusty sword stained with what appeared to be blood was found in Briggs's cabin, the attorney general's suspicions turned to murder.

The board of inquiry headed by Sir James Cochrane, chief justice of Gibraltar, began on December 18, 1872. Solly-Flood pushed hard for his theories of conspiracy or foul play, but the court decided they could not be substantiated. (According to the testimony of a local surgeon, the stains on the sword turned out to be from rust or vegetable residue.)

The court ended up granting payment to the *Dei Gratia*'s salvagers, but only one-sixth of the $46,000 for which the ship and cargo had been insured, suggesting its members were not entirely convinced of the salvagers' innocence.

DEVELOPING STORY

TOP THEORIES

1 Briggs and Morehouse concocted an insurance-based conspiracy.

Some believed Solly-Flood's contention that Briggs and Morehouse conspired to share the salvage spoils from the *Mary Celeste*, and that Briggs, his family, and the crew hid aboard the *Dei Gratia* until the case could be settled.

2 The *Mary Celeste* were victims of piracy.

Another theory held that the *Dei Gratia*'s captain and sailors—or unknown pirates—murdered all aboard the *Mary Celeste* and threw their bodies overboard, or forced them to walk the plank. But there was no sign of a struggle aboard the ship, and pirates would presumably have been more interested in taking the ship and its valuable cargo, rather than the crew.

3 One or more of the ship's crewmen could have risen up in mutiny against the captain.

At one point, suspicion fell on the Lorenzen brothers, as apparently none of their belongings were found on the ship. But the motive for mutiny was weak—Briggs was known to be experienced and fair—and it seemed unlikely that mutineers would leave behind a seaworthy vessel, its cargo, and supplies.

4 An alcohol explosion, or some other crisis, led captain and crew to abandon ship.

According to one popular recent theory, alcohol vapors expanded in the heat and blew open one or more of the ship's hatches, or at least released strong fumes, leading the captain and his family and crew to abandon ship. If the rope connecting the ship with the yawl (sailboat) they took refuge in was then severed in some way, they would have been left adrift

FRINGE THEORIES

Bermuda Triangle: The notorious region has been cited in relation to the *Mary Celeste*, even though the ship was found in an entirely different part of the Atlantic.

Assault by giant octopus or sea monster: Although giant squid have been known to attack boats, this one can also be summarily dismissed.

Alien abduction: This theory can probably be chalked up to the weirdly pristine condition of the *Mary Celeste* when it was found. (According to one persistent myth, tea was still boiling on the stove and lukewarm food was on the table.)

N HIS REPORT TO THE US DEPARTMENT OF STATE months after the Gibraltar inquiry concluded, Horatio Sprague wrote: "This case of the *Mary Celeste* is startling, since it appears to be one of those mysteries which no human ingenuity can re-create sufficiently to account for the abandonment of this vessel, and the disappearance of her master, family, and crew, about whom, nothing has ever transpired."

Nearly 150 years later, the mystery continues. For a 2007 documentary, *The True Story of the* Mary Celeste, a team led by filmmaker Anne MacGregor tried to trace backward from the moment when the *Dei Gratia* found the *Mary Celeste* drifting to the last entry in its log. As reported in *Smithsonian*, the team analyzed data about the water temperatures and wind speeds and directions on those days, concluding that the ship might actually have been 120 miles west of where Captain Briggs thought it was, because the chronometer was inaccurate. In this case, if they did have to abandon ship (due to a clogged pump, an explosion on board, or some other reason) and were cast adrift in some way, eight men, a woman, and a young child would have been left to die in a tiny lifeboat.

HISTORY'S OTHER "GHOST SHIPS"

Rosalie (1840)

The French ship *Rosalie*, bound from Hamburg to Havana, was reputed to be an early victim of the Bermuda Triangle, that infamous stretch of the Atlantic between Florida, Bermuda, and Puerto Rico. The ship was reportedly found abandoned and adrift, with its cargo intact; none of the crew was ever found.

Resolven (1884)

Dubbed the "Welsh *Mary Celeste*," the *Resolven* had been transporting fish and timber between Wales and Canada. The Royal Navy's HMS *Mallard* found the *Resolven* floating off the Newfoundland coast; the captain and crew were nowhere to be seen.

Carroll A. Deering (1921)

This commercial schooner was found run aground off the North Carolina coast, emptied of all of its crew, their personal belongings, and the ship's log, anchors, and navigation equipment. Some claimed it fell victim to the Bermuda Triangle, while others pointed to mutiny against the ship's new captain as the more likely explanation.

Joyita (1955)

A merchant vessel that patrolled in Hawaii during World War II, the *Joyita* went missing in the South Pacific after leaving Apia, in Samoa, for the Tokelau Islands, some 270 miles away. The ship was later found partially submerged, with all twenty-five crew and passengers missing, along with three life rafts.

UNSOLVED OR CASE CLOSED?

Engraving from the sheet music to "The Phantom Ship from Legendary Ballads" by Thomas Moore, circa 1860. Library of Congress

LASTING IMPACT

Poster art from *Phantom Ship* starring Bela Lugosi. Photofest

Arthur Conan Doyle. Library of Congress

A FTER THE COURT'S INQUIRY, THE *MARY CELESTE* would go on to sail under several different owners, until in 1885 its last captain deliberately ran it aground in Haiti as part of an attempted insurance fraud. (In 2001, novelist and adventurer Clive Cussler claimed to have found the wreck of the *Mary Celeste* off the Haitian coast, but later analysis of the timbers retrieved from the ship he found showed the wood was still living at least a decade after the *Mary Celeste* sank.)

Thus ended the ghost ship's unfortunate history—but its legend would endure. Into the void of the 1872 court's conclusions, sensationalized coverage of the *Mary Celeste*'s disappearance wasted no time in providing various theories as to what exactly happened. This process began in 1884, when Arthur Conan Doyle (not yet famous as the creator of Sherlock Holmes) anonymously published the short story "J. Habakuk Jephson's Statement," in which an ex-slave captures the *Mary Celeste* as an act of vengeance. Such vivid myths kept the *Mary Celeste* alive in popular culture, feeding the enduring speculation as to what its fate really might have been.■

THE *MARY CELESTE* IN LITERATURE, FILM, AND TV

Around the same time Conan Doyle published his story, Bram Stoker made a less-explicit reference to the *Mary Celeste* in his famous novel, *Dracula.* The ship that carries Dracula to London is also a "ghost ship," and arrives without its crew.

In 1935, the horror film *Phantom Ship* starred Bela Lugosi as a vengeful, murderous sailor (rather unfairly based on the Lorenzen brothers) who kills off the rest of his ship's crew one by one during a storm.

Thirty years later, the *Mary Celeste* showed up in an episode of the British sci-fi TV hit, *Doctor Who,* entitled "The Chase." After the mutant Daleks appear, the entire crew of the ship jumps overboard.

Conan Doyle himself appears as a minor—but important—character in Valerie Martin's 2014 novel, *The Ghost of the* Mary Celeste, which uses a range of different points of view to explore the ghost ship's haunting story.

Detroit Free Press

ON GUARD FOR 146 YEARS

Friday, August 1, 1975

LAST SEEN OUTSIDE RESTAURANT

Jimmy Hoffa Is Missing

Investigators Probing Mystery Appointment

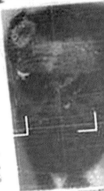

F.B.I. CHECKING TIP OF HOFFA'S 'BURIAL'

SPECIAL TO THE NEW YORK TIMES   AUG. 17, 1975

DETROIT, Aug. 16 (AP)—The Federal Bureau of Investigation searched a construction site in northern Lower Michigan, and the family of James R. Hoffa unveiled a bumper sticker campaign today in efforts to find the former president of the international Brotherhood of Teamsters.

F.B.I. agents and the state police checked a state Highways Department garage under construction near Marion in Osceola County last night after having received a tip that Mr. Hoffa could be found buried there. But Keith Sturgis, an F.B.I. agent, said more information would be needed before a search of Mr. Hoffa...

THE HEADLINES

Jimmy Hoffa glad-handing union workers shortly before his disappearance in 1975.
Photofest

JIMMY HOFFA 1975

WHEN JIMMY HOFFA DISAPPEARED IN JULY 1975, HE was one of the most famous labor leaders in American history. The former boss of the International Brotherhood of Teamsters, Hoffa had built the union into the nation's largest, wealthiest, and most powerful labor organization, becoming the hero of millions of people in the process. But he also created an unholy alliance between the Teamsters and the Mafia, which may have ultimately led to his disappearance and (assumed) death.

Thanks to a dedicated campaign by his sworn enemy, Attorney General Robert F. Kennedy (who assembled a "Get Hoffa" squad of investigators and prosecutors), Hoffa was convicted in two separate trials of jury tampering and defrauding the union's pension fund, and sent to prison in 1967. Prohibited by law from serving as Teamsters president for five years after President Richard Nixon commuted his sentence in 1971, Hoffa was gearing up to grab power again when he scheduled a meeting with two men at a restaurant in Bloomfield Hills, Michigan, on July 30, 1975. After calling his wife from a pay phone to say he had been stood up, Hoffa vanished without a trace.

IN OTHER NEWS

In late July/August 1975:

During an official trip to Poland, Gerald Ford became the first US president to visit Auschwitz, the largest of the Nazi concentration camps during World War II.

In Finland, representatives from more than thirty nations signed the Helsinki Final Act, which aimed to reinforce the flagging détente between the Soviets and the United States and its allies.

Stevie Wonder signed a new seven-year, $13 million contract with Motown Records, in the biggest deal ever for a recording artist at the time.

WHAT DID WE KNOW?

HOFFA MOVED TO DETROIT WITH HIS MOTHER AND three siblings at the age of seven, after his father died. At fourteen, he dropped out of school to begin working. Hoffa rose steadily through the Teamsters' ranks, and was elected vice president of the entire union in 1952. He won the presidency five years later.

Hoffa centralized power in the union's international office and built the Teamsters into the nation's largest labor union. In early 1964, he brought nearly all of North America's truck drivers under one contract for the first time. As his influence grew, Hoffa's ties to organized crime drew the attention of the FBI and Robert F. Kennedy, who pursued Hoffa as chief counsel to the Senate Rackets Committee, and later as US attorney general. Soon after the trucking agreement, Hoffa was convicted in separate trials of jury tampering and misusing union pension funds, and sentenced to thirteen years in federal prison.

Even after his conviction, Hoffa was reelected as Teamsters president; he eventually agreed to resign in exchange for Nixon's pardon in late 1971. While in jail, Hoffa clashed with former loyalist Frank Fitzsimmons, who had succeeded him as Teamsters president. Hoffa soon set about trying to regain his former position in the Teamsters, starting with the local branch in Detroit.

CHRONOLOGY

1913	James Riddle Hoffa was born on February 13, 1913, in Brazil, Indiana.
1924	He moved to Detroit.
1931	At eighteen, he organized his first labor strike.
1932	Hoffa became an organizer for the International Brotherhood of Teamsters.
1936	He married Josephine Poszywak; they would have two children, Barbara and James.
1952	Hoffa was elected vice president of the International Brotherhood of Teamsters.
1957	He was elected president of the Teamsters; he faced his first major criminal investigation under a Senate subcommittee headed by Senator John McClellan (known as the Senate Rackets Committee).
1964	Hoffa was convicted of jury tampering and misuse of union pension funds.
1967	He entered Lewisburg Federal Penitentiary to begin serving a thirteen-year sentence; he appointed Frank Fitzsimmons as acting Teamsters president.
June 1971	He resigned his Teamsters presidency.
December 1971	Hoffa was released from prison.
1974	Hoffa filed a federal appeal to reverse ban on participating in union activities until 1980, but the court upheld the ban.

Hoffa's nemesis, Attorney General Robert F. Kennedy, testifying before a Senate subcommittee on crime in 1963. Library of Congress

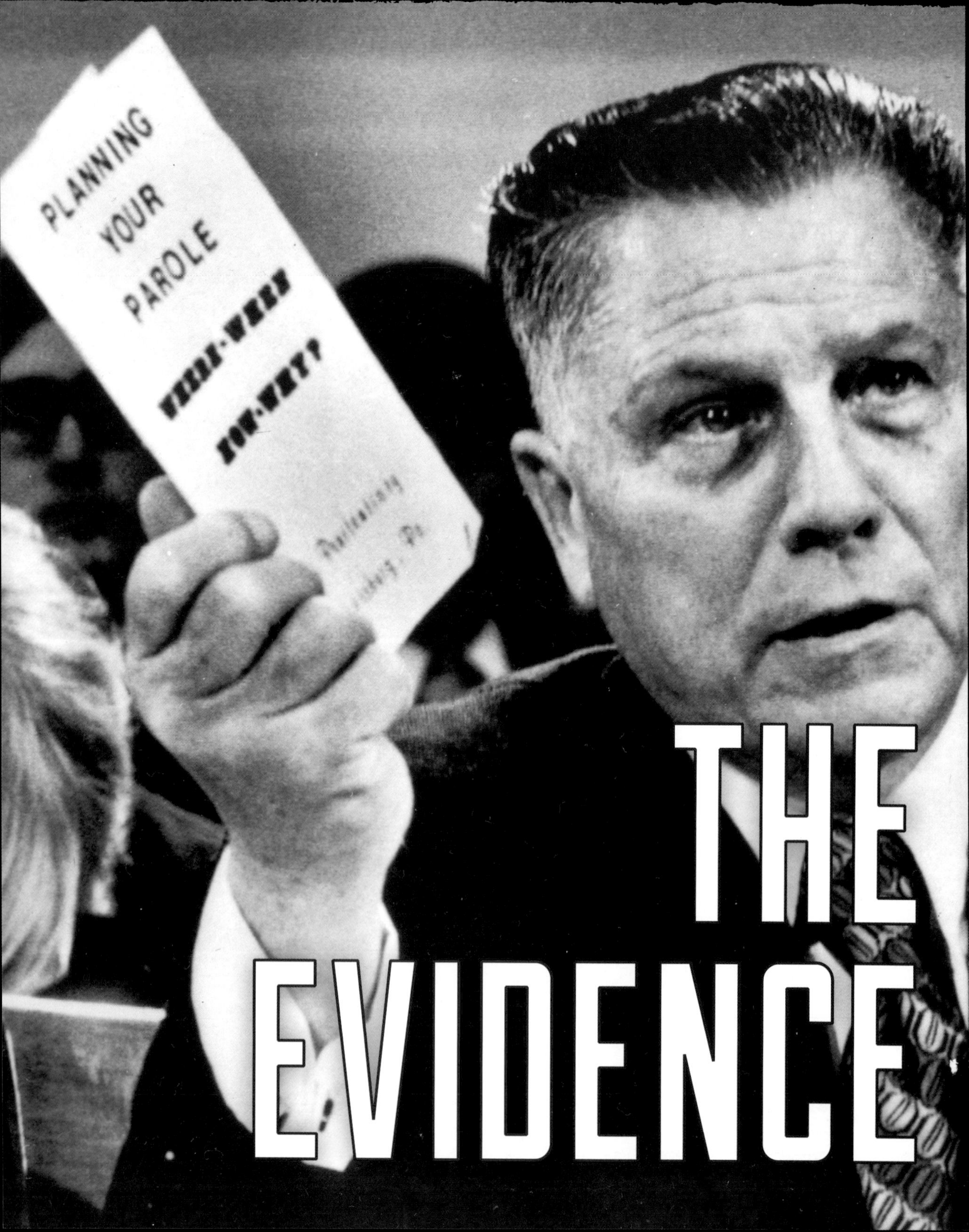

PLANNING YOUR PAROLE

WHERE·WHEN

HOW·WHY?

THE EVIDENCE

After agreeing to stay away from union activities until 1980, Hoffa was pardoned by Richard Nixon in 1971. Nevertheless, he continued to consort with union officials and had intended to see New Jersey union boss "Tony Pro" Provenzano on the day he disappeared. Photofest

HOFFA AND THE FBI

Hoffa's disappearance launched one of the biggest investigations in FBI history, lasting more than twenty -five years and generating nearly two thousand pages of FBI files.

But the FBI's interest in Hoffa didn't begin on July 30, 1975; it stretched back some two decades, starting when he became president of the Teamsters in 1957.

That year, FBI surveillance cameras recorded Hoffa paying off a New York attorney (who was working with the government) to get confidential documents from a Senate commit-tee investigating racketeering.

He was acquitted of these charges in a jury trial, the first of several federal prosecutions he beat before his conviction in 1964.

After he was released from prison, the FBI continued to monitor Hoffa—including his behind-the-scenes maneuvers to regain influence with the Teamsters—up until the day he vanished.

A T 2:00 P.M. ON JULY 30, 1975, HOFFA SHOWED UP AT the Machus Red Fox restaurant in Bloomfield Hills, Michigan. He planned to meet two men there: Anthony "Tony Jack" Giacalone, a Mafia captain in Detroit, and Anthony "Tony Pro" Provenzano, a New Jersey Teamsters official and a capo in the Genovese crime family. Hoffa waited in front of the restaurant until 2:15, then called his wife from a phone booth to say he'd been stood up. He never returned home.

When police went to the Red Fox, they found Hoffa's 1974 green Pontiac Grand Ville, unlocked, with an empty trunk. As Arthur A. Sloane recorded in his 1991 biography of Hoffa, Hoffa's son arranged to meet Giacalone—whom he immediately suspected of having something to do with his father's disappearance—at an intersection close to Bloomfield Township on August 1, but Giacalone stood him up as well.

On August 3, the FBI took over the investigation. As was widely publicized at the time, rewards totaling some $275,000 were offered to anyone with meaningful information about Hoffa's whereabouts. Giacalone and Provenzano, the two main suspects at the outset, denied they had plans to meet Hoffa, and both had solid alibis. Witnesses saw Giacalone in a steam room at the Southfield Athletic Club, while a number of people claimed to have seen Provenzano playing cards in a Teamsters office in New Jersey.

PLEADING THE FIFTH

As Dan Moldea, author of *The Hoffa Wars*, recounted on the fortieth anniversary of Hoffa's disappearance, the first big public break in the case came in December 1975.

After Ralph Picardo, a former driver for Provenzano then serving time for murder in a New Jersey prison, spoke to the FBI, four longtime associates of Tony Provenzano—Salvatore and Gabriel Briguglio, and Stephen and Thomas Andretta—appeared before a federal grand jury.

Picardo told investigators that the Andretta brothers had visited him in prison a few days after Hoffa's disappearance and told him the Provenzano group had been responsible for killing Hoffa.

When they appeared before the jury, all four men invoked their Fifth Amendment rights rather than answer any questions about Hoffa's murder.

INVESTIGATORS SUSPECTED HOFFA HAD FALLEN VICTIM to an old Mafia trick: get someone the victim trusted to lure him to his murder. After a witness reported seeing a maroon 1975 Mercury Marquis leaving the Red Fox parking lot on July 30, the FBI tracked down the car and found fingerprints belonging to Charles "Chuckie" O'Brien, a young man whom Hoffa had helped raise after the death of O'Brien's father. In recent years, the relationship had soured; O'Brien was now close with Giacalone and appeared loyal to Fitzsimmons, the new Teamsters president.

O'Brien admitted he had borrowed the car from Tony Giacalone's son that day, but said he hadn't seen Hoffa. His alibi? He'd been delivering a frozen forty-pound salmon steak to the home of a Teamsters official. (In 2001, investigators matched DNA from a strand of hair found in the Marquis's backseat to Hoffa, but didn't have enough evidence to pursue an indictment.)

A federal grand jury convened in September 1975 called some fifty witnesses to testify; no charges were ever brought. Over the next decade, more than two hundred FBI agents worked on the Hoffa case in Detroit, New Jersey, and elsewhere. Meanwhile, six suspects in Hoffa's disappearance—including Giacalone and Provenzano—were convicted on unrelated charges.

DEVELOPING STORY

Tony Provenzano and his associates carried out a hit on Hoffa.

According to the most widely accepted theory of Hoffa's fate, his efforts to regain influence within the Teamsters led Mafia leaders to order his murder. In this version of events, Russell Bufalino, Tony Pro's boss, gave the order to kill Hoffa, and Provenzano (who hated Hoffa) gladly followed it. O'Brien likely helped get his former mentor in the car in the Red Fox parking lot, then one of Provenzano's associates killed Hoffa, whether in the car or after transporting him to some destination.

The murder took place near the restaurant, or at a Michigan horse farm.

Ralphie Picardo said the murder went down at a house near the Red Fox, while Dan Moldea believes Hoffa was most likely killed at a horse farm in Wixom, Michigan, owned by Rolland McMaster, a Teamsters official. The FBI dug up the site in 2006, after a tip from one of McMaster's associates, but they found nothing; Moldea believes Hoffa's body was transported to New Jersey and buried in a landfill.

Different possible triggermen have been named.

Enforcer Salvatore "Sally Bugs" Briguglio has long been rumored to be the man who actually killed Hoffa. But on his deathbed in 2003, Frank "the Irishman" Sheeran, a Teamsters official from Delaware and right-hand man to Bufalino, confessed to killing Hoffa. His lawyer, Charles Brandt, later included the claim in a book about Sheeran, *I Heard You Paint Houses*. Moldea believes Sheeran was involved, but doesn't think he was the triggerman.

THE TOP THEORY

ALTERNATIVE THEORIES

According to Mob historian and author Andy Petepiece, Ralph Picardo's story threw FBI and other historians off track.

Writing on the website Gang Land News in 2016, Petepiece argued that Tony Giacalone and other Detroit mobsters got rid of Hoffa on their own without the help of their East Coast counterparts, and buried him somewhere in Detroit.

In 2013, after former Detroit Mafia boss Anthony Zerilli told a TV reporter he knew where Hoffa's body was buried, the FBI went on a massive dig on a property in Oakland Township.

Zerilli claimed Hoffa had been clubbed on the head with a shovel and buried on the property, which belonged to Zerilli's cousin—but the FBI turned up nothing after two days of excavation.

Zerilli died in 2015, at the age of eighty-seven.

One of the leading theories behind Hoffa's disappearance claimed that his body had been transported to New Jersey and buried in a landfill beneath the Pulaski Bridge, shown above.
Library of Congress

EXCLUSIVE: New evidence emerges on Jimmy Hoffa's possible fate, suggests feds were on right track search N.J. dump

DAILY NEWS

Is Detroit Dig Latest Search for Jimmy Hoffa's Body?

J IMMY HOFFA WAS DECLARED LEGALLY DEAD IN 1982. The consensus theory among law enforcement officials was that Mafia leaders, concerned about Hoffa's efforts to regain influence in the Teamsters organization, ordered his murder. As early as 1976, the FBI prepared a report stating its belief that organized crime figures likely murdered Hoffa in order to prevent him from revealing the Mob's infiltration of the Teamsters and the union's pension funds.

In 1989, seven years after Hoffa was declared legally dead, the former Detroit FBI head Kenneth Walton told a newspaper that he pretty much knew who killed Hoffa, "but it's never going to be prosecuted because…we would have to divulge informants, confidential sources."

The complete lack of evidence (no body, no solid witnesses) suggests that Hoffa's murder was a highly professional operation by experienced criminals. According to the leading theory, advanced by Ralph Picardo's testimony to the feds, Hoffa's killers placed his body in a fifty-five-gallon steel drum and drove it from Michigan to New Jersey in a Gateway Transportation truck soon after his murder. The probable destination was a toxic-waste dump then owned by Phillip "Brother" Moscato, who was an associate of the Genovese crime family.

The feds searched the dump, located under the Pulaski Skyway in Jersey City, back in 1975, but failed to find the drum or any of Hoffa's remains. But, according to Dan Moldea, who recorded several interviews with Moscato before he died in 2014, the late mobster admitted that a 55-gallon drum with Hoffa's body inside had in fact been buried at the landfill.

WHERE ARE THEY NOW?

Most of the leading suspects in Hoffa's murder are now dead themselves.

While awaiting trial in 1978 for the murder of another Provenzano rival, Anthony Castellito, Sal Briguglio was shot by two unidentified men outside a restaurant in New York's Little Italy.

Tony Provenzano died in 1988 of a heart attack, while serving twenty years in a California prison for labor racketeering.

In 1976, Tony Giacalone was convicted of tax evasion and sentenced to ten years in prison. He died in 2001, while facing federal indictment for racketeering and other charges.

As he told an Associated Press reporter in 2006, Chuckie O'Brien was banned from the Teamsters for his alleged Mob ties, went to Florida, and spent some time in prison for minor offenses. He continued to deny any involvement in or knowledge of what happened to Hoffa.

UNSOLVED OR CASE CLOSED?

Jimmy Hoffa's son, James P. Hoffa Jr., continued his father's work with the International Brotherhood of Teamsters up through the 2010s. He is shown here with Los Angeles D.A. Gil Garcetti sometime in the 1990s.
Eric Garcetti via Wikimedia Commons

Jimmy Hoffa's legacy and mysterious disappearance were the subject of the 1993 film Hoffa. In this scene Hoffa (Jack Nicholson) confronts Robert F. Kennedy (Kevin Anderson). Photofest

The former Giants Stadium in the New Jersey's Meadowlands, where many claim Hoffa's remains are buried. Nicky Pallas via Wikimedia Commons

WHERE IS JIMMY HOFFA?

Over more than forty years, the list of proposed locations for Hoffa's remains has stretched almost long enough to deserve a book of its own. But here's a (small) sample:

Hoffa's body was buried under the west end zone of the former New York Giants stadium at the Meadowlands in East Rutherford, New Jersey.

His body was ground up, shipped to Florida, and thrown in a swamp—or encased in the foundation of a public garage in Cadillac, Michigan.

After a dispute with a West Coast businessman, Hoffa was killed and buried in the foundation of a restaurant/poker club in Gardena, California.

Hoffa's body was crushed by a machine in a Detroit factory and added to steel used for manufacturing automobile parts.

Hoffa wasn't murdered, but checked into a hotel under an alias/ran off to Brazil with a go-go dancer/moved to a suburban neighborhood under a new identity.

LASTING IMPACT

TO DATE, NO CHARGES HAVE EVER BEEN FILED against anyone for the murder of Jimmy Hoffa. On the fortieth anniversary of Hoffa's disappearance in 2015, the *Detroit Free Press* reported that most investigators were convinced no one would ever be charged with Hoffa's death. The city's US attorney at the time reportedly declined to comment on the case, beyond saying it was "inactive, but not closed."

Hoffa's supporters within the Teamsters carried on the battle against Fitzsimmons and his backers after the former president's disappearance. In May 1999, Hoffa's son James P. Hoffa was sworn in as president of the Teamsters after a bitter election campaign ended in his victory over Ron Carey, a longtime critic of his father. Under his leadership, the Teamsters joined the Service Employees International Union in breaking from the AFL-CIO, the national trade union center, in 2005.

Jimmy Hoffa's disappearance on July 30, 1975, remains one of the most famous and enduring mysteries of the twentieth century. His story has been the subject of at least two features (the 1983 TV movie, *Blood Feud*, starring Robert Blake, and the 1992 big-screen biopic, *Hoffa*, starring Jack Nicholson), as well as the basis of numerous pop-culture references, from music to video games. ∎

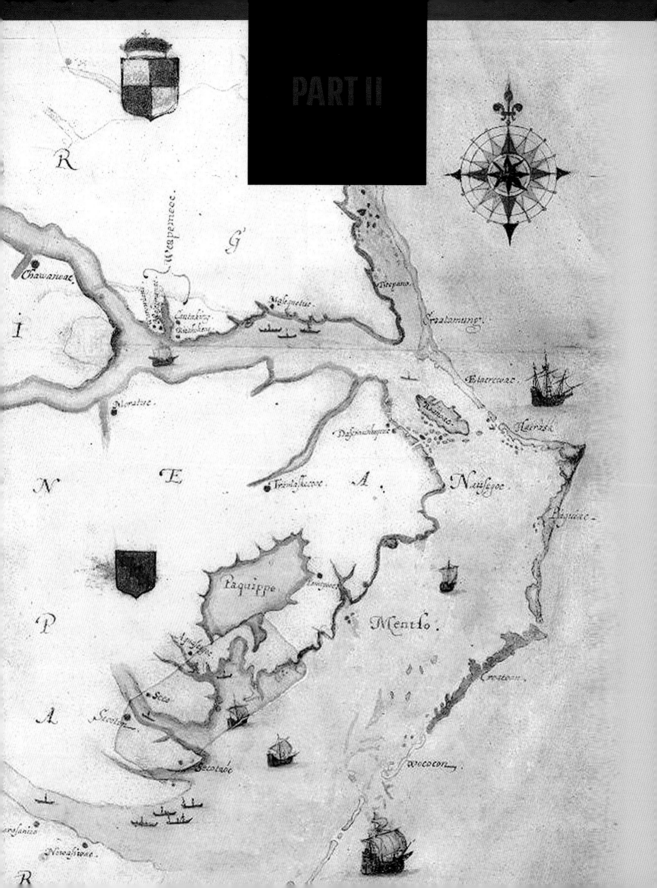

PART II

THE FIRST DISAPPERANCE

THE ROANOKE COLONY

Excerpts from *John White, The Principal Navigations, Voyages, Traffiques, and Discoveries of the English Nation,* 1590

At our first coming to anchor ... we saw a great smoke rise in the isle of Roanoke.

Coming to the fire, we found the grass & sundry rotten trees burning about the place.

We saw in the sand the print of the savages' feet of 2 or 3 sorts trodden in the night. The shore of Roanoke Island as

We passed toward the place where they were left in sundry houses, but we found the houses taken down ... and 5 feet from the ground in fair capital letters was graven CROATOAN without cross or sign of distress.

THE HEADLINES

THE ROANOKE COLONY 1590

O N AUGUST 18, 1590, THE ENGLISH ARTIST AND explorer John White arrived on Roanoke Island, one of a chain of barrier islands off the coast of today's North Carolina, a geographical feature now known as the Outer Banks.

White had been to Roanoke Island before. The celebrated adventurer Sir Walter Raleigh had appointed him governor of a settlement—the first attempt at a permanent English colony in North America—founded there in 1587. A mere six weeks after the earlier expedition's arrival, White had sailed back to England to retrieve additional supplies. When war between England and Spain broke out, however, Queen Elizabeth I called on every available British ship to face the mighty Spanish Armada. Nearly three long years passed before White was able to return to Roanoke Island, where he had left his wife, daughter, and infant granddaughter, Virginia Dare, the first English child born in the Americas.

When he landed, White found the colony abandoned, with precious few clues as to where the colonists might have gone. More than four hundred years later, the inexplicable disappearance of the Lost Colony of Roanoke remains America's most enduring mystery.

IN OTHER NEWS

In February 1587, Mary, Queen of Scots, was executed for her role in a Catholic plot to assassinate her cousin, Queen Elizabeth I of England.

Meanwhile, the daring privateer Sir Francis Drake had been gleefully raiding Spanish possessions in North and South America, loading up on treasure and damaging Spanish morale.

Such actions would lead Spain's King Philip II to declare war on England in 1588—a conflict that would delay John White's return to the Roanoke colony.

WHAT DID WE KNOW?

Sir Walter Raleigh. National Portrait Gallery, London

B Y THE LATE 1500S, ENGLAND HAD FALLEN BEHIND Spain and France in New World exploration and colonization. But the nation was anxious to make up ground. Two English expeditions landed in the coastal region known to Native Americans as Ossomocomuck before 1587; one even built a fort on Roanoke Island. But when John White and his fellow colonists (including seventeen women and nine children) arrived, they found the fort abandoned, apart from the bones of one of the garrison's soldiers. White had orders to move further north and settle in the Chesapeake Bay area. Yet the ship's captain was apparently eager to return to sea, and insisted they disembark on Roanoke. With only a few months' worth of supplies, the colonists made the best of it. They started repairing the fort's buildings and erecting new cottages of brick and tile. In mid-August 1587, the settlers celebrated the arrival of the first baby born to English parents in the Americas: White's granddaughter, Virginia Dare.

Amid uneasy relations with local Native Americans—one settler had been found dead outside their camp, his body pierced with sixteen arrows—the settlers decided White (who had the most experience in the region) would be the one to report to Raleigh on the colony's progress and come back with fresh supplies. Though reluctant to go, White was soon on his way to England, pledging to return within three months. He would not keep that promise.

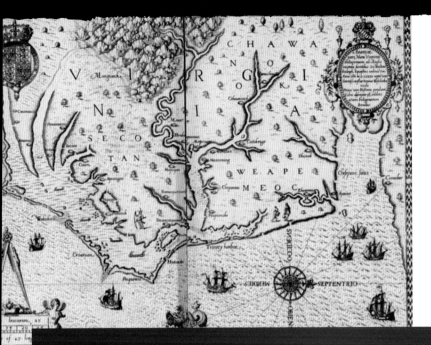

CHRONOLOGY

1578	Queen Elizabeth I granted Sir Humphrey Gilbert a patent to form a colony in North America.
1583	Gilbert died at sea; his half-brother Walter Raleigh inherited his colonizing mission.
1584	The first Raleigh-sponsored exploration party landed in the Outer Banks of present-day North Carolina.
1585	A second expedition to the region, led by Sir Richard Grenville, built a fort on Roanoke Island.
July 22, 1587	John White and some 116 men, women, and children landed in the Outer Banks and found the Roanoke fort abandoned.
July 28, 1587	Colonist George Howe was found dead two miles from camp, his body beaten and pierced with arrows.
August 9, 1587	After learning that Roanoke Native Americans killed the fort's soldiers as well as Howe, a party of colonists attacked the town of Dasemunkepeuc.
August 27, 1587	White sailed for England.
1588	The Spanish Armada attacked England and was defeated.
August 1590	White finally made it back to Roanoke Island, but found the colony abandoned.
October 1590	After a failed attempt to find the colonists, White returned to England.

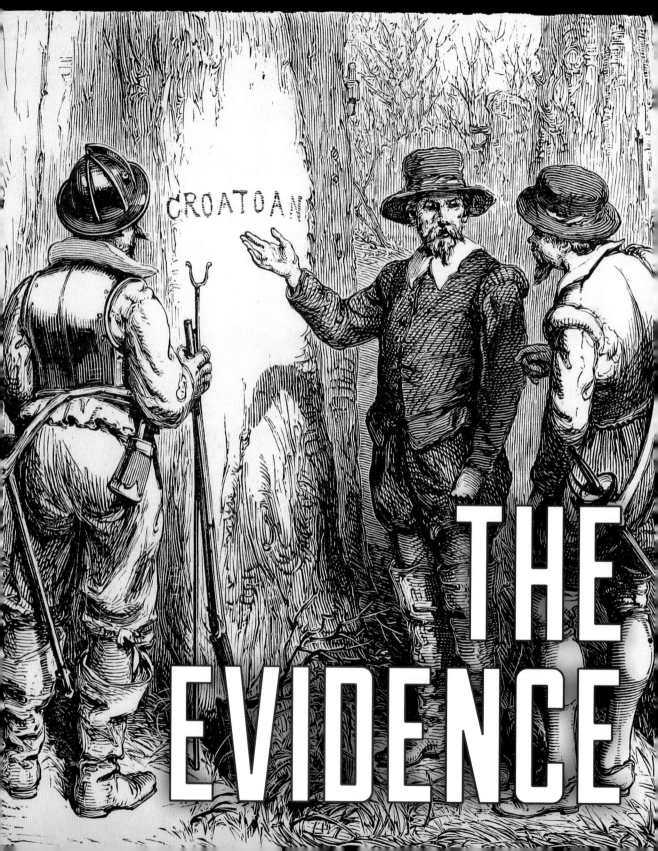

THE EVIDENCE

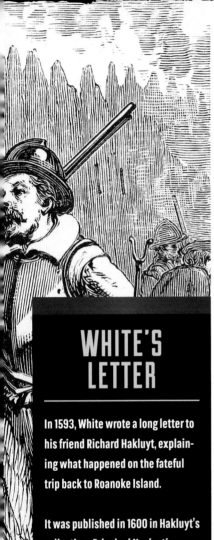

The discovery of the "Croatoan" carving as imagined by a nineteenth-century artist for *A Popular History of the United States* by William Cullen Bryant and Sydney Howard Gay. Wikimedia Commons

WHITE'S LETTER

In 1593, White wrote a long letter to his friend Richard Hakluyt, explaining what happened on the fateful trip back to Roanoke Island.

It was published in 1600 in Hakluyt's collection, *Principal Navigations, Voyages, Traffiques, and Discoveries of the English Nation*, and contains much of what we know about the Lost Colony's disappearance.

White placed blame for the colony's fate largely on the original expedition ship's captain, Simon Fernandez, who had insisted on leaving the colonists in Roanoke, where it was known not to be sustainable, instead of going on to the Chesapeake Bay region.

DELAYED BY ENGLAND'S WAR WITH SPAIN, WHITE finally got passage with an expedition of privateers back across the Atlantic in 1590. When White and a group of sailors landed on Roanoke on August 18, Virginia Dare's third birthday, they found the colony abandoned and its buildings gone. The only clue as to the settlers' fate was a single word—"CROATOAN" —carved into a wooden post, along with three letters—"CRO"— scratched into a tree trunk.

Croatoan, also spelled Croatan, was the name of an island around fifty miles southeast of the Roanoke settlement (now Hatteras Island), as well as the name of the Native American tribe that lived there. According to White, he and the other settlers had agreed that if they needed to move while he was gone, they would indicate their destination by making just such a carving. If they were under attack or in some other kind of distress, they should carve a cross over the letters or name. As White saw no such cross, he initially felt relieved, and assumed the colonists had gone to live with the Croatoans, one of whom—a man named Manteo —had served as an interpreter for the English settlers. Though White's group tried to sail for Croatoan, a storm drove the ships out to sea, and he was forced to return to England without finding his fellow colonists.

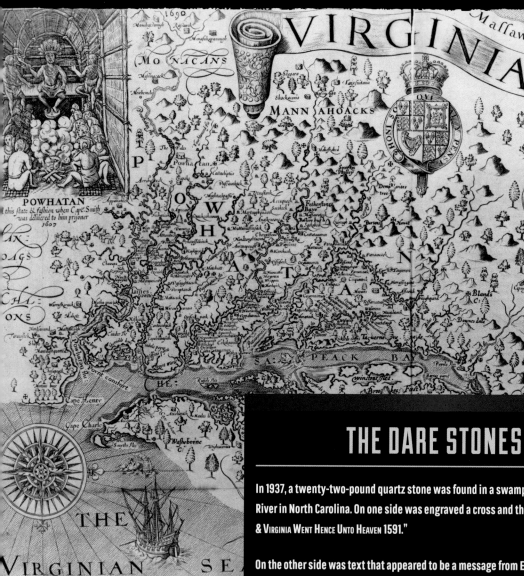

John Smith's 1606 map of Virginia. Library of Congress

THE DARE STONES

In 1937, a twenty-two-pound quartz stone was found in a swamp along the Chowan River in North Carolina. On one side was engraved a cross and the words "Ananias Dare & Virginia Went Hence Unto Heaven 1591."

On the other side was text that appeared to be a message from Eleanor White Dare to her father, John White, about a Native American attack that had driven surviving colonists inland.

Over the next few years, some forty more "Dare Stones" were found, with similar inscriptions about the Lost Colony's fate.

After a flurry of press attention, a reporter for the *Saturday Evening Post* did an exposé in 1941, dismissing the stones as a hoax, and they've been largely discredited since.

But experts say the first stone, found along the Chowan River, is quite different from the others—in the type of rock, engraving style, and word usage—raising the possibility that it may be authentic.

S EVERAL RESCUE MISSIONS FOR THE LOST ROANOKE COLONISTS CONDUCTED BETWEEN 1590 and 1603 came up empty-handed. Then, in 1607, some 105 settlers sailed into the Chesapeake Bay and founded the colony of Jamestown.

In late 1607, the Jamestown colonists sent Captain John Smith to negotiate for provisions with Native Americans along the James River. From them, Smith heard reports of "people clothed at Ocanahonan" and a land farther south called "Anone, where they have abundance of Brass, and houses walled as ours." Convinced these clothed people in houses were the lost colonists of Roanoke, Smith set out to find them, but was unsuccessful.

A Powhatan man named Machumps, who had traveled briefly to England with one of the Jamestown settlers, provided another account of the lost colonists' fate. He claimed the Roanoke colonists had moved north and lived peacefully with the Chesepian (Chesapeake) Native Americans for some years. Then, around the same time the first fleet arrived at Jamestown, Powhatan warriors attacked the English colonists, slaughtering all but seven of them.

DEVELOPING STORY

A "Dare stone," likely a **hoax.** Library of Congress

TOP THEORIES

1 The colonists went to live with the Croatoan (Croatan) people on a nearby island.

This was John White's first theory, after he saw the words CROATOAN and CRO carved at the site of the colony, though he was unable to travel to Croatoan (now Hatteras) Island to confirm. Manteo, who had served as liaison between the Natives and the English, was from Croatoan Island, and White thought the settlers could have gone with him. Some members of the Lumbee tribe, now living in the Outer Banks, believe they are descended in part from the Roanoke colonists as well as the Croatans. Efforts are now ongoing to collect and analyze DNA from local families to confirm such ties.

2 The settlers went north toward the Chesapeake Bay region, where most of them were killed in a massacre by 1609.

According to this theory, the colonists left Roanoke Island and traveled north to the region in which they were originally supposed to settle. After they lived with friendly Native Americans for nearly twenty years, Powhatan tribesmen under Chief Wahunsonacock reportedly attacked them, killing all but a small group. According to Jamestown secretary William Strachey's version of events, included in his history of the Jamestown colony in 1612, the survivors included a "young mayde," possibly Virginia Dare. Jamestown colonists reported sightings of pale-skinned Indians in the surrounding area, including a "savage boy" with yellow hair and "a reasonable white skinne" who ran away before the settlers got a chance to talk to him.

John White's 1585 depiction of Secotan Indians dancing. National Park Service

FRINGE THEORIES

Other possible fates for the Lost Colonists (with less evidence and fewer adherents) include:

They were killed by Spaniards who came north from Florida: It appears the colonists avoided such a fate—perhaps narrowly. Recently surfaced evidence shows that a raiding party from St. Augustine arrived on Roanoke in June 1588, but found the colony already abandoned.

They fell victim to diseases.

They tried to sail back to England on their own and got lost at sea.

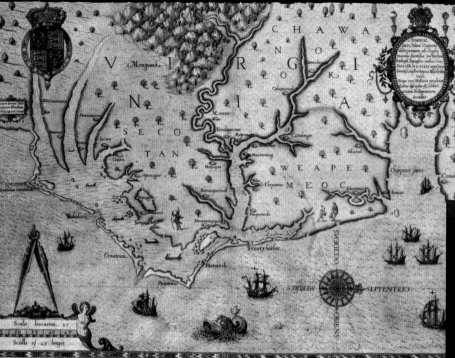

An engraving by Theodor de Bry, based on a map John White drew of the coast of Virginia and North Carolina, circa 1585–86. (The engraving appeared in Thomas Hariot's 1588 book, *A Briefe and True Report of the New Found Land of Virginia*.)

"LA VIRGINEA PARS"

John White painted this map of the East Coast of North America, from Chesapeake Bay to Cape Lookout, on his earlier voyage to the New World in 1585–86.

In 2012, at the urging of the First Colony Foundation, researchers using X-ray spectroscopy and other imaging techniques spotted a tiny four-pointed star concealed under a patch of paper White had used to make corrections to the map.

The star was thought to mark the location of a site some 50 miles inland, which White alluded to in testimony given after his failed return to the colony.

If such a site did exist, historians assumed, it would have been a reasonable destination for the displaced Roanoke settlers.

EVEN AFTER JAMESTOWN OFFICIALS REPORTED TO THE Crown their conclusion that Powhatans had murdered the Roanoke colonists around 1607, John Smith and others continued to search for survivors for decades. They didn't believe that the "official" version of events marked the end of the Lost Colony.

In recent years, archaeological excavations at two separate sites have appeared to support the conclusion that the Roanoke colonists split up shortly after White left in 1587, with most moving inland and a smaller group heading to Croatoan Island. One of the two sites, Cape Creek on Hatteras Island, was a major Croatoan center in the late sixteenth century. Beginning in the late 1990s, archaeologists uncovered many non–Native American artifacts there, including a signet ring, flintlocks from a sixteenth-century rifle, and metal fragments believed to be of European origin.

A watercolor map that John White drew in 1585, known as "La Virginea Pars," inspired the search at the second site, known as Site X. Excavations at the North Carolina site, located some 50 miles inland near what was once a small Native American town, Mettaquem, revealed shards of pottery of a style called Border Ware. Similar to pottery that has been dug up on Roanoke Island, as well as at Jamestown, the style was no longer imported to the New World after the early seventeenth century.

UNSOLVED OR CASE CLOSED?

LASTING
IMPACT

THE SPECTACULAR FAILURE OF THE ROANOKE COL-
ony provided lessons for the Jamestown colonists, who
managed to achieve what the Roanoke group could not:
founding the first permanent English settlement in the New
World. Though the colony was teetering on the brink of collapse
by the winter of 1607, some five hundred more settlers arrived in
Virginia in 1609, and within a decade large-scale tobacco production had begun along the James River.

More than four hundred years after the Lost Colony's disappearance, its mysterious story continues to enthrall. Since August
1937, the 350th anniversary of Virginia Dare's birth, visitors to
the Outer Banks have been able to view annual productions of
The Lost Colony, a play by Paul Green based on a 1921 silent movie of the same name. (President Franklin D. Roosevelt attended
the inaugural production in 1937.) In 2016, the cable network FX
debuted the sixth season of its anthology drama series, *American
Horror Story: Roanoke*. ∎

ANOTHER DISAPPEARANCE

When John White did not return as promised, it seems likely that his family and the
other Roanoke colonists turned to the people they had relied on (and feared) as long
as they had been in the New World: Native Americans.

They lived peaceably with some, but faced attacks from others.

Eventually, they may have blended into Native communities throughout the region.

In the centuries to come, just as the Lost Colony disappeared into history, so—to a
great extent—did the Native Americans of the region, as they were pushed out of
their homeland by ever-expanding settlement.

The Waterside Theater at Fort Raleigh National
Historic Site, where *The Lost Colony* has been
playing continuously since 1937. National Park
Service

PART III

THE RICH AND THE FAMOUS

THEODOSIA BURR ALSTON, DOROTHY ARNOLD, JIM THOMPSON, AND SEAN FLYNN

MYSTERY OF AARON BURR'S DAUGHTER BAFFLES A CENTURY

Her Disappearance Just One Hundred Years Ago Caused a Worldwide Sensation---Went to Sea and Was Never Heard of Again---Was She Forced to Walk the Plank by Pirates, or What Was Her Fate?

THE ORIGINAL "WHITE HOUSE" WHEN AARON BURR WAS VICE-PRESIDENT AND HIS DAUGHTER, THEODOSIA, WAS A BELLE IN DIPLOMATIC SOCIETY—1801–5.

THEODOSIA BURR-ALSTON WHOSE TRAGIC DISAPPEARANCE 100 YEARS AGO IS STILL UNSOLVED.

- WASHINGTON - 100 YEARS AGO.

DOLLY MADISON, WHO DOMINATED WASHINGTON SOCIETY WHEN THE DISAPPEARANCE OF THEODOSIA BURR ALSTON WAS A NATIONAL MYSTERY.

AARON BURR

THE HEADLINES

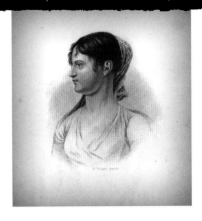

Aaron Burr and Theodosia Burr Alston. Museum of American Finance via Wikimedia Commons

"Tomorrow it will be three weeks since, in obedience to your wishes, Theodosia left me. It is three weeks, and not yet one line from her. My mind is tortured."
—*Letter from Joseph Alston to Aaron Burr, January 19, 1813*

THEODOSIA BURR ALSTON 1812

AS THE CHERISHED DAUGHTER OF DISGRACED former US vice president Aaron Burr and the wife of South Carolina's newly elected governor, Joseph Alston, Theodosia Burr Alston moved in the most eminent circles of the post–Revolutionary War era. Thanks to her father's close attention to her schooling, she was also one of the best-educated women in the country. But as the year 1812 drew to a close, twenty-nine-year-old Theodosia was also in dismal health after a decade of medical problems and mired in grief after the recent death of her ten-year-old son.

Despite her husband's concerns for her well-being (the United States was again at war with Britain at the time), Theodosia insisted on making the journey north to reunite with Aaron Burr, recently returned from several years of European exile. On December 30, she boarded the schooner *Patriot* for the risky journey from South Carolina to New York. But somewhere off the coast of North Carolina, the *Patriot* disappeared, taking with it Theodosia, her fellow passengers, and the ship's entire crew. The unknown fate of one of America's most accomplished young women captivated the attention of the nation, launching a colorful legend that would soon eclipse the reality of Theodosia's brief but extraordinary life.

IN OTHER NEWS

In January 1813:

US troops clashed with a joint British–Native American force in Frenchtown, Michigan Territory. After the United States had initial success, the Battle of Frenchtown ended in a decisive victory by the British and Native Americans.

A group of musicians, composers, and other music lovers gathered in London to form the Philharmonic Society, later the Royal Philharmonic Society.

Jane Austen's *Pride and Prejudice* was published in the United Kingdom.

Aaron Burr's home at Richmond Hill, New York.
New York Public Library Digital Collections

CHRONOLOGY

June 21, 1783	Theodosia Bartow Burr was born in Albany, New York.
1794	Her mother, Theodosia Prevost Burr, died.
1800	Aaron Burr lost a contentious US presidential race to Thomas Jefferson and became vice president.
1801	Theodora married Joseph Alston; the couple honeymooned in Niagara Falls.
1802	Aaron Burr Alston was born.
1804	Burr killed Alexander Hamilton in a duel in Weehawken, New Jersey.
1806	Theodosia, her husband, and their son traveled down the Ohio River.
1807	Burr was tried for treason in Richmond, Virginia; he was acquitted, but his reputation was in ruins.
May 4, 1812	Traveling under an alias, Burr returned to New York after four years living in Europe.
June 18, 1812	President James Madison signed Congress's declaration of war against Great Britain, beginning the War of 1812.
June 30, 1812	Young Aaron Burr Alston died of malaria.
December 10, 1812	Joseph Alston was elected governor of South Carolina.

AFTER HER MOTHER DIED WHEN SHE WAS ONLY TEN years old, Theodosia became her father's closest confidante. Under Aaron Burr's supervision, his daughter studied not only the conventional subjects for well-bred girls (French, music, dancing) but also arithmetic, English composition, and foreign languages. By the age of fourteen, she was hosting parties for political VIPs at Richmond Hill, Burr's country estate (located in what is now New York City's SoHo neighborhood).

In 1801, Theodosia married Joseph Alston, heir to a South Carolina rice fortune. The couple moved to the Oaks, Alston's ancestral home near Georgetown, South Carolina, where Theodosia gave birth to a son, Aaron Burr Alston, in 1802. The difficult labor caused lingering medical problems that would plague her for the rest of her life.

In 1804, Burr fatally shot his political nemesis, Alexander Hamilton, in a duel. Though charged with murder in New York and New Jersey, he would escape punishment. A few years later, Burr hatched a plot to split the Western states from the rest of the country, invade Mexico, and form an empire (with himself as emperor and his daughter as empress). After this scheme was discovered, Theodosia rushed to her father's side during his highly public trial for treason, which ended in acquittal.

Meanwhile, her health continued to decline, including uterine infections, rheumatism, and nervous complaints. With Burr in self-imposed exile in Europe and Alston busy with his rice planting and political career, Theodosia's son became her only solace.

Artist's depiction of the 1804 duel between Aaron Burr and Alexander Hamilton, from *Our Greater Country: Being a Standard History of the United States from the Discovery of the American Continent to the Present Time* by Henry Davenport Northrop (1901). Library of Congress

WHAT DID WE KNOW?

THE EVIDENCE

A 1794 map of thesoutheastern United States with South Carolina outlined in red. Winyah Bay, Georgetown, is roughly two-thirds of the way up the South Carolina coast. Library of Congress

WHAT DID THEODOSIA HAVE ON BOARD?

In addition to her clothing and other personal belongings, Theodosia brought with her a number of sealed tin boxes.

Inside were many of Aaron Burr's personal and professional papers, which he had left with his daughter for safekeeping while he was in Europe.

It has also been reported that she carried a portrait to give her father as a gift (later linked to a painting that allegedly washed up on the North Carolina coast), but no documentary evidence supports this conclusion.

ON JUNE 30, 1812, AARON BURR ALSTON DIED AFTER contracting malaria, and Theodosia fell into a deep depression. Aaron Burr, who had returned to the United States earlier that year, urged his daughter to join him in New York, and she was determined to go. As Joseph Alston could not accompany Theodosia—the War of 1812 was on, and he was a commander of the state militia, not to mention the recently elected governor of South Carolina—Burr enlisted his friend, Dr. Timothy R. Greene, to accompany his daughter and look after her fragile health during the journey.

Late on the afternoon of December 30, Theodosia boarded the schooner *Patriot*, commanded by Captain William Overstocks, in Winyah Bay, Georgetown's harbor. Accompanying her were Dr. Greene, Theodosia's French maid, and possibly her cook. Soon after they boarded, the ship lifted its anchor and set sail. As Joseph Alston later wrote to Aaron Burr, the weather seemed to be agreeable, and "The wind was moderate and fair."

The British war ship *Shannon* captures the USS *Chesapeake* in this scene from the War of 1812. Could the same fate have befallen the *Patriot*?
Library of Congress

FEARS OF BRITISH CAPTURE

During the War of 1812, British war ships patrolled the Atlantic coast en masse, blockading harbors and raiding coastal settlements and plantations.

In one such raid—on October 14, 1812—the British took eight US warships as prizes in Charleston Harbor.

Before his wife sailed, Governor Alston reportedly gave Captain Overstocks a letter intended for the admiral of the British fleet, then blockading South Carolina's coast.

The letter appealed to the man's chivalry and asked him to give Theodosia safe passage.

But after the *Patriot* disappeared, fears lingered that British war ships might have captured the ship and carried off Theodosia as a prize of war.

"Your letter of the 10th, my friend, is received.... Authentic accounts from Bermuda and Nassau, as late as January 30, connected with your letter from New-York of the 28th, had already forced upon me the dreadful conviction that we had no more to hope."

—Letter from Joseph Alston to Aaron Burr, February 25, 1813

R EPUTED TO BE A SWIFT BOAT, THE *PATRIOT* WAS SUPPOSED TO COMPLETE THE journey from South Carolina to New York in five to six days, but after two weeks there was still no sign of it at its destination, or anywhere along the way. Aaron Burr stalked the docks of New York Harbor and sent inquiry letters to ports stretching from New York to the Caribbean (including Nassau and Bermuda), with no results. He and Alston, both crazed with worry, wrote letters back and forth as they tried to dismiss their worst fears about Theodosia's fate. But as the weeks passed with no word, it grew difficult to sustain hope.

After previously seeing service as a privateer, harassing British commercial vessels and capturing their cargoes, the *Patriot* had been returning to New York with its guns dismounted and stowed. In his book *Theodosia Burr: Portrait of a Prodigy*, Richard N. Côté wrote that the *Patriot*'s owner reportedly told Aaron Burr that the ship's officers and crew never intended to return to New York, but instead had returned to privateering. This raised Burr's hopes that they had deposited his daughter in some port somewhere, and she might still return. This theory never panned out, and by the end of February Burr and Alston were left only with their mutual grief.

DEVELOPING STORY

TOP THEORIES

1 Theodosia's ship was captured by pirates.

Pirates had been known to prowl the Outer Banks, off the coast of North Carolina, for centuries, and the idea that some might have captured the *Patriot* inspired all sorts of bloody stories over the years. In 1820, the *Mercantile Advertiser* reported that two captured pirates, Jean Desfarges and Robert Johnson, had confessed to murdering Theodosia Burr Alston and the crew of the *Patriot*. The two men were supposedly tried and convicted by a US court and executed aboard a navy war ship in the Mississippi. According to Côté, this was the most credible of all the various pirate-related theories that surfaced to explain Theodosia's fate, which would only get more lurid and detailed over the course of the nineteenth century.

2 The ship sank in a storm after a run-in with the British.

According to Jacob Motte Alston, Theodosia's great-nephew by marriage, the family later learned that the British fleet stopped the *Patriot* off Cape Hatteras on January 2, 1813, three days after its departure. Thanks to Governor Alston's letter, the British admiral let Theodosia's ship pass, but later that night a violent storm arose, scattering the British fleet. The British assumed the *Patriot*, and all aboard, went down in the storm. According to Motte Alston, whose account was first published in 1902, "This was the first reliable information which had been received, and the family accepted it as absolutely true." But Côté cited the work of South Carolina archaeologist James L. Michie, whose search through British Admiralty records found that the war ship believed to have stopped the *Patriot* was in fact anchored in Bermuda at the time.

Wreckers—Coast of Northumberland by J. M. W. Turner (1775–1851). Yale Center for British Art

THE "WRECKERS"

In addition to pirates and privateers, another group threatened travelers along the Atlantic coast off the Carolinas: the "wreckers," who flourished especially near the Outer Banks.

These coastal residents made their living by salvaging cargo and other materials from the many ships that wrecked in the region.

In some cases, the wreckers were thought to neglect, or even murder, shipwreck survivors in their salvaging efforts.

In 1869, near Nag's Head (a beach on the Outer Banks), Dr. William Gaskins Pool acquired an oil painting of a woman, possibly Theodosia, from the widow of a wrecker, who said her husband had acquired it from a nearby shipwreck in early January 1813.

Though Pool spent the rest of his life trying to determine the portrait's origins and authenticity, he was ultimately unsuccessful.

"Were she alive, all the prisons in the world could not keep her from her father. When I realized the truth of her death, the world became a blank to me, and life then lost all its value."
—Letter from Aaron Burr to a friend, 1813

Engraving of Aaron Burr's grave at Princeton, New Jersey. New York Public Library Digital Collections

THOUGH ARCHAEOLOGIST JAMES L. MICHIE FOUND no evidence in British Admiralty logbooks that a British ship stopped the *Patriot* and then let it pass in January 1813, he did find accounts of a vicious storm off the Carolina coast on January 2–3. According to Michie's calculations, the *Patriot* might have been just north of Cape Hatteras when the storm reached its height. Even if it managed to survive the storm itself, the schooner would have faced winds of near hurricane force in the hours that followed.

In all, despite the more colorful theories involving enemy ships, mutiny, pirates, and wreckers, the most probable conclusion seems to be that Theodosia Burr Alston met the very fate her father had envisioned. Though the exact circumstances remain a mystery more than two hundred years later, she likely perished at sea, sinking below the waves along with the rest of the *Patriot*'s crew, passengers, and cargo.

THE MEN WHO LOVED HER

Despite the lurid headlines, Aaron Burr steadfastly refused to believe rumors that pirates had captured and killed his beloved daughter, but remained convinced that she died at sea.

Burr lived another twenty-three years after his daughter's disappearance; he even remarried—and later divorced—wealthy widow Eliza Jumel. But after such a tumultuous life and career, the loss of Theodosia had broken Burr's heart and spirit.

As for Joseph Alston, he made it through a single term as South Carolina's governor, but then succumbed to illness and depression.

He died in 1816, at just thirty-seven years old.

UNSOLVED OR CASE CLOSED?

LASTING IMPACT

Theda Bara—born Theodosia Burr Goodman—as Cleopatra (1917). Photofest

ANOTHER FAMOUS THEODOSIA

Among the many little girls named for Theodosia Burr Alston was one of the leading actresses of the silent film era.

According to the marketing campaigns for early films like *A Fool There Was* (1915) and *Cleopatra* (1917), Theda Bara was "the daughter of an Arab sheik and a French woman, born in the Sahara." In reality, she was born Theodosia Burr Goodman in Cincinnati, Ohio, in 1885.

Bara's success helped to build the foundations of Twentieth Century Fox, the future movie empire.

Her persona played on the image of the exotic femme fatale, and her stage name was supposed to be an anagram for "Arab Death."

BY THE MID-NINETEENTH CENTURY, THEODOSIA Burr Alston's life and the mystery surrounding her presumed death had made its way into hundreds of newspaper and magazine accounts. Her beauty, intellect, and celebrity, combined with the circumstances of her disappearance, elevated Theodosia to the highest ranks of America's tragic heroines. Though her given name is certainly not common today, numerous women inspired by her story named their daughters after her.

As Richard Côté recounted in his biography of Theodosia, the first "overtly fictional" story of her life was published in 1872. Since then, various novelists have written fictional accounts about Theodosia, including Charles Felton Pidgin (*Blennerhassett and The Climax: Or, What Might Have Been*), Anya Seton Chase (*My Theodosia*), and Anne Colver (*Theodosia, Daughter of Aaron Burr*). Gore Vidal's bestselling *Burr: A Novel* (1973) threw coals on the fire of history, linking the Burr–Hamilton duel to Hamilton's suggestion of an incestuous element to Burr and Theodosia's relationship. (There's no evidence of incest, and Vidal later admitted that he invented the whole concept.)

More recently, Theodosia—but not her tragic fate—reentered the public consciousness with the success of *Hamilton*, Lin-Manuel Miranda's Tony-winning hip-hop musical. In one scene, set just after the Revolutionary War, the character of Aaron Burr sings "Dear Theodosia," a tender song addressed to his newborn daughter. ∎

MISSING HEIRESS MAY BE DISGUISED
DENY RELIGIOUS LINE IN SENATORIAL FIGHT

WEATHER—Fair to-night and Friday.

WEATHER—Fair to-night and Friday.

The Evening Edition World.

FINAL EDITION

FINAL EDITION

"Circulation Books Open to All."

"Circulation Books Open to All."

PRICE ONE CENT.

Copyright, 1911, by The Press Publishing Co. (The New York World.)

NEW YORK, THURSDAY, JANUARY 26, 1911.

20 PAGES

PRICE ONE CENT.

PERILS OF LONG HATPINS TOLD BY THE CLUBWOMEN IN PLEAS TO ALDERMEN

Committee Gives a Hearing on Ordinance Providing for Protection...

SIX IN AEROPLANE,

RECORD OF FLIGHTS WITH PASSENGERS

First passenger flight, Leon Delagrange, March 22, 1908, Paris, biplane.

March 30, 1908, Rheims, biplane. Four passengers, Henry Farman and the Master, monoplane and biplane, France, Aug. 1, 1910, biplane.

Six passengers, Louis Breguet, France, Aug. 23, 1910, and M. Farman, Chalons, France, Nov. 9, 1910, biplane.

First American passenger flight, Wilbur Wright, Kitty Hawk, N.C., May 14, 1908, biplane.

Four passengers American record, Charles P. Willard, Mineola, L. I., Aug. 14, 1910.

JURY DEADLOCKED

IN SCHENK CASE

WOMAN HOPEFUL

BOLTERS ALL DENY FIGHTING SHEEHAN ON CHURCH ISSUE

Declare That Statement by Bishop Ludden of Syracuse Was Uncalled For.

BIG ROW IN THE SENATE.

Brackett Takes Up Cudgels for Roosevelt, Whose Clerk Was Bounced.

EIGHTH BALLOT IN ALBANY ON SENATORSHIP.

(Special to The Evening World.)

ALBANY, N. Y., Jan. 26.—The result of the joint session for United States Senator was:

Sheehan	22	82
Kernan	5	10
Connan	1	
Gerard		1
O'Farrell	1	
Atkinson	1	
Slynn		1
Lieb		1
Fae		1
Herrick		1
Van Eastwood		1
Taylor		1
Douglass		2
O'Brien		1
Depew	67	77

Total vote cast to-day ... 180
Necessary to choice to-day ... 91
Absentees ... 13

(Special from a Staff Correspondent of The Evening World.)

ALBANY, N. Y., Jan. 26.—Senator Elsher P. Brackett announced to-day that he intends to offer a resolution instructing the Committee on Privileges and Elections of the Senate to investigate the charges that Charles F. Murphy, through Patrick E. McCabe, the Senate clerk, has been attempting to influence the action of legislators by using the power of patronage.

The statement came as a result of the resolution of Senator Franklin D. Roosevelt directing the Senate clerk to appoint Morgan Hoyt clerk of the committee on Forest, Fish and Game. Senator Roosevelt's resolution brought on a bitter fight in the Senate. Republican Leader Brackett immediately took up the cudgels for young Roosevelt.

"I want to give notice now," he said, "that later I shall offer a resolution directing the Committee on Privileges and Elections to investigate the outside interference in the distribution of Senate patronage. This is contempt of the Senate and we should resent the interference of Tammany or any other half...

GIRL SEEKING DISGUISE MAY BE LOST HEIRESS

Three Latest Photographs Of Missing Dorothy Arnold

River Front Merchant Certain Millionaire's Daughter Tried to Buy Man's Clothes and Was Afraid of Identification.

ASKED ABOUT STEAMERS SAILING FROM HOBOKEN

Many False Clues Telephoned by Persons Who Locate Dorothy Arnold in Various Points Are Run Down Vainly by Her Distracted Father.

Except for one clue, which may or may not be worth anything, the first day of the public search for Miss Dorothy H. C. Arnold, the girl who disappeared so completely in broad daylight of Dec. 12, an hour after leaving the home of her father, Francis R. Arnold, the importer, has been no more productive of results than was the private search which preceded it.

YOUNG ASTOR'S ICE YACHT RUNS DOWN A WOMAN

Mrs. Henry Kipp Badly Injured in Accident on Hudson, Near...

MISS ARNOLD NOT IN CHICAGO.

Though It Will Be Hard to Convince Three Women there She Is Not Selling Shoe Polish.

Special to The New York Times.

CHICAGO, Feb. 2.—Mrs. Charles Kusel, wife of a real estate operator living at 4,521 Michigan Avenue; Mrs. Harriet Lauer of the same address, and Mrs. C. W. Whitney of 4,001 Grand Boulevard believe that Dorothy Arnold is in Chicago.

A well-dressed young woman resembling Miss Arnold's description called at Mrs. Kusel's house yesterday, offering shoe polish for sale, and told a story of privation caused by the loss of her baggage and money since her arrival in the city. She was advised to go to the Young Women's Christian Association, and did so.

Mrs. Kusel read later a description of Miss Arnold, and was convinced that her caller was the missing New York girl. The pictures of Miss Arnold, she says, show an astonishing likeness to the girl who sold the shoe polish. Mrs. Lauer says so, too.

Mrs. Whitney gave the same details of the girl's story as told by Mrs. Kusel. Mrs. Whitney added, however, that the girl said she had a cousin at the University of Chicago, and gave his name. When the cousin was seen to-night he said that the girl had not given her real name to Mrs. Kusel or Mrs. Whitney.

"My cousin has run away from home," he explained. "I admit that, and I admit that the name she has given these women is not her real one. But I refuse to disclose who she is. It is not Miss Dorothy Arnold."

THE HEADLINES

The portrait of Dorothy Arnold that many press outlets reproduced after her disappearance.
Library of Congress

DOROTHY ARNOLD 1910

IN LATE JANUARY 1911, THE WEALTHY PERFUME IMPORTER Francis R. Arnold called reporters into his office in New York City and revealed that his daughter, Dorothy, had been missing since the previous December 12. The disappearance of the rich New York socialite (a niece of Rufus Peckham, the late US Supreme Court justice) made headlines all over the United States and Europe. Gossip-worthy revelations followed—a secret boyfriend, a covertly opened post office box, thwarted literary aspirations—along with multiple reported sightings of Miss Arnold everywhere from Boston to Chicago to Europe.

Despite an avalanche of leads and several scandalous theories, Dorothy Arnold was never found. The case would captivate the public's attention for decades, however, hinting at the shadows that lurked beneath the gilded surface of upper-class New York society.

IN OTHER NEWS

Also in January 1911, a South Pole expedition led by Roald Amundsen landed on the Ross Ice Shelf.

A would-be assassin fired two shots at French prime minister Aristide Briand in front of the French Assembly.

Congress weighed a "special message" from President William Howard Taft over a proposed reciprocity agreement with Canada.

The US Navy destroyer USS *Terry* made the first rescue of an airplane at sea, fishing pilot John McCurdy out of the water after he crashed off the coast of Havana, Cuba.

WHAT DID WE KNOW?

ABOUT 11:30 ON THE MORNING OF DECEMBER 12, 1910, Dorothy Arnold left her family's home at 108 East 79th Street. She told her mother she was going shopping for a new gown to wear at her sister Marjorie's coming-out party on December 17. Her mother offered to accompany her, but Arnold said she preferred to go alone.

She walked to Fifth Avenue and turned south, traversing the twenty blocks downtown on foot despite raw winter weather and icy patches on the sidewalk. At 59th Street, she went into Park & Tilford's candy store and bought a box of chocolates, charging it to her father's account.

Dorothy then walked thirty-two more blocks south to Brentano's bookstore, where she browsed the aisles and purchased a book of stories called *Engaged Girl Sketches*. She ran into a friend, Gladys King, outside the store and they chatted for a bit before going their separate ways sometime after 2:00 p.m. Dorothy headed up Fifth Avenue, after telling Gladys she was going for a walk in Central Park.

Dorothy Arnold at about the time of her disappearance. Library of Congress.

A YOUNG LADY OF PRIVILEGE AND WEALTH

Dorothy Harriet Camille Arnold seemed to enjoy all the privileges that wealth and high social standing afforded in early twentieth-century New York.

Her father traced his lineage back to the *Mayflower*, his sister had married Rufus Peckham, who became a Supreme Court justice. Dorothy's mother, the former Mary Parks, was similarly well connected.

But despite her shiny pedigree, Dorothy was far from a frivolous socialite. A studious Bryn Mawr grad, she spoke several languages fluently and was trying to launch a writing career.

Fifth Avenue near 57th Street circa 1910, showing the historic Vanderbilt Mansion and Plaza Hotel. Wikimedia Commons

THE EVIDENCE

A PRIVATE INVESTIGATION

At first, the Arnold family opted for a discreet private investigation rather than going directly to the police.

Dorothy's brother called on a friend, a lawyer named John Keith, who searched morgues, hospitals, and jails in New York, Philadelphia, and Boston, with no results.

As Allen Churchill wrote in a 1960 article about Dorothy's disappearance in *American Heritage*, Keith recommended the Arnolds call the Pinkerton Detective Agency, which sent a circular to police departments around the country offering a $1,000 reward for information.

The NYPD presumably received one, but refused to act until contacted directly, according to protocol. The family finally contacted the police in late January, six weeks after Dorothy had vanished.

O N THE DAY SHE VANISHED, DOROTHY ARNOLD was expensively and fashionably dressed in a well-tailored blue serge coat and matching hobble skirt. She carried a large fox-fur muff and a silk handbag, and topped off the outfit with her hair in a full pompadour under a black velvet hat with two blue roses. The day before, Arnold had withdrawn $36 from her bank account for a lunch-and-matinee outing with some friends; she was thought to have the remainder ($25 or $30) on her. (She had reportedly been receiving a monthly allowance of some $100.)

When family friend John Keith searched Arnold's room the day after she went missing, he found a pile of personal letters, some with foreign postmarks; two brochures from transatlantic steamship companies; and a small pile of burned papers in the fireplace. Her father suggested this might be the rejected manuscript of a short story Dorothy had recently submitted to *McClure's* magazine. (Police later discovered she had secretly rented a post office box a few months before she vanished, presumably to avoid sharing news of future literary rejections with her family.)

The packet of letters contained a bombshell: Dorothy had been secretly dating George C. Griscom Jr., a forty-something engineer from a wealthy family in Pittsburgh. The two had recently spent a weekend in Boston together, during which Arnold told her family she was visiting some college friends.

The Chicago Daily Tribune.

WEDNESDAY, FEBRUARY 15, 1911—TWENTY PAGES. ★ ★ PRICE ONE CENT.

THE ELEPHANT—"I'LL HAVE TO HURRY IF I GET ANYWHERE BY MARCH FOURTH."

CARDINAL GIBBONS SAYS EDISON HAS A MAIMED MIND

Declares Inventor's Religious Sense Atrophied by Devotion to Mechanics.

SIMILAR TO DARWIN'S CASE

Cites Example of Electrical Genius' Dogmatism in Speaking of Intelligent Cells.

SOUL SURELY IS IMMORTAL

E. F. DUNNE TELLS WHY HE WOULD BE MAYOR.

RECIPROCITY BILL PASSED BY HOUSE IN BITTER FIGHT

Regular Republicans Beaten in Hard Contest When Insurgents and Democrats Unite.

FINAL VOTE 221 TO 92

DOROTHY ARNOLD IS FOUND IN A NEW YORK HOSPITAL?

DOROTHY ARNOLD IN LOS ANGELES, CLAIM

Father of Missing Girl Doubts Truth of Story.

BURIED DOROTHY ARNOLD, WEST POINT, SAYS CONVICT

Carried From New Rochelle and Interred in West Point Cellar, Is His Story.

TELLS OF MAN WHO PAID

DOROTHY ARNOLD IN GENEVA?

Her Parents Expected There—May Be Teacher in Girls' School.

Special Cable to THE NEW YORK TIMES.

GENEVA, Aug. 19.—Mr. and Mrs. Arnold of New York are expected here in search of their daughter Dorothy, who suddenly disappeared from her New York home last year.

It would be an easy matter for a young woman like Miss Arnold to obtain a post as teacher...

WHERE IS DOROTHY ARNOLD?

One year ago to-morrow DOROTHY ARNOLD, daughter of a merchant of large means dwelling in this city, a young woman with a host of friends and acquaintances, disappeared suddenly. She was last seen walking on Fifth Avenue. She had made purchases in a bookshop and a grocery store. Many tales supposed to be related to her disappearance have since been told, but not one of them has proved well-founded. All sorts of theories have been advanced, but all have been discredited. Miss ARNOLD vanished and, so far as is known, no trace of her has ever been discovered. The family has been gravely accused of knowing where she is, and refusing to tell. That is natural yet most un-reasonable.

I AM DOROTHY ARNOLD

In the months after she vanished, reports poured in placing Dorothy everywhere from Italy to Chile, not to mention numerous American cities.

A long list of people came forward claiming to be the vanished heiress, hoping to claim the reward money offered by her wealthy family.

In February 1911, the Arnolds received a postcard with a NYC postmark reading only "I am safe," and signed "Dorothy." Though the handwriting matched hers, the family believed it was copied from published samples and was just a cruel joke.

Over the years, the family received various letters from women claiming to be Dorothy. In just one example from 1914, an attorney in Los Angeles claimed that Dorothy was living there under the name Ella Nevins. Like other such reward-based claims, it was investigated and found to be false.

The view from West Point, New York at about the time of Dorothy Arnold's disappearance.
Library of Congress

R EACHED BY TELEGRAM IN FLORENCE, ITALY, JUNIOR Griscom (as he was known) denied any knowledge of or involvement in Arnold's disappearance. In mid-January 1911, Arnold's mother and older brother traveled to see Griscom in Florence. The meeting reportedly got violent; according to some reports, John Arnold thrashed Griscom in his hotel room. Junior produced a letter from Dorothy saying a magazine had rejected one of her short stories; he implied Arnold was depressed as a result, and may have harmed herself.

When Griscom returned home in February, he placed personal ads in New York papers signed "Junior," imploring Dorothy to communicate with him. He got no response. Meanwhile, tips poured in of possible sightings in various cities (and countries), none of which panned out.

Then, more than five years after Arnold vanished, a Rhode Island convict named Edward Glennoris claimed that he had helped bury her body under a house outside West Point, New York. According to Glennoris, Arnold had died in the house after being taken there unconscious from New Rochelle, where a man called "Doc" had operated on her. Glennoris said an unnamed man had paid him $250 to help transport Arnold from New Rochelle to West Point, then return and bury her body. Police followed up on the story by searching the basements of several houses in the area, but found no human remains.

DEVELOPING STORY

TOP THEORIES

1 Arnold was kidnapped and murdered.

From the day he announced his daughter's disappearance, Arnold's father maintained she had been abducted and murdered, her body dumped in the Central Park reservoir. Francis Arnold persisted in this stubborn belief, and he and Mary Arnold, who both died in the 1920s, made no provision for Dorothy in their wills, writing they were "satisfied that she is not alive."

2 Arnold committed suicide.

Could Dorothy have been so depressed about her literary setbacks and family drama that she took her own life? Some press reports suggested she might have followed the example of Junior's young cousin, whom Arnold had met at Bryn Mawr. Andrew Griscom leapt from the deck of a transatlantic liner after his parents refused to let him marry an English governess. (After all, Dorothy had left those steamship brochures on her desk when she disappeared.) But she hadn't seemed depressed, and no steamboat passengers were reported missing in the days after she vanished.

3 Arnold died after a botched abortion.

According to one widespread rumor, Arnold had become pregnant, and died during or after a botched abortion. In April 1914, detectives raided a private hospital in Pittsburgh run by a Dr. C. C. Meredith. They found an operating table and two furnaces in the house, believed to be an illegal abortion clinic. Meredith reportedly claimed that Dorothy Arnold had died there after a procedure, but Arnold's father and Keith vehemently denied the story, as they denied Glennoris's claims two years later.

FRINGE THEORIES

She staged her own disappearance: Shortly before she vanished, Dorothy asked her parents' permission to move out of their home and get an apartment in the literary neighborhood of Greenwich Village. Her father flatly refused. Perhaps this rejection, combined with her family's insensitivity to her failed stories, drove her to take off and start a new life somewhere else.

She fell and hit her head, and suffered amnesia: Suspecting that Arnold might have been injured and unable to recall her own identity, investigators checked area hospitals for anyone matching her description, but came up empty.

Her family had something to do with it: Perhaps inevitably, suspicion fell on those closest to Arnold: her own family, who had initially hushed up the fact of her disappearance. "The family has been gravely accused of knowing where she is, and refusing to tell," the *New York Times* reported a year after she'd vanished. But no evidence ever surfaced to support such suspicions, and the possibility seems highly unlikely.

DOROTHY ARNOLD STORY.

Arrests in Pittsburgh Private Hospital Elicit Remarkable Tale.

Special to The New York Times.

PITTSBURGH, April 9.—Headed by Chief Clark and Assistant District Attorney John N. Dunn, detectives raided a private hospital conducted by Dr. C. C. Meredith in Bellevue this afternoon. Meredith and Lucy Orr, a nurse, were arrested there and Dr. H. E. Lutz, was later arrested at his office in this city.

In the Bellevue house were found an operating table and in the cellar were two large furnaces.

In a statement made to District Attorney R. S. Jackson this afternoon, Lutz said that Meredith had told him that a well-known young woman from New York had once been traced to his office, but had disappeared from sight. Later, he said, Meredith admitted the person to whom he referred was Dorothy Arnold, the missing heiress. When asked what had become of the Arnold girl, Meredith, according to Lutz, intimated that she had been taken to the Bellevue house and cremated.

District Attorney Jackson says he expects some developments in this story tomorrow.

Lutz also told of M ... taken a Mrs. ... in the search for the missing New York girl. The engagement (Lutz's) ... feature was also contradicted, it developing that Mr. Griscom, Jr., was merely a friend of the family.

After returning to this country, and aiding in the search, Griscom, Jr., returned with his parents to this city, the family again making their home at the Kenmawr Hotel. He made no effort whatever to conceal his whereabouts, going about the city openly and making trips East and abroad. A few months ago he took up his residence in London, England, where he is at present the representative for several Pittsburgh manufacturing firms.

Dorothy Arnold's Father Does Not Believe Story

[SPECIAL TELEGRAM TO GAZETTE TIMES.]

NEW YORK, April 9.—The dispatches concerning the reported visit of Dorothy Arnold to Pittsburgh were repeated in brief to Francis A. Arnold, her father, tonight at his home here. Mr. Arnold insists that the story was not true and described it as absurd.

"The story is ridiculous," said Mr. Arnold, "and absolutely untrue. I told you frankly when the report came from Los Angeles about my daughter being there that I had heard of that months before and I did not credit it. My statement was proved correct, and now I tell you that the present dispatches are not correct.

"I never sent private detectives to Pittsburgh. I never even received any clue leading to Pittsburgh, and I do not believe a word of this.

"I believe my daughter is dead. I believe she died the day she disappeared or almost immediately afterward. The one theory to which I always have leaned is that she was kidnaped and made away with in a short time."

ARNOLD LAWYER TALKS.

Tells of Trip Here to Run Down Alleged Baseless Rumor.

NEW YORK, April 9.—J. S. Keith, attorney for the Arnold family, said this evening he had investigated more than three years ago the story that Miss Arnold was in a sanitarium in Pittsburgh, had actually seen the girl reported to be Miss Arnold and had found that the rumor was without foundation.

"I was called up on the long-distance telephone in January or February following the disappearance of Miss Arnold by a lawyer of Pittsburgh," he said. "This lawyer told me he had been assured by a woman client who had come to him that she had seen Miss Arnold and that the woman had identified herself as Dorothy Arnold.

"I accordingly went to Pittsburgh without the knowledge of Mr. Arnold and, hiring two detectives, I went to the sanitarium in question. I stationed them outside the building and, going in, de ...

... ceived from other sources. I believe the house was one of the main institutions of its kind in this district."

regarded in New York. collection of 124 paintin ...

RECEPTION FOR HUMPHREYS.

Head of Stevens Institute Holds Levee in Art Gallery.

About 400 persons attended the reception in honor of Dr. Alexander C. Humphreys, president of the Stevens Institute of Technology, last night in the art galleries of the Carnegie Institute. In the receiving line were Mr. and Mrs. Taylor Allderdice, Director and Mrs. John W. Beatty, Dr. and Mrs. Humphreys and Dr. and Mrs. Arthur A. Hamerschlag. Among the notable out-of-town people present were the eight members of the international art jury, William M. Chase, Robert Henri, W. Elmer Schofield, W. L. Lathrop and Cecelia Beaux, all of New York; Daniel Garber of Lumberville, Pa.; Julius Olsson of Cornwall, England, and H. Caro-son of Delvaille of Paris, France. Paul Dougherty of New York, the marine landscape painter, who has a special exhibition of 30 paintings to open at the same time as the international exhibit, was also present. Of the fine arts committee those in evidence comprised Director Beatty and Mr. Alderdice, Martin Leisser and A. Bryan Wall. W. N. Frew of the committee is ill at his home and William McConway, another member, is not in the city at present. Judge John B. Shafer, vice president of the institute board of trustees, was in the throng. Secretary Samuel Harden Church of the board was likewise present.

Among the guests were Herbert DuPuy.

As, ag ...
or for a ...
worry ...
pany co ...
Mortg ...
tured ...
tates, ...
cures ...

THE
Capital,

A SIMPLE WAY TO REMOVE DANDRUFF

DOROTHY ARNOLD MYSTERY SOLVED, SAYS CAPT. AYERS

Announces in Lecture That Girl Is No Longer Listed by Police as Missing.

CONTRADICTED BY LAWYER

Family Still in Ignorance of Fate of Daughter, He Declares.

PARTICULARS ARE WITHHELD

Police Official Refuses to Say Whether the Girl Is Dead or Alive.

The fate of Dorothy Arnold, whose disappearance on Dec. 12, 1910, provided one of the greatest mysteries of the last decade, has been known to the Police Department for many months, according to a statement made last night by Police Captain John H. Ayers, head of the Bureau of Missing Persons, in a lecture on the Police Department at the High School of Commerce, in West Sixty-fifth Street.

Captain Ayers refused to tell whether Miss Arnold was alive or dead, saying that this was a confidential matter of the Police Department. "All I can say is that it has been solved by the department," he said in reply to questions from the audience. "Dorothy Arnold is no longer listed as a missing person."

Emphatic denial of Captain Ayers's statement was made by John S. Keith, attorney for Francis R. Arnold, Dorothy Arnold's father, at his home in the Hotel Commodore. Mr. Keith declared that Captain Ayers's statement that the case had been solved was a "damned lie," and said the mystery of the girl's disappearance was as great as it had been the day she disappeared.

Mr. Keith declared that he would write a letter of complaint to Police Commissioner Enright and ask him to take suitable action against Captain Ayers.

Captain Ayers's reference to the status of the case after he had been told of the Police Department and invited questions. "Line" on the murder had been obtained in the Elwell case. Captain Ayers replied that this was a mystery even greater than before. Charles S. Whitman for investigation and it would not be proper for him to discuss it.

Statement of Captain Ayers.

"In my statements about missing girls," continued Captain Ayers, "I wonder how many of you have ever heard of the case of Dorothy Arnold. I recall that some time ago the search for her ceased apparently? Her relatives and friends, who had been led to follow in all directions clues, multitudes of letters, suddenly ceased their activity."

A man seated on the platform asked if it was an intricate case. "All I can say is that it has been solved by the department," Captain Ayers replied. "Dorothy Arnold..."

DOROTHY ARNOLD MYSTERY SOLVED

Continued from Page 1, Column 5.

lice had done good work in clearing up the case.

Controversy Deepens Mystery.

The direct conflict in the statements of the official at the head of the Bureau of Missing Persons and the lawyer representing the missing girl's family had the effect of making the case more of a mystery than ever.

Many clues have been run down by the police and private investigators, and thousands of dollars have been spent since Dorothy Arnold left her home at 108 East Seventy-ninth Street, a little before noon on Dec. 12, 1910, after telling her mother that she intended to buy an evening gown. So far as ever became known, Miss Arnold's home life at that time was happy. Since her graduation from Bryn Mawr College, she had been socially active in New York. She had written two stories for a magazine, but did not seem to have been disheartened by their rejection. By the statements of her father, her mother, her brothers, John and Hinckley Arnold, and her younger sister, Miss Martha Arnold, there was no known reason for her disappearance.

When she left her home, Miss Arnold, according to the police description later sent broadcast, wore a blue tailor-made suit, a long blue coat, a small black velvet hat, with a hat pin of lapis lazuli with earrings to match. She carried a black fox muff with white points. The day was mild for the season and she wore no other furs.

Only twice after she left her home was a trace of Miss Arnold found by investigators. She purchased a box of candy at the Fifty-ninth Street store of Park and Tilford and later bought a book, entitled "An Engaged Girl's Sketches," at Brentano's. At both places, so far as the salesmen could...

DOROTHY ARNOLD

The mystery of whose disappearance, Dec... to have been solved...

DOROTHY ARNOLD MISSING 40 YEARS

Disappearance, Still a Police Case, as Much a Mystery as When It Occurred

Dorothy Arnold disappeared forty years ago yesterday. Each year on this date the few known facts about one of New York's greatest mysteries are brought out at police headquarters and there is general agreement among police officials that the case is in a class by itself.

The 25-year-old and attractive daughter of a wealthy importer waved to a friend...

...the police confronted with anything like so strange a case.

Miss Arnold, who lived with her family at 108 West Seventy-ninth Street, was not the type of person that would disappear without trace, yet disappear she did. She would be about 65 today if she were alive—and there is no legal proof that she is not alive.

Acting Capt. John Cronin, in charge of the Missing Persons Bureau, said that since the police had no proof of her death or that she had gone away of her own free will, the case was listed as open.

Today, there is nobody at police headquarters who was there when Dorothy Arnold disappeared. Captain Cronin was 9 years old at that time.

THE FOUNDING OF THE NYPD'S MISSING PERSONS SQUAD

In February 1917, barely six years after Arnold disappeared, eighteen-year-old Ruth Cruger went missing after bringing her ice skates to be sharpened at a local motorcycle shop in Upper Manhattan.

Owner Alfredo Cocchi admitted seeing Cruger, but said he didn't know where she went after leaving his shop. After some police officers vouched for him, the NYPD let the case drop, concluding that Cruger had gone off of her own accord.

But her disappearance fueled fears that girls in cities nationwide were being forced into "white slavery," or prostitution.

Cruger's father hired lawyer/investigator Grace Humiston, who convinced the police commissioner to have Cocchi's shop searched again that June. Cruger's body was subsequently found buried under the floor.

The ensuing investigation revealed a corrupt arrangement in which officers sent traffic violators directly to Cocchi's shop instead of court, pocketing the fines.

Cocchi, who had fled to Italy soon after Cruger disappeared, later confessed to her murder; Italian courts sentenced him to twenty-seven years in jail.

The badly mishandled case led the NYPD to create the Bureau of Missing Persons, now the Missing Persons Squad.

UNSOLVED OR CASE CLOSED?

IN 1921, NYPD CAPTAIN JOHN H. AYERS MADE A SPEECH TO THE STUDENT BODY OF THE High School of Commerce in which he claimed that police had known the real truth about Arnold's fate for many months, and that "Dorothy Arnold is no longer a missing person." Speaking for the Arnold family, John Keith fiercely denied Ayers's statement, calling it a "damned lie." Ayers later denied that he had ever made the claim.

After Mary Arnold's death in 1928 (Francis Arnold had predeceased her), their family friend and lawyer John Keith, who was involved in the case from the beginning, went public for the first time with his own theory of Dorothy's disappearance. He believed that the young woman, distraught over the rejection of her stories, had taken her own life.

According to Churchill's *American Heritage* account, even in 1935, twenty-five years after her disappearance, police said tips were still coming in about Dorothy Arnold. Close to the fortieth anniversary in December 1950, a report in the *New York Times* noted that "Each year on this date the few known facts about one of New York's greatest mysteries are brought out at police headquarters, and there is general agreement among police officials that the case is in a class by itself."

LASTING IMPACT

THE STRANGE AND TRAGIC CASE OF DOROTHY Arnold, still one of the most sensational missing persons cases in New York City history, may have had one lasting positive consequence. According to reports, a young Englishwoman named Agatha Christie became intensely interested in Arnold's disappearance, and followed it closely in the press. Just twenty years old, Christie seemed to empathize with the socialite and aspiring writer, and Arnold's mysterious vanishing act is said to have inspired Christie to begin writing her now-classic mystery novels.

The link between Dorothy Arnold and Agatha Christie seemed to get even stranger in December 1926, when Christie herself vanished under strange circumstances. After packing an attaché case with clothing, she walked out of her opulent country home in Berkshire, England, on a stormy night, got into a two-seater sports car, and drove away. The next morning, police found the car abandoned.

A massive search ensued, including as many as fifteen thousand volunteers, and people came up with multiple theories ranging from suicide to kidnapping to murder at the hands of someone she had fictionalized as a villain in one of her novels. The scandal ended in undramatic fashion, after a fellow guest recognized Christie at a luxury spa in Yorkshire. ■

MRS. CHRISTIE FOUND AT HARROGATE

Dramatic Re-union With Husband in Famous Hydro.

"HER MEMORY GONE"

How Missing Novelist Spent Time While Police and Public Looked for Her

Mrs. Christie, the missing inventor of detective stories, was traced last night to the Hydro, Harrogate, by her husband, Colonel Christie.

In an interview after a dramatic meeting between the pair, Colonel Christie told the DAILY HERALD that his wife had suffered from the " most complete loss of memory." She did not even recognise him, he added.

"She does not know why she is here."
—Col. Christie

Mrs. Christie

Col. Christie

Thai Silk Company Thrives as Founder Is Sought

By PETER BRAESTRUP
Special to The New York Times

BANGKOK, Thailand, April 29—While the search continues in Malaysia for James H. W. Thompson, missing wealthy American "father of the Thai silk industry," his saddened business associates have reported business as usual.

"Once everything was carried in Mr. Thompson's h...

The company's directors, who include both Thais and Americans, are scheduled to hold their annual general meeting next month.

It is almost certain, Sheffield said, that they will vote to defer any decisions for two months, pending the conclusion ...search for the ... er.

...rted Better

...doctors, tele-...rs flood the ...rognostications ...s fate, work ...Thompson's silk ...Sheffield re-...s in the local ...better than ...on. "It may ...riosity, in-...ade or our ...e no way of ago.

...S. lk's Mail
...O countries ...States, nor ...des shades of ...ffected by ...npearance, ...some of ...hat Mr. ...74 years at ...well; a va...turquoise ...ings, has homes.
...ands of ...the com-...f 4,000 ...weights, ...s new ...to be ...ices, ...y of ...Thai ...local

field, according to local bankers. It produces half a million yards of silk a year, employs 3,000 workers, and stresses quality control. Thai Silk has shares in two other companies, Thaibok of Hong Kong.

Mr. Thompson believed in profit-sharing with his weavers, who own much of the company stock.

It is a measure of Mr. Thompson's success, industry sources said, that his disappearance is unlikely to affect Thailand's $12-million-a-year silk sales. Indeed, as his own admirers here are quick to point out, Mr. Thompson's contribution was to revive and organize the Thai silk industry and introduce it to the Western world. That happened 16 years ago.

Attended Schools in East

Jim Thompson was born in Greenville, Del., on March 21, 1906. He attended Eastern schools—St. Paul's School, Concord, N. H., and Princeton, Class of 1928. A man who inherited wealth, he subsequently earned a degree in architecture at the University of P... and practiced in ...York, mostly designing priv...

He went into the Army before the United State... entered World War II and w... a commission in Officers' Ca... didate School. He later serve... in the Office of Strategic Ser... first in the Mediterranea... theater, then in Southeast Asia... When the Pacific war ended in August 1945, he was ... my

Ceylon planning a parachute operation into Japanese-occupied Thailand to join the free Thai forces. His associates here said he got to Thailand after the war ended.

He served as an attaché, according to reports in intelligence work, to the United States diplomatic mission in Bangkok before regular diplomatic relations were established with Thailand, a wartime ally of Japan.

Joined Diplomatic Mission

Traveling widely, he saw traditional Thai silk being woven in the up-country villages—an art that had virtually ceased to exist in Bangkok. At that time no organized Thai silk industry existed, there were no brilliant colors, exports, and quality control. Mr. Thompson, an art buff, began selling the silk for Thai weavers in his room at the Oriental Hotel, which he and others sought to enlarge and remodel after the war. The big break came when he sent a friend to the United States with a suitcase full of Thai silk for Mrs. Edna Woolman Che...

CLUES ARE SOUGHT ON LOST AMERICAN

Friends Believe Thompson Was Abducted in Malaysia

Special to The New York Times

BANGKOK, Thailand—Friends and business associates of John W. Thompson are piecing together evidence to suggest that he is not lost in the Malaysian jungle but has been abducted.

Mr. Thompson, a 61-year-old American who lived here and who made a fortune selling Thai silk, was last seen on the afternoon of Sunday, March 26, at a bungalow in the Cameron Highlands of Malaysia, a resort area.

An intensive search—involving the Malaysian police, units of the British Army, close friends including Brig... Ed... F. Blac... of the United ...es Arm... a... h...reds of ...n... teer...ha... fa...ed to f... r. Th... R... s office... or info... a...t him... al $12,...0.

Th... p...e h...e work... the... t... e Ameri...n b... nes... an... rem... a... lk got lost. Those who favor the abduction theory believe that Mr. Thompson was seized by someone whom he had arranged to meet, or by that person's agents. They offer these points in support of that theory:

¶Mr. Thompson was a chain smoker. Yet he supposedly went for a walk leaving his cigarettes

THE HEADLINES

Jim Thomson. Wikipedia Commons

JIM THOMPSON 1967

ON EASTER SUNDAY IN 1967, PROMINENT AMERICAN businessman Jim Thompson headed out for a walk while staying with friends at the northern Malaysian resort of Cameron Highlands. Despite an exhaustive search effort, he would never be seen or heard from again.

Thompson's wealth and fame—he was celebrated across Southeast Asia and beyond as the "Thai Silk King"—ensured that his disappearance would make headlines worldwide. So did his colorful past, as a former officer in the Office of Strategic Services (the precursor to the CIA) who was sent to Bangkok at the end of World War II and decided to stay on. Thompson tried out several business ventures before settling on handwoven Thai silk. By the mid-1950s, he had almost single-handedly turned production of the lustrous fabric from a dying cottage-based industry into a thriving export empire, with outposts worldwide.

After he mysteriously vanished into the Malaysian jungle, Thompson's legendary status only grew, along with the frenzied and enduring speculation about his fate.

IN OTHER NEWS

United Nations Secretary General U Thant made public proposals for peace in Vietnam.

Jimi Hendrix burned his guitar for the first time onstage in London.

After Muhammad Ali (who had recently changed his name from Cassius Clay) refused induction into the US Army, boxing organizations stripped him of his world heavyweight championship title.

The Soviet Union objected to a proposed United States treaty to halt the spread of nuclear weapons.

CHRONOLOGY

1906   James Harrison Wilson Thompson was born in Greenville, Delaware.

1928   Thompson graduated from Princeton University and entered architecture school at the University of Pennsylvania.

1930s He worked as a practicing architect in New York City.

1940   He volunteered for the US Army, and won a commission in Officers' Candidate School.

1942   Thompson married Pat Thraves, a former model; six months later, he was shipped overseas as part of an OSS group working with French forces

1945   Shortly after V-E Day, Thompson volunteered to go to the Pacific; he was named OSS station chief in Bangkok, and was on his way there when Japan surrendered.

1946   Thompson returned to the United States to receive his military discharge, and his wife informed him she wanted a divorce.

1948   Having decided to stay on in Bangkok, Thompson established Thai Silk

1951   Thai silk appears on Broadway in costumes for *The King and I*.

1959   He moved into the "Jim Thompson Thai House"; Thai silk was used for all principal costumes in the movie *Ben-Hur*.

1960s By the 1960s, the Thai Silk Company had representatives in thirty-five countries worldwide, and Thompson built a new Bangkok shop.

1962   The Thai government awarded Thompson the Order of the Royal Elephant in recognition of his service to the country and its people.

WHAT DID WE KNOW?

J AMES HARRISON WILSON THOMPSON'S FATHER WAS president of a textile company; he was named for his maternal grandfather, a US Civil War general. After prep school and Princeton, Thompson studied architecture at the University of Pennsylvania. In 1940, when World War II was escalating in Europe, he left his job as an architect in New York City to volunteer for the Army, and was assigned to the Office of Strategic Services (OSS).

Thompson became OSS station chief in Bangkok just as the war in the Pacific drew to a close. He decided to stay on in Thailand, banking on a postwar boom in Southeast Asian leisure tourism. Plans to reorganize and renovate the old Oriental Hotel fell through, and Thompson soon refocused on handwoven Thai silk, known for its striking, lustrous texture and contrasting colors. He would play a crucial role in reviving the silk industry, introducing modern dyes, better looms, and higher quality standards. He also allowed his weavers (many of them women) to share in the company's profits.

THE
EVIDENCE

Moonlight Cottage. Wikipedia Commons

THE MANHUNT

Some 325 policemen, including members of the Malaysian Field Force Police, took part in the search, along with British Army troops and several Royal Army Air Corps helicopters.

US Army Brig. Gen. Edwin F. Black, Thompson's good friend in Bangkok, and commander of US support forces in Thailand, flew in to assist in the search, along with other senior colleagues.

About thirty aborigines in the region, who knew the most about the trails and possible dangers, were enlisted as guides.

The official search for Thompson lasted ten days, involved more than four hundred people, and made headlines all around the world—but did not turn up a single clue about Thompson's fate.

IN MARCH 1967, THOMPSON AND HIS LONGTIME FRIEND Connie Mangskau were visiting Dr. and Mrs. T. G. Ling of Singapore in the Lings' summer bungalow, "Moonlight Cottage," in Cameron Highlands. On the afternoon of Sunday, March 26, the group returned to the bungalow after a picnic, and Mangskau and the Lings retired for a nap. Around 3:30 p.m., Dr. Ling heard footsteps crossing the stone terrace; he told his wife Thompson was probably heading out for a solitary stroll, as he liked to do.

Close to 4:00 p.m., a servant from a nearby cottage saw a man resembling Thompson admiring a rose garden along the road. If the woman's account of the timing was correct, she was the last known person to see Thompson. When he failed to return by nightfall, the Lings called the authorities. A search party spent the night combing the nearby jungle, but turned up nothing.

Over the next week, the search for Thompson morphed into the largest manhunt in the region's history, including Malaysian police, British Army units, and hundreds of volunteers. The Thai Silk Company offered a reward of 20,000 Malaysian dollars (about $7,000) for any information; the reward later grew to the equivalent of some $25,000.

Main house of Jim Thompson. Wikipedia Commons

COLLATERAL DAMAGE?

In a gruesome footnote to Thompson's vanishing, his eldest sister was found beaten to death at her home near Philadelphia just before Labor Day in 1967.

At age seventy-four, Katherine Thompson Wood was divorced, and lived alone. She had two unfriendly guard dogs, a German shepherd and a golden retriever, in the house with her at the time.

There were no signs of a break-in, and the sensational case would remain unsolved.

Though Wood's murder was never officially linked with her famous brother's disappearance, conspiracy theorists suggested the murderer was searching for some documents concerning Thompson, or that his kidnappers might have killed Wood to force him to do what they wanted.

I N LATE APRIL 1967, THE THAI SILK COMPANY PAID Richard Noone—a former British adviser to Malaysian aborigines, and the planning officer for the Southeast Asia Treaty Organization (SEATO) in Bangkok at the time—to go to Malaysia on their behalf. Noone spoke the local language, and had a special connection to the case: His brother had been lost in the same area in the late 1940s, and Noone had gone into the jungle and found his grave. After two days in the Highlands jungle, speaking with the natives, Noone said he was "fully convinced" that Thompson was not lost in the jungle.

Around the same time, Peter Hurkos, a psychic famous from working on the Boston Strangler case, "saw" that Thompson had been drugged and abducted by a group of men and flown to the Cambodian jungle. Hurkos said a man Thompson knew named "Bebe," or "Preebie," who was probably Thai, had aided in the abduction. (This raised some eyebrows, as one of Thompson's old political friends was Pridi Phanomyong, the exiled former prime minister of Thailand.) Cambodia had no diplomatic relations with the United States or Thailand at the time, however, and investigating Hurkos's theory was a nonstarter.

DEVELOPING STORY

TOP THEORIES

1 Thompson got lost and/or had an accident and died in the jungle.

The possibilities of having an accident in such difficult jungle terrain were endless, but critics of this theory had many reasons to reject it. Most importantly, it seemed unlikely that either Thompson, or his lifeless body, could still be in the jungle and remain undiscovered by either the massive search effort or the local aborigines.

2 Thompson was kidnapped for ransom purposes.

Early on, the Malaysian police announced that they suspected kidnapping, probably by one of the well-organized gangs in the region that often preyed on wealthy Chinese vacationers. But no one ever came forward with a ransom demand or any valid evidence about his whereabouts.

3 Thompson was a victim of a politically motivated kidnapping/murder.

Hurkos's Cambodia theory opened the floodgates to all sorts of sinister suggestions about the possible political motives behind Thompson's disappearance. Many such theories remained pretty vague, and none were backed up with solid evidence. Most agreed that Thompson's fate had something to do with his work with the OSS (or possibly even in the CIA), his association with former prime minister Pridi Phanomyong, or his sympathy for dissident nationalists from Vietnam or Laos.

FRINGE THEORIES

Thompson disappeared on purpose: One tipster claimed that Thompson was living undercover in Malaysia. This turned out to be a hoax, but the idea that the former spy may have vanished of his own accord and gone off to start a new life somewhere has endured.

Thompson was mauled to death by a wild animal: Tales of tigers were common in the region, along with leopards and wild boars. But the fact that no blood or remains were found tends to detract from this theory, though one inventive man suggested that perhaps Thompson had been swallowed whole by a python.

Thompson was killed (or seduced) by an aborigine: One Malaysian businessman earnestly suggested that an amorous aboriginal tribeswoman had abducted the Thai Silk King, after which he fell under her spell. According to other theories, an aborigine hunter shot Thompson with a dart, or he stumbled into one of the pits the tribesmen used to trap animals.

FIFTY YEARS AFTER HE VANISHED, THE FATE OF THE Thai Silk King remains unknown, although the legend has only continued to grow. Two recent books about Thompson have delved more deeply than ever into the mystery.

In his book *The Ideal Man: The Tragedy of Jim Thompson and the American Way of War* (2010), Joshua Kurlantzick suggested that local business rivals might have had the motive and means to abduct Thompson, and could have bribed the local police not to investigate extensively.

William Warren became friends with Thompson in Thailand in the 1960s and has reported on his disappearance from the beginning. Near the end of his most recent book, *Jim Thompson: The Unsolved Mystery* (1998), Warren evaluated the most prominent theories that have emerged over the years about Thompson's vanishing (including suicide, kidnapping for ransom or political purposes, and jungle accident). "They all share the considerable disadvantage of being unsupported by the smallest shred of evidence, even circumstantial, which might make one substantially more attractive than the others," Warren concluded. In this shadowy realm of doubt, the Jim Thompson legend lives on.

WAS IT SUICIDE?

Some have speculated that Thompson may have decided to go into the jungle and kill himself in such a way that his body couldn't be found.

Suicide theories focus on possible depression over his failing health (he had a serious gallbladder condition).

But his friends' impressions of Thompson's good spirits in the days before his disappearance went against this theory, as did a report from his doctor, claiming that Thompson was still extremely active and had his illness under control.

UNSOLVED OR CASE CLOSED?

JIM THOMPSON'S BANGKOK HOUSE—WHICH HE BUILT in 1959 from six different styles of traditional Thai houses—remains one of the city's top tourist attractions. Its distinctive red peaks rise amid lush greenery on the banks of the *khlong* (canal), across from where Bangkok silk weavers live and work. Inside, visitors can admire Thompson's vast collection of Southeast Asian art and antiques, much of which he rescued from junk shops.

If anything, Thompson's sensational disappearance, and the mystery that swirled around him, only increased the success of the company he founded. By the early twentieth century, the Thai Silk Company was doing some $80 million in business each year. Today, it is the world's biggest producer of handmade fabrics, operating in some thirty countries with more than three thousand employees. ■

LASTING IMPACT

HOME / NEWS / WORLD / ASIA

AP Associated Press

CIA past of Bangkok's American 'Silk King' emerges

FILE - In this undated file photo, Jim Thompson smiles shortly before he disappeared. Thompson mysteriously disappeared while going for a walk on Easter Sunday, March 26, 1967 in the Cameron Highlands of Malaysia. It's the cloak and dagger stuff, rather than the glitz and glamor, that's the focus of a recent book "The Ideal Man: The Tragedy of Jim Thompson and the American Way of War" by Joshua Kurlantzick, an author on Asian affairs with the New York-based Council on Foreign Relations. (AP Photo/File)

By Denis D. Gray
Associated Press / January 18, 2012

BANGKOK—Forty-five years after vanishing into a jungle without a trace, "Silk King" Jim Thompson remains a daily presence in Thailand: Shoppers crowd his elegant stores and the American expatriate's antique-rich residence is one of the capital's top tourist attractions.

Credited with the revival of a now booming silk industry, Thompson attained legendary status, enhanced by a bon vivant lifestyle at a time when Thailand was still truly exotic -- and by his mysterious death. But little has been known about Thompson's intensely political, darker side -- his freelance backing of Asia's insurgencies, clashes with Washington's Cold War warriors and his connections to the U.S. Central Intelligence Agency, which to this day reportedly refuses to release his complete file.

It's the cloak and dagger stuff, rather than the glitz and glamor, that's the focus of "The Ideal Man: The Tragedy of Jim Thompson and the American Way of War" by Joshua Kurlantzick, an author on Asian affairs with the New York-based Council on Foreign Relations.

The book provides no new clues about Thompson's vacation walk into a Malaysian jungle in 1967 from which he never returned. Numerous theories range from his having been eaten by a tiger to abduction by U.S. intelligence agents.

But Kurlantzick says he uncovered a trove of other information from the Federal Bureau of Investigation, departments of Defense and State and other U.S. government agencies through the Freedom of Information Act as well as unclassified material available, but mostly untapped, in the National Archives.

From this, emerges a portrait of Thompson as a U.S Army officer in the Office of Strategic Services, forerunner of the CIA, who stood ardently behind America's immediate post-World War II policy of championing democracy and ridding the world of colonialism. He believed Vietnam's Ho Chi Minh was a nationalist who should be supported, and almost worshipped Pridi Banomyong Thailand's

THAI SILK ON BROADWAY

By 1951, just three years after Thompson founded the Thai Silk Company, the lustrous fabric made its way to Broadway.

It was first used in the musical revue *Michael Todd's Peep Show*, which featured an original jazz composition by none other than His Majesty the King of Thailand.

Then, influential costume designer Irene Sharaff sparked a fashion and interior-design craze when she chose vibrant Thai silk for her Tony-winning costumes in *The King and I*.

The musical about Ann Leonowens, who worked as a governess for the future King Chulalongkorn (Rama V) when he was a child, became a movie in 1956, winning Sharaff an Academy Award for costumes and set design.

By the time the movie came out, silk had become Thailand's best-known export.

In 1951 Thai silk made its Broadway debut in the original production of *The King and I*, starring Yul Brynner and Gertrude Lawrence.
Wikimedia Commons

Silk print block and ceramic display at the Jim Thompson House Museum in Bangkok.
Wikimedia Commons

THE CASE OF SEAN FLYNN, 1970

A S THE HANDSOME SON OF THE DASHING Australian-born actor Errol Flynn, most famous for his swashbuckling heroics in 1938's *The Adventures of Robin Hood*, Sean Flynn seemed to have an inside track on his own Hollywood career. But after a brief foray into acting in the early 1960s, he went an entirely different way, following his passion for photojournalism into the danger zones of the Middle East and Southeast Asia.

In 1970, the twenty-eight-year-old Flynn was on assignment in Cambodia during the Vietnam War when he and fellow photojournalist Dana Stone learned of a checkpoint nearby that was guarded by the North Vietnamese communist soldiers known as the Vietcong. Breaking apart from a group of journalists headed for Saigon, the two men rode off on motorcycles in search of the checkpoint—and presumably a good picture or two. They were never seen or heard from again.

FAST FACTS

Born in May 1941, Sean Flynn was the son of actor Errol Flynn and his first wife, French actress Lili Damita.

In late 1942, Errol Flynn was charged with two counts of statutory rape and underwent a public trial; he was eventually acquitted, but he and Damita divorced that same year.

As a teenager, Sean Flynn appeared in an episode of his father's TV show, *The Errol Flynn Theatre* (1956).

In 1959, Errol Flynn died from a heart attack at the age of fifty.

Sean Flynn, who bore a striking resemblance to his father, appeared in the 1960 film *Where the Boys Are* and played the lead role in *The Son of Captain Blood*, a 1962 sequel to *Captain Blood* (1938), which made his father a star.

After a few other films, Sean ditched Hollywood in late 1964 and headed to Africa to work as a safari and big-game hunting guide.

WHAT DO WE KNOW?

SEAN FLYNN TRAVELED TO SOUTH VIETNAM AS A FREE-lance photographer in 1966. Over the next several years, he didn't hesitate to throw himself in harm's way to capture the conflict with his camera. Along with other daredevil photojournalists, he parachuted into combat zones with US troops and spent time embedded with Special Forces units fighting in the Vietnam War, all the while taking photographs for outlets like *Time* magazine, *Paris Match*, and United Press International.

In 1970, after the conflict in Vietnam spilled over into neighboring Cambodia, Flynn traveled to the country on assignment for *Time*. On April 6, Flynn and Dana Stone, a photographer then working for CBS News, were leaving Phnom Penh, the Cambodian capital, along with a group of fellow journalists on their way to a press conference in Saigon (now Ho Chi Minh City), organized by the government. After they got word of a checkpoint on nearby Highway 1 manned by Vietcong, Flynn and Stone broke off from the group and rode rented motorbikes toward the highway, rather than the large limos favored by the press corps.

Stephen Bell, then a reporter for ABC News and a future anchor of *Good Morning America*, took a photograph of the two men as they set out. "We headed back to Phnom Penh and no one ever saw them again," Bell told the *Independent* in 2010. "I think they were among the first to go missing. It had not reached the point where we knew quite how dangerous it was."

SEARCH EFFORTS

A FTER RIDING OFF TOWARD THE CHECKPOINT that day, Flynn and Stone vanished completely. Search efforts began almost immediately to determine the two journalists' fate, and Lili Damita, Flynn's mother, would spend huge sums of money over the years on efforts to find her son.

The most widely accepted theory holds that the Vietcong held the two men captive for a while before turning them over to the Khmer Rouge, the radical communist rebels fighting against the US-backed Cambodian government.

As Perry Deane Young, Flynn's friend and fellow Vietnam War correspondent, and author of *Two of the Missing: Remembering Sean Flynn and Dana Stone*, recounted in 2010, famed CBS anchorman Walter Cronkite led an international group of journalists in negotiations aimed at freeing their captured colleagues in Southeast Asia. The group's investigations concluded that Stone and Flynn were likely executed out of expediency, perhaps as long as six months after they were captured.

Cambodia's rice fields. Wikimedia Commons

2 More Newsmen Slain by Reds in Cambodia

By HENRY KAMM
Special to The New York Times

PNOMPENH, Cambodia, Oct 29—Two journalists were found dead on the side of a highway today, bringing to seven the total of newsmen known to have been killed while reporting on the war on Cambodia. The latest victims were Jesse Frank Frosch, chief of the Pnompenh bureau of United Press International, and Kyoichi Sawada, a Pulitzer Prize-winning photographer for U.P.I. They were evidently gunned down by Vietnamese or local Communist troops yesterday afternoon about 20 miles south of here.

The bodies of Mr. Frosch, who was 28 years old, and Mr. Sawada, 34, were found by Cambodian soldiers. The car in which they had been riding was riddled with bullet holes and had swerved off the road and crashed against a tree.

The bodies were lying in a paddy field many feet apart, the nearest more than 20 feet from the car. Both men had been shot repeatedly through the chest. No blood stains were found in the car.

The conclusion drawn was that Mr. Frosch and Mr. Sawada had been taken out into the rice paddy by the ambushers, after their fire had caused the car to crash, and had been shot at close range.

There is no chance that they could have been mistaken for soldiers because their car, a small sedan, was bright blue and both men were wearing brightly colored civilian clothing.

Others Killed in Same Area

The scene of the ambush, on Route 2 leading to Takeo and a few miles north of the village of Chambak, is only slightly to the east of the village of Tramkhmar, where last May 31 two American reporters for the Columbia Broadcasting System and an Indian cameraman were killed in a similar ambush.

The missing newsmen include three Americans: Dana Stone, a freelance cameraman working for the Columbia Broadcasting System; Sean Flynn, a photographer on assignment from Time magazine and a son of the late actor Errol Flynn, and Welles Hangen, correspondent for the National Broadcasting Company. Mr. Flynn and Mr. Stone were captured on April 6, Mr. Hangen on May 31.

Eight Japanese newsmen, including five employed by American television networks, and four Frenchmen, including two who worked for American news organizations, are also among those listed as missing and believed to be held by the enemy.

A number of other newsmen, including Mr. Sawada, were released by the Communist forces after having been captured. Among them were Richard Dudman of The St. Louis Post-Dispatch, Elizabeth Pond of The Christian Science Monitor, and Michael Morrow of Dispatch News Service, who were captured last May 7 and freed on June 15, and Robert Anson of Time magazine, who was captured Aug. 3 and released on Aug. 23.

PRIZE W...
picture...
wading a...
of the w...

Mr. Sawad...
were attemp...
safe for tra...
Mr. Sawad...
United Pres...
Indochina fo...
was regarde...
best, as we...
boldest, photo...
the Pulitzer...

UNSOLVED OR CASE CLOSED?

SEAN FLYNN WAS OFFICIALLY DECLARED DEAD IN 1984, more than a dozen years after his disappearance. His mother died ten years later.

In 1990, twenty years after Flynn and Stone's disappearance, the prominent British photographer Tim Page returned to Cambodia to search for their final resting place. Page, who covered the wars in Southeast Asia alongside Flynn, has a daredevil reputation of his own; he is said to be the inspiration for Dennis Hopper's character in *Apocalypse Now*. As chronicled in the 1991 documentary *Danger on the Edge of Town*, his search for Flynn turned up some promising remains—but DNA testing later revealed they belonged to two other foreigners who disappeared around the same time.

Then in 2010, two amateur archaeologists made headlines when they uncovered a gravesite in Cambodia's eastern Kampong Cham province that they believed was Flynn's. Again, however, forensic analysis showed the remains did not match DNA on file from the Flynn family. To date, neither Flynn's nor Stone's remains have been found. ∎

LASTING IMPACT

At the time Flynn and Stone vanished, not much was known about the Khmer Rouge, but their brutality would later be revealed.

In 1975, after five years of civil war, the Khmer Rouge successfully attacked Phnom Penh and established a national government under the rebels' military leader, Pol Pot.

Over the next four years, the regime would be responsible for the murder of some 1.7 million Cambodians.

The images Sean Flynn, Dana Stone, and their fellow photojournalists captured helped inform the American public as to what was going on in Southeast Asia and stoke the fires of protest against US military involvement there.

But many of them paid the ultimate price: At least thirty-seven journalists were killed or went missing in Cambodia during the 1970–75 war, many of them vanishing along the same stretch of highway where Flynn and Stone disappeared.

PART IV

FRANKLIN

THE EXPLORERS

SIR JOHN FRANKLIN AND PERCY FAWCETT

Statue of Sir John Franklin on Waterloo Place, London. Wikipedia Commons

THE HEADLINES

Sir John Franklin—Last News from Him.
From The Journal of Commerce.

The last tidings had of this distinguished navigator were contained in his letters written on the 9th and 12th of July, 1845, in Baffin's Bay, off the west coast of Greenland. In one of them, addressed to a Col. Sabine, he says, "I hope my dear wife and daughter will not be over-anxious, if we should not return by the time fixed upon; and I must beg of you to give them the benefit of your advice and experience when that arrives, for you know well, that even after the second winter, without success in our object, we should wish to try some other channel, if the state of our provisions and the health of the crews justify it." He must then have crossed that wide Bay (Baffin's) and entered Barrow's Strait on the north coast of the continent, and proceeded through it to Beechy Island, on the north side of the Strait; for here the traces recently met with, of the missing expedition were found.

None of the expeditions have proceeded far beyond this locality. Capt. Parry navigated a few miles to the West of it; the Grinnell expedition a few miles to the North. Capt. Ross, during one whole season, was able to advance only two or three miles from the spot near it, at which he had wintered. Sir John Franklin must have proceeded either in a direction towards the Pole, up Wellington Straits, (our expedition took this route) or westward in the direction taken by Capt. Parry. The most remarkable season, for its openness, ever known in the Polar seas, was the one in which Capt. Parry proceeded a short distance west of Beechy Island. It may be that Sir John Franklin found one still more favorable for progress, and proceeded beyond any of those localities. It will be recollected that the *Advance* and *Rescue* were frozen in on the 19th September, and were not liberated until the 10th of August, dates which show the length of the Winter. The Summer is consequently but little over a month in duration, and it constitutes the limit with which vessels propelled by wind can do anything for discoveries in those seas. As he supposed that the Northern ice-cap, or the Polar ice, was the great barrier surrounding the Pole, Capt. Penny, (referring to Sir John Franklin's letters) says that he found an open sea, and believed to that sea, which he would reach by sledges or other means, any navigator would be carried; and believe that such an expedition would reach the north wind; and concur in the opinion that... always present the history of exploration reached those open waters, or was caught in the intermediate ice, is matter for conjecture. It is improbable that it ever returned to Barrow Straits or Baffin's Bay, as no traces of it were ever found. The course of the pack ice is Eastward and Southward, through those channels, toward the Atlantic. The *Advance* and the *Rescue*, soon after reaching the seat of Arctic discovery, remained locked in it for ten months, and were carried 1,070 miles toward the Ocean. They were unable to recover their position in time for the second summer. It is very evident that a steam vessel, or propeller, is the only one capable of doing effective service in those regions. The English talk of sending one, accompanied by two sailing vessels to supply her with coal, and it is the opinion of some of those connected with the *Advance* and *Rescue* that the plan is feasible

Sir John Franklin. Wellcome Library, London

Francis Crozier, Franklin's second-in-command on the ill-fated voyage. Wikimedia Commons

SIR JOHN FRANKLIN 1845

IN 1845, SIR JOHN FRANKLIN SET OUT WITH TWO SHIPS and a crew of some 128 men on an expedition to find the Northwest Passage, the sea route linking the Atlantic and Pacific Oceans through the frozen Arctic. At the age of fifty-nine, Franklin was a Royal Navy officer whose three previous expeditions had made him one of the most celebrated Arctic explorers of the nineteenth century.

After two years went by without a word from Franklin or any of the expedition's members, the British Admiralty (with help from Franklin's wife, Lady Jane Franklin) sent out the first search parties. Thus began the greatest rescue operation—and one of the greatest mysteries—in the history of exploration. More than thirty land- and sea-based expeditions would comb the Canadian Arctic over the next two decades, charting vast swaths of territory and mapping the route of the Northwest Passage Franklin had been searching for.

Sir John Franklin's ships were sailed by experienced crews, equipped with the latest technology, and loaded with years' worth of provisions, yet the expedition stands as the worst disaster in the history of British polar exploration. What led to its tragic end?

WHAT DID WE KNOW?

CHRONOLOGY

April 16, 1786	Sir John Franklin was born in Spilsby, Lincolnshire.
1801–03	Franklin accompanied Matthew Flinders on an exploratory voyage to Australia.
1805	He served in the Battle of Trafalgar.
1815	He served in the Battle of New Orleans.
1818	Franklin commanded the HMS *Trent* on an Arctic expedition led by Captain David Buchan.
1819–22	He led his second Arctic expedition.
1823	Franklin published *Narrative of a Journey to the Shores of the Polar Sea, in the Years 1819, '20, '21, and '22.*
1825–27	He led his third Arctic expedition.
1828	Franklin married his second wife, Jane Griffin; published *Narrative of a Second Expedition to the Shores of the Polar Sea, in the Years 1825, 1826, and 1827.*
1829	He was knighted by England's King George IV and received the first gold medal bestowed by France's Geographical Society.
1836–43	He served as governor of Van Diemen's Land (now Tasmania).
May 1845	Franklin sailed from England with two ships, *Erebus* and *Terror*, and 128 men in search of the Northwest Passage.

John Wilson Carmichael, *HMS* **Erebus** *and* **Terror** *in the Arctic* **(oil on canvas), 1847.** National Maritime Museum, Greenwich, London

JOHN FRANKLIN JOINED THE ROYAL NAVY AT THE TENDER AGE OF FOURTEEN, AND JUST three years later went along on an exploratory voyage to Australia. He served Britain in the Battle of Trafalgar (the Napoleonic Wars) and the Battle of New Orleans (the War of 1812), but would become best known for his travels to the Arctic, which began in 1818. His second such expedition, from 1819 to 1822, was an overland voyage from the western shore of the Hudson Bay, during which his party ran out of food and struggled to survive. Franklin's next expedition, to the same region, was far more successful: It mapped some 1,200 miles of coastline and collected a wealth of information on geology, weather, and plant life.

By 1845, sufficient progress had been made in exploring the Arctic coastline that people were optimistic about the chances of finally locating the elusive Northwest Passage. Franklin wasn't the first choice to head the 1845 expedition, as he was nearly sixty years old and had been retired from Arctic exploration for some two decades. But the British Admiralty ended up giving him the job. On May 19, 1845, amid much fanfare, the HMS *Erebus* and HMS *Terror* set sail from Kent, England, with Franklin and 128 other officers and crew.

Poster offering reward from the British Admiralty to help find Sir John Franklin's expedition.
Wikimedia Commons

£20,000 REWARD

WILL BE GIVEN BY

Her Majesty's Government

TO ANY PARTY OR PARTIES, OF ANY COUNTRY, WHO SHALL RENDER EFFICIENT ASSISTANCE TO THE CREWS OF THE

DISCOVERY SHIPS

UNDER THE COMMAND OF

SIR JOHN FRANKLIN,

1.—To any Party or Parties who, in the judgment of the Board of Admiralty, shall discover and effectually relieve the Crews of Her Majesty's Ships "Erebus" and "Terror," the

£20,000.

OR

2.—To any Party or Parties who, in the judgment of the Board of Admiralty, shall discover and effectually relieve any of the Crews of Her Majesty's Ships "Erebus" and "Terror," or shall convey such intelligence as shall lead to the relief of such Crews or any of them, the Sum of

£10,000.

OR

3.—To any Party or Parties who, in the judgment of the Board of Admiralty, shall by virtue of his or their efforts first succeed in ascertaining their fate,

£10,000.

W. A. B. HAMILTON,

Admiralty, March 8th, 1850.   Secretary of the Admiralty.

SIR JOHN FRANKLIN'S EXPEDITION.

[From the *Cornwall Chronicle*, Van Diemen's Land, March 9.]

Sir J. Ross, Sir J. Richardson, and Mr. Kerr, master of the whaler *Chieftain*, have just arrived in London from the Arctic seas. Sir J. Ross and Sir J. Richardson went out, the one by sea, the other overland, to endeavour to discover Sir John Franklin. Captain Kerr, it will be remembered, was the ship-master who met with the Esquimaux Indian, upon whose authority it is held that the Arctic navigators are still in existence. In the autumn of last year, Sir J. Ross penetrated a little to the westward of Leopold Island, when the ships were obliged to take up their winter quarters at Port Leopold (entrance of Prince Regent's Inlet.) In the spring of this year Sir James Ross with a party traversed the north coast of North Somerset, beyond Capes Rennel, Gifford, Bunny, and finding the land extend nearly due south, he followed it to that part of the western coast opposite Kerswell Bay ; the total distance traversed being about 500 miles.

Another detachment was sent down Prince Regent's Inlet, as far as the spot at which the provisions of the *Fury* were left ; they reached it, and found them in a perfect state of preservation. This party then crossed over to the opposite side to Port Bowen, and returned across the inlet to the ships. A third party went from the ships, across Barrow's Strait, but they found it at that time impenetrably blocked with ice.

Meeting with no vestige of any kind, and no flag-staff or marks, the probability is that Sir John Franklin's ships passed through towards Cape Walker, without any obstruction.

Sir James Ross having wintered at Leopold Island, and searched all around in every direction, next cut a canal of [...] half in length, with the inte[...] ing the search, and proceed[...] ward, to Melville Island ; [...] after getting out of this ca[...] got into a flue of ice, in w[...] frozen up, and were thus c[...] the field, at the rate of abou[...] through Lancaster Sound, [...] Pond's Bay, much after th[...] which Back's the ship the Te[...] Southampton Island in [...] however, the gale and the [...] up the ice, the ships, as soon as [...] leased, stood over to the other side. It was now too late in the season to return to Leopold Island, and Sir James, therefore, [...]

In 1848, Sir J. Richardson proceeded from Mackenzie, eastward to the Coppermine[...] forming depots of provisions at different part[...] of the coast. He describes an open sea t[...] the north, all the way as far as his vision ex[...] tended, until his arrival at the Dolphin a[...] Union Straits, which were blocked with ic[...] His companion Dr. Rae, was to proceed wi[...] a party of select men down the Coppermi[...] in this manner to penetrate as far north as [...] could, and endeavour to advance betwe[...] Woollaston, and Victoria Islands, where i[...] believed there is an opening, as the tide [...] eastward and westward through Dease's Str[...] and the Dolphin Straits. This route will [...] tersect the course which Franklin would [...] probably steer from Cape Walker, the [...] test distance to which point is 400 miles [...]

The latest news from the third exped[...] that by Behring's Straits, is to the tim[...] Majesty's ship *Herald*, Captain Hellet, C.B.[...] sailed from Oahu on the morning of the 19th[...] May last, loaded with provisions of all kinds [...] from a hired transport sent from Valparaiso.

None of the Esquimaux had been on board Sir James Ross's ships, and from the communication of Mr. Kerr, of the *Chieftain*, who had been examined by the Lords of the Admiralty, it would appear that there is a slight discrepancy between his statement and that of Captain Parker of the *Truelove*, inasmuch as the Esquimaux had told Captain Kerr, that they had been on board the ships; nor in the Esquimaux sketch was there any track from ship to ship, both of which were inferences, the one from the Esquimaux having said they were all well, the other from there being a line on the sketch which might be meant for the bowsprit of one of the ships, or any other long article. [...] respect to Sir J. Franklin, it is sta[...]

THE EVIDENCE

Portrait of Lady Jane Franklin by Thomas Bock, 1838. Wikimedia Commons

LADY FRANKLIN'S ROLE IN THE SEARCH

In addition to a figure of international sympathy (e.g., the popular ballad "Lady Franklin's Lament"), Jane Franklin became an important figure in polar exploration in her own right, thanks to her relentless efforts to find her husband.

With the British government preoccupied by the Crimean War (1853–56), it was up to Lady Franklin to keep the search alive.

Between 1850 and 1857, she financed five search missions through contributions from others; later, she even bought her own ship.

According to one newspaper of the time period, "What the nation would not do, a woman did."

In 1857, long after the Admiralty and Crown had given up, Lady Franklin persuaded Captain Francis McClintock to command one final mission to find her husband.

ON JULY 26, 1845, THE CAPTAIN OF A BRITISH WHALING ship saw the *Erebus* and *Terror* in Baffin Bay, off the southwest coast of Greenland. Franklin's ships were waiting for ice to clear at the entrance to Lancaster Sound. It would be the last time he or any of the 128 other men on the expedition were seen alive.

After two years without a word from Franklin or his crew, the explorer's wife, Lady Jane Franklin, joined members of Parliament and the press in urging the British Admiralty to send out a search party. The Admiralty dispatched three rescue missions, but found no trace of Franklin, his men, or the two ships.

In 1850, after Lady Jane's appeals to the US government for assistance stalled in Congress, New York shipping tycoon Henry Grinnell financed the first American attempt to search for Franklin. Led by navy lieutenant Edwin De Haven, the two ships of the Grinnell Expedition coordinated with several British expeditions to identify the first real signs of Franklin's party: the remnants of a winter campsite on the shores of tiny Beechey Island, in the Barrow Strait. The searchers found three graves at the site belonging to crew members of the *Erebus* and *Terror*, but no documents or records of what happened to the rest of the expedition. By 1854, after several other unsuccessful search missions, the British Admiralty declared the two ships' officers and crew officially dead, with their wages to be paid to surviving relatives.

The note found in a rock cairn by Francis Leopold McClintock's Expedition on King William Island in 1859, detailing the fate of the Franklin Expedition. Wikimedia Commons

THE GRUESOME TRUTH

The expedition's survivors would have been weakened and starving. No evidence exists to suggest they made it to the outpost.

Inuit reports, as well as bones later discovered at various sites related to the expedition, suggest that some of the men resorted to cannibalism in their efforts to survive.

The revelations shocked and horrified Victorian-era Britain, but served to underscore the desperate situation in which the men found themselves.

IN 1859, FOLLOWING TIPS FROM LOCAL INUIT, MC-Clintock's mission found relics from Franklin's expedition, along with human remains, on King William Island in northern Canada. Inside a sealed tin stashed in a rock cairn on the island, the searchers discovered a piece of paper that remains the only written record of the Franklin expedition's fate.

A standard British Admiralty form, the document had notes in the margin, dated April 25, 1848. The scribbled notes told a sad story. After ice trapped the *Erebus* and *Terror* in Victoria Strait in September 1846, the crew had made their way across the ice to Point Victory on King William Island the following spring.

Lady Franklin's hopes of finding her husband alive were in vain, as it turned out: The note recorded Sir John Franklin's death on June 11, 1847. The following April, with the ships still stuck fast, Captain F. R. M. Crozier, Franklin's second-in-command, ordered them abandoned. Leaving behind the still-plentiful food stores on the ships, the surviving 105 officers and crew had decided to set out on foot for the nearest Hudson's Bay trading post, some one thousand miles away, along Back's Great Fish River (now Back River).

DEVELOPING STORY

TOP THEORIES

1 **Their deaths were caused by lead poisoning.**
In 1981, a landmark study led by Owen Beattie of the University of Alberta found that while pneumonia and tuberculosis probably killed the Franklin expedition's crew, severe lead poisoning—likely due to the poorly soldered cans in which their food was kept—played a role as well. The study found high lead levels in the remains buried on Beechey Island, and suggested that lead poisoning could also have sickened the surviving crew members to the point where they decided on the ill-fated plan of setting off along Back's Great Fish River. A variation on the above theory argued that the internal pipe system on the ships, not the cans, may have caused the lead poisoning that led to the sailors' illness, debilitation, and death.

2 **Their deaths weren't caused by lead poisoning; contributing factors could have included extreme cold, hunger, and malnutrition.**
In 2013, a team of chemists at the University of Western Ontario used updated technology to analyze bone samples from the Franklin crew members; although they confirmed a high level of lead in the bones, they concluded any lead poisoning would have begun prior to the expedition's departure, and wasn't caused by the cans. Another study, published in the *Polar Record* in 2014, found that the level of lead in the three men's bodies varied significantly, as did those in seven other skeletons of men from the expedition who died later. While these and other scientific studies argue against lead poisoning from the cans or pipes as the cause of the sailors' disorientation and death, they don't establish a definitive alternative theory. Instead, they point to extreme hunger, severe cold, and ailments such as scurvy (lack of vitamin C) as contributing factors to the expedition's grim fate.

Memorial to the Franklin Expedition at Greenwich Hospital, UK. Wikimedia Commons

FACTS ON LEAD POISONING

Humans have been exposed to lead for thousands of years in thousands of ways, from the pipes used to transport water in ancient Rome to the paint on the brushes of Renaissance artists like Michelangelo.

The all-important element wasn't really known to be toxic until the early nineteenth century—and even after that, we kept using it.

High levels of lead were common in Victorian times, when food and drinking water were often contaminated, and some medicines contained lead as well.

Lead poisoning causes abdominal pain, confusion, headache, and anemia; in more severe cases, it can cause seizures, coma, and even death.

The threat of lead poisoning is ongoing even today: In 2014–15, more than 100,000 residents of Flint, Michigan (including some 9,000 children under the age of six), were potentially exposed to high levels of lead in their drinking water.

ALTHOUGH THE NOTE FOUND ON KING WILLIAM Island confirmed Lady Franklin's fears that her husband died in the Arctic, she continued to send vessels in the hopes of recovering his written records from the journey. A final expedition set sail in June 1875, weeks before she died.

The spirit of Jane Franklin's search remains alive and well today. The Canadian government began looking for the lost ships of Franklin's 1845 expedition in earnest in 2008, as part of an effort to reassert the country's supremacy in the Arctic and to develop the region's natural resources. The searchers were aided in their work by global warming and the acceleration of melting polar ice, which made the Northwest Passage newly accessible. Images taken in the Victoria Strait, just off King William Island, showed the wreckage of a ship on the ocean floor, and in 2014 Prime Minister Stephen Harper confirmed that it was indeed the *Erebus*.

Then in September 2016, a team from the Arctic Research Foundation discovered the *Terror*—in pristine condition, with even its windows intact—resting in its watery grave just eighty feet below the surface. Intriguingly, the wrecks of both of Franklin's ships were found far south of where experts believed that ice had trapped them, raising the possibility that the stranded, desperate crew members might have reboarded at least one of them and attempted to sail their way to safety.

Lady Franklin Bay in Arctic Canada, named in honor of the explorer's wife's unflagging search for artifacts from the Franklin Expedition. This photo shows an American ship that was part of the International Polar Expedition (1881-1884) that established a meteorological station there as well as collected astronomical and and polar magnetic data. Library of Congress

DISAPPEARING ARCTIC ICE

According to scientists, over the last several decades the Arctic landscape has been changing at a record pace, as the average annual temperature rises at twice the rate of lower latitudes.

Although sea ice has actually been increasing in the Antarctic area, that growth has not been enough to offset the losses in the Arctic region.

A study conducted by the National Aeronautics and Space Administration (NASA) in 2015 concluded that since 1979 the planet has been losing sea ice at an average annual rate of 13,500 square miles—the equivalent of losing an area of ice larger than the state of Maryland each year.

UNSOLVED OR CASE CLOSED?

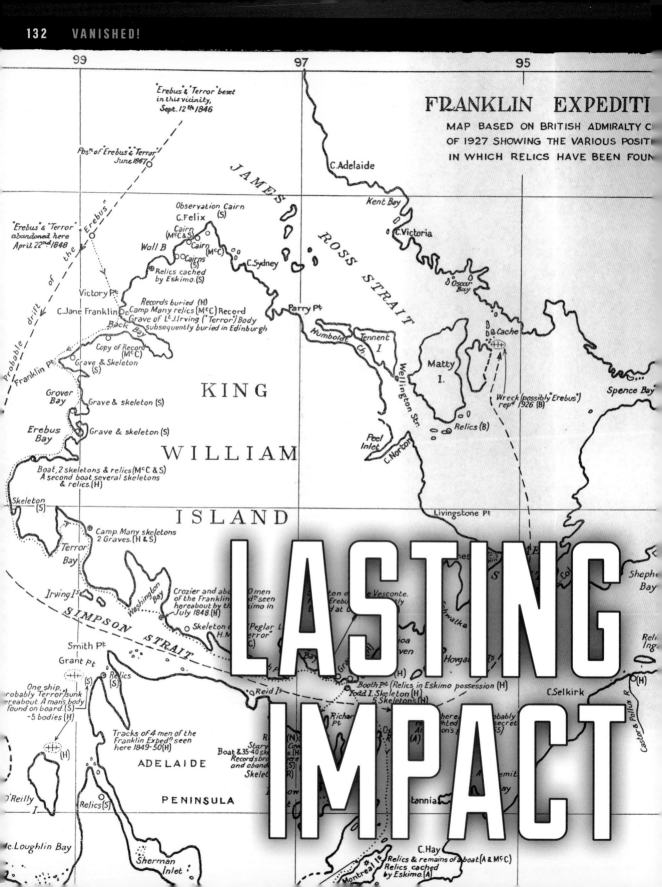

FRANKLIN EXPEDITI

MAP BASED ON BRITISH ADMIRALTY C
OF 1927 SHOWING THE VARIOUS POSITI
IN WHICH RELICS HAVE BEEN FOUN

LASTING
IMPACT

A British Admiralty chart from 1927 showing where various artifacts from the Franklin Expedition had been located. Wikimedia Commons

THE FRANKLIN EXPEDITION IN SONG

"Lady Franklin's Lament," a traditional folk ballad that first appeared around 1850, contained the verse "In Baffin's Bay where the whale fish blow/The fate of Franklin no man may know/The fate of Franklin no tongue can tell/Lord Franklin alone with his sailors do dwell."

In 1981, the Canadian folk musician Stan Rogers invoked Sir John Franklin and the lost expedition in his song "Northwest Passage," sometimes called the unofficial Canadian national anthem.

Singer-songwriter James Taylor's 1991 song "Frozen Man" was reportedly inspired at least in part by a photograph of the exhumed body of one of the Franklin expedition's sailors, buried on Beechey Island.

FRANKLIN'S DOOMED FINAL EXPEDITION, THOUGH tragic, wasn't a total loss. Many of the explorers sent to look for the vanished sailors ended up making their own discoveries, documentations, and other contributions. To name just a few: a record of flora and fauna in the Canadian Arctic; a survey of Greenland's west coast; and even the long-sought Northwest Passage, which Sir Robert McClure discovered on a Franklin search expedition financed by the British Navy in 1850. In addition, Lady Franklin's efforts to enlist American explorers in the search for her husband sparked greater US involvement in polar exploration, laying the groundwork for Robert Edwin Peary's historic North Pole expedition in 1908–09.

Sir John Franklin himself was celebrated as a hero, despite the failure of his final expedition and the gruesome reports of cannibalism among its sailors. The National Maritime Museum in London now houses all the artifacts from the 1845 expedition.

Along with the continuing search for the lost ships, the mystery surrounding the expedition's fate has fueled the creations of many artists over the years, beginning with playwright Wilkie Collins's *The Frozen Deep*, first performed in the 1850s. ■

THE HEADLINES

PERCY FAWCETT 1925

W HEN THE FIFTY-EIGHT-YEAR-OLD EXPLORER Percy Fawcett disappeared into the Brazilian jungle in 1925, many people assumed that he had found the object of his obsession—the mysterious City of Z—and decided to remain there. After all, Fawcett had made his name surveying land in South America in the early years of the twentieth century. He was known for spending years in the jungle, ingratiating himself with local tribesmen who had never before seen a white man.

Along the way, Fawcett became captivated by tales of El Dorado, the legendary lost city that had entranced treasure-seeking Europeans since the sixteenth century. Combining his love of exploration with his spiritual beliefs, Fawcett developed a theory about what he called the City of Z, a vast stone metropolis hidden in the heart of the jungle. His first attempt to find it, in 1921, failed miserably. But four years later, Fawcett set out again, accompanied by his twenty-one-year-old son, Jack, and Raleigh Rimell, Jack's school friend.

In late May 1925, from the depths of the Brazilian jungle, Fawcett would send the final dispatch of their journey. After that, they were never heard from again. Fawcett's disappearance made headlines in the United States and around the world, inspiring numerous rescue missions and efforts to determine his fate.

Percy Fawcett in 1911

IN OTHER NEWS IN MAY 1925:

A grand jury in Tennessee indicted science teacher John Scopes for violating the state's Butler Law, the first law in the United States to ban the teaching of evolution.

Virginia Woolf published *Mrs. Dalloway*.

Famed Norwegian polar explorer Roald Amundsen launched an expedition to fly over the North Pole.

Los Angeles police officers arrested three people for plotting to kidnap movie star Mary Pickford and hold her for ransom.

1915 map pf Bolivia showing the Percy Fawcett Expedition. Board of Regents of the University of Wisconsin System

WHAT DID WE KNOW?

CHRONOLOGY: LIFE OF AN EXPLORER

August 18, 1867	Colonel Percy Harrison Fawcett was born into an upper-class family in England.
1886	At the age of nineteen, Fawcett headed to the British colony of Ceylon (now Sri Lanka) to join the Royal Artillery (British Army). (In Ceylon, Fawcett would be introduced to Madame Blavatsky's Theosophy movement, the teachings of which also influenced Mohandas Gandhi, Thomas Edison, and Sir Arthur Conan Doyle.)
1900	Fawcett took his first training course at the Royal Geographic Society (RGS) in London.
1901	Fawcett married Nina Paterson, whom he had met in Ceylon; they would have two sons.
1906	The RGS invited Fawcett to survey the Brazil–Bolivia frontier.
1914	At nearly fifty years old, Fawcett volunteered for military service during World War I.
1916	The RGS awarded Fawcett its Founder's Medal.
1921	After years of preparation, Fawcett launched his first expedition to search for Z, which failed due to rain, illness, and other setbacks; a solo follow-up journey later that year also failed.

I N 1906, BRITAIN'S ROYAL GEOGRAPHICAL SOCIETY HANDPICKED FAWCETT TO SURVEY
part of the border between Brazil and Bolivia. He spent eighteen months in the Mato Grosso, a province in central Brazil on the edge of the Amazon basin. Once, confronted by a group of hostile native
tribesmen, Fawcett played music on a small accordion, and made friends with his would-be attackers.

In 1911, natives in Peru guided Hiram Bingham to a spectacular discovery: the lost Inca city of Machu
Picchu. News of this windfall, along with spectacular photographs published in *National Geographic*,
inspired Fawcett's own dreams of a lost jungle city. Sometime after 1913, he developed his theory
of Z (pronounced "Zed," in the British fashion), and wrote about it in his journals. Fawcett was a
follower of the Theosophy movement and its founder, Madame Blavatsky, who believed in a race of
enlightened "master" priests living in hidden cities around the world, including in South America. In
1920, in the National Library of Rio de Janeiro, Fawcett stumbled on a document called Manuscript
512: an eighteenth-century account by Portuguese explorers of a walled city deep in the jungle, and
pale-skinned natives paddling a canoe nearby.

FAWCETT'S SECRET ROUTE

Throughout his journey, Fawcett kept his route a secret in order to keep rival explorers from finding Z first.

In *Exploration Fawcett*, a collection of his writings first published in 1953 by his son, Brian, Fawcett wrote: "Our route will be from Dead Horse Camp, 11º 43' south and 54º 35' west, where my horse died in 1921."

But, as Fawcett's family confirmed years later, these were false coordinates, written in code to conceal the camp's true location.

The ruse worked on some later explorers who attempted to follow Fawcett's route, only to go significantly off course.

O N FEBRUARY 11, 1925, PERCY AND JACK FAWCETT and Raleigh Rimell set out from Rio de Janeiro, Brazil. Traveling via train and riverboat, they arrived in Cuiabá, Mato Grosso's capital, in early March. Armed with .30-caliber rifles and 18-inch machetes, they traveled with two native porters and guides. Along the way, Fawcett sent dispatches that native runners carried through the jungle; these were tapped out on telegraph machines and printed on every continent. To raise money for the expedition, news rights had been sold to papers around the world, including the North American Newspaper Alliance, a consortium of the *New York World*, *Houston Chronicle*, *Los Angeles Times*, and other publications.

In mid-May, they arrived at Bakairí Post, considered the region's "last point of civilization." Late that month, after nine days hacking through the jungle, they arrived at the site Fawcett called Dead Horse Camp (on his previous expedition to find Z, his horse had expired there).

At that point, the explorers were approaching the territory of warlike tribes such as the Suyás and Kayapós. But Fawcett remained confident in his eventual success. "It is obviously dangerous to penetrate large hordes of Indians traditionally hostile," he wrote in his final dispatch on May 29. "But I believe in my mission and in its purpose. The rest does not worry me, for I have seen a good deal of Indians and know what to do and what not to do." To his wife, Nina, he offered reassurance: "You need have no fear of any failure."

Rio de Janeiro, Brazil, at about the time of Fawcett's ill-fated quest to find the legendary City of Z. Library of Congress

THE EVIDENCE

DEVELOPING STORY

DENIES JUNGLE INDIANS MURDERED FAWCETT

Brazil Press Rejects Accusations of Leader of Search Party for Lost British Explorer.

Special Cable to THE NEW YORK TIMES.

RIO DE JANEIRO, Sept. 26.—
fact that an Indian has been
in the Brazilian jungle wear
white man's shirt is not proof
he committed murder, argues
the newspapers joining in t
tional editorial objection to
nouncement made by Com
George M. Dyott, who heade
pedition to find Colonel P.

ritish explorer, and
Colonel
an Ind
s are
hander
ians m
r, whos
unsol
ating
paper
azilia
out
ustom
se goin
osso
lowe
that
unexplo

COL. FAWCETT'S SILENCE.

NO NEWS FOR TWO YEARS.

More than two years have passed since news
was received of Colonel P. H. Fawcett, who set
out in the early part of 1925, in face of great
risks, on an expedition to the interior of Brazil.
Dr. J. G. Hogarth, in his presidential address
to the Royal Geographical Society at the Æolian
Hall yesterday, referred to the long silence which
had followed Colonel Fawcett's departure, and
said:

"We hold ourselves in readiness to help any
competent and well accredited volunteer party
which may propose to proceed on a reasonable
plan to the interior of Brazil in order to try for
news of Colonel Fawcett. Before his departure
Colonel Fawcett stated that he proposed to go
where none but he could hope to penetrate and
pass. He insisted that no uneasiness need be
if nothing was heard of his fortunes for two
whole years or even more. His line was to
strike north from Cuyaba, in the province of
Matto Grosso, to the head-waters of the Xingu,
and on reaching the seventh parallel of south
latitude to turn across more than one thousand
miles of unknown country to the Atlantic. Almost
from the start his expedition had to be hoped to live
solely on the country, although this is, in part, of
more or less desert character. Further on he
would have to make contact with the wildest of
Indian tribes out of reach of white races. Since
Colonel Fawcett more than two years ago left the
Bakairi post all has been dark. No mission or
search could attempt to follow him far beyond
that point, for if the party that he had could not
penetrate and push through, much less can anyone
else. The only thing to do will be to prospect
in various directions, just as far as is consistent
with reasonable prospects of safe return, and
gather from native such information of what is
beyond as may be procurable."

The president said he hoped this year would see
the founding of a private lecture hall for the use
of the society.

The following awards were made by the
society:

Founder's Medal to Major Kenneth Mason (formerly
of India) for his connection between the surveys of India
and Russian Turkistan through the surveys of the Pamirs
and organisation and conduct of the Shaksgam Expedition
of 1926.

Patron's Medal to Dr. Lauge Koch, of Copenhagen,
for his many years' exploration of Northern Greenland
in continuation of the work of Sir Charles Clos for his
contribution to the knowledge of Northern Greenland.

Victoria Medal ... paragraph,
Murchison Grant to Mr. John Mathieson for his survey
of Spitsbergen and special studies during his surveys
with the Ordnance Survey and his long service.

Back grant to Captain ... in the hydrographical
survey of the British ...

JUNGLE HOLDS COL. FAWCETT

Noted Explorer Is Found As Recluse In S. America

ESTABLISHES FARM

Engineer Tells of Meeting After Absence Since 1925

LIMA, Peru., Sept. 12.—
Roger Courteville, the Brazilian engineer, who claims to
have found Colonel P
Fawcett

HEADED EXPEDITION

COURTEVILLE was on an automobile expedition in the interests of
his government, which intends to
construct a highway that will make
possible a trip from the Pacific to
the Atlantic in 14 days.

Starting from Rio de Janeiro September 12, 1926, the engineers reached Lima August 10, and claims the
distinction of being the first man to
traverse by automobile the jungles of
Brazil and Bolivia. It was while
crossing Matto Grosso state last November. Courteville reported, that he
found Colonel Fawcett living with
his son and another white man on
a farm about 63 miles from Diaman-
tina, state of Matto Grosso, in the
geographical centre of South America.

When Colonel Fawcett arrived at
Cuyaba, capital of the state of the
same name, the engineer, related,
the explorer received £6,000 from the
state government to search for an
ancient, lost city, placed somewhere
in Matto-Grosso territory. The city
is said to have been founded
Indians, and alth
seen b

FASCINATED BY JUNGLE

Courteville's story is that Cole
Fawcett, unable to find the city,
son afflicted with malaria and
party experiencing trouble with
Indians, returned to the start
point of the expedition. There he
tablished himself as a "fazendeir
or farmer, in a region described as
veritable paradise land.

Courteville described Color
Fawcett as a man of dull spirit ar
a misanthrope. He said that th
explorer had become fascinated b
the sorcerous jungle, and wished
know nothing from the civilize
world and its people. He spends h
time fishing in the rivers and shoot
ing wild cattle, game and the mar
velously feathered tropical birds, an
appears to be enjoying his paradis
cal existence.

The Fawcett farm settlement
which was cultivated by the explor
er and his aids, Courteville said, i
not far from the River of Doubt, dis
covered by the late Theodore Ro
velt.

Noted British Explorer, Long Missing, Is Discovered Living in Jungle Paradise

LIMA, Peru, Sept. 11.—(By Associated Press) Roger Courteville, the
Brazilian engineer who claims to have
found Colonel P. H. Fawcett, noted
British explorer, has given further details of his meeting with Colonel Fawcett, who has not been heard from since
May, 1925. Courteville was on an automobile expedition in the interests of
his government, which proposes to construct a highway that will enable a

same name, the engineer related, th
explorer received $6,000 from the stat
government to search for an ancien
lost city, placed somewhere in Matt
Grosso territory. The city is said t
have been founded by white India
and although never seen by a whi
man, the legendary story of its exte
ence has often been told. It is su
posed to have great quantities of go
diamonds and other riches.

FAWCETT HAD WARNED HE MIGHT BE OUT OF contact for months in the jungle, so when his dispatches suddenly stopped, no one was too concerned. In September 1927, after more than two years without a word from the expedition, French engineer Roger Courteville claimed to have encountered Fawcett while traveling in Mato Grosso. According to him, the explorer was not being held hostage, but had decided to stay in his jungle paradise rather than return to reality. Nina Fawcett flatly refused to believe Courteville's claims, however, and others followed her lead.

In early 1928, the RGS launched the first official rescue mission, led by explorer George Miller Dyott and sponsored by the North American Newspaper Alliance. After choosing his team from some twenty thousand volunteer applicants, Dyott headed into the Amazon complete with a film crew and wireless radio, which he used to send regular reports that fed the media frenzy in the United States and around the world. After trekking for nearly a month north from Bakairí Post, Dyott's group beat a sudden, hasty retreat down the Xingu River. Dyott concluded that the "Fawcett expedition perished at the hand of hostile Indians," a gruesome fate his own group had only narrowly avoided.

Not everyone was convinced by this "official" explanation, and the search continued. In 1932, Swiss trapper Stefan Rattin reported meeting an English colonel held hostage in Mato Grosso by a native tribe. Though his description rang true to some close to Fawcett, Rattin and two companions disappeared that year after mounting a search party into hostile Indian territory. In April 1933, Fawcett's compass was found in Bakairí Post, which Nina took as a sign that her husband was still alive.

"KING OF THE WILD"

In 1933, English actor Albert de Winton, who had appeared in Hollywood B-movies like King of the Wild, launched his own search for Fawcett.

Vowing to find the British explorer dead or alive, Winton spent months in the jungle of Mato Grosso.

He emerged in 1934 and was photographed in tattered clothes, emaciated, before disappearing again into the Xingu region.

That September, an Indian runner brought a note out from the forest that said Winton had been captured by a tribe, and begged for help.

Years later, Brazilian officials learned that members of the Kamayura tribe had killed Winton in order to steal his rifle.

EXPLORER'S BODY REPORTED FOUND

Brazil Jungle Mystery

The remains of Colonel Percy Harrison Fawcett, the British explorer who vanished 25 years ago in the Brazilian jungle with his son John and an American friend, Mr. Raleigh Rimmel, were reported yesterday in Rio de Janeiro to have been found by Brazilian explorers (states Reuter).

The Brazilian official news agency stated that explorers of the Central Brazil Foundation had exhumed Fawcett's bones in the area between the Kuluene and Tanuiro rivers in the Rio Das Mortes region of the Matto Grosso. The region is inhabited by the Calapalo Indians.

The Central Brazil Foundation are a Governmental body charged with the development of the central region of Brazil.

The Brazilian explorers said, according to the official report, that both Fawcett's son John and his friend were thrown into the river, they had been killed by the Indians. Colonel Fawcett was buried by them, all the ritual due to an elder and chief whom they revered because of his age and his courage in the face of death.

The mystery of Colonel Fawcett has intrigued fellow explorers and scientists over many years. He was never convinced of his death, several expeditions went in search of the party. Although Colonel Fawcett was generally presumed to be dead, reports circulated for some years that he was living with an Indian tribe.

TOP THEORIES

1 **Fawcett was killed by hostile Indians.**

In 1951, Brazilian explorer Orlando Villas Boas announced that the Kalapalo Indians of the Xingu had confessed to killing Percy Fawcett, Jack Fawcett, and Raleigh Rimell. Boas even claimed to have found Colonel Fawcett's bones buried in the forest between the Kuluene and Tanguro Rivers. But Brian Fawcett, the explorer's surviving son, traveled to Brazil to visit the Kalapalos and examine the bones, concluding—as did the Royal Anthropological Institute in London—they were not his father's.

2 **Fawcett died after suffering some kind of accident or disease (or he starved to death).**

Fawcett and his fellow explorers faced all kinds of dangers in the Amazon jungle, from drowning to starvation to infection by some kind of parasite. Swarming mosquitoes, bloodsucking ticks, and other insects plagued the group, and could have caused them to contract malaria or some other illness. (By the time they reached Dead Horse Camp, Rimell was suffering from an infected insect bite on his foot, but had refused to let the others go on without him.) According to another variation on the accidental death theory, jaguars could have attacked and eaten the three men, leaving no evidence behind.

3 **Fawcett was attacked in the jungle by robbers and killed.**

A 2011 episode of the PBS documentary series *Secrets of the Dead* probed the mystery of Fawcett's fate, and presented a third theory. In the months surrounding Fawcett's expedition, there had been a revolution in the region. Reports had surfaced of rebel soldiers hiding out in the jungle who had harassed, robbed, or even murdered travelers. As Fawcett's party was widely known to be traveling with weapons and other valuable items, it might have been a tempting target for such an attack.

OCCULT THEORIES

Desperate for information about Fawcett's fate, his wife (and some of his friends) turned to psychics, soothsayers, and séances, looking for clues to his fate.

Encouraged by Fawcett's own longtime belief in mysticism, some spiritualists and occultists decided that he had used Z to disappear into an alternate reality or "invisible world" (to quote Fawcett's own essays, published in magazines such as *Occult Review*).

As David Grann described in *The Lost City of Z*, several religious cults formed in Brazil during the 1960s began worshiping Fawcett as a kind of god.

One of the cults, the Magical Nucleus, even attracted Fawcett's great-nephew, but disbanded in 1982, after its leader's prediction that the world would end that year failed to come to fruition.

As late as 2005, a Greek explorer announced plans for an expedition to find the Fawcett portal, billing the trek as an "Expedition of No Return in the Ethereal Place of the Unbelief."

AS EARLY AS 1936, MOST PEOPLE (INCLUDING RALEIGH Rimell's family) had come to the conclusion that all three explorers were dead. But Nina Fawcett continued to believe her husband and son might return, up until her own death in 1953. By that time, Brian Fawcett had published *Exploration Fawcett*, a collection of his father's logbooks, diaries, and other papers edited into a single volume. In 1955, Brian conducted his own widely publicized expedition to South America, but came back empty-handed.

In the decades that followed, Fawcett's story continued to draw explorers to the Amazon; by one estimate, as many as one hundred people have disappeared in the attempt to trace his route.

In 2005, David Grann, a staff writer for *The New Yorker*, launched his own quest to follow in Fawcett's footsteps, later chronicled in his book *The Lost City of Z* (2009). With the help of a guide, Grann ventured into the Amazon, stayed with some of the tribes Fawcett encountered, and collected their stories. From some Kalapalo Indians (members of the very tribe whom Villas Boas said confessed to killing Fawcett's party), he heard a tale passed down for generations, about the three Englishmen who arrived in their village. They had warned Fawcett about the dangers of the "fierce Indians" occupying the territory to the east, the Kalapalo said, but the explorer was determined to move in that direction. For the next five nights, the Kalapalo watched the smoke from the Fawcett expedition's campfire. Suddenly, on the sixth night, it disappeared, as if it had been snuffed out—a sign, they assumed, that the Suyás or another warlike tribe had killed Fawcett, Jack, and Rimell.

COUNTERPOINT

At least one respected expert in the field doesn't buy the heroic version of Fawcett portrayed in *The Lost City of Z*.

Just after the release of the movie version of Grann's book in 2017, Canadian explorer John Hemming wrote in the *Spectator* that calling Fawcett one of Britain's great explorers is "an insult to the huge roster of true explorers."

Like many an English colonial official of the day, Hemming argued, Fawcett's writings displayed friendliness toward the native peoples he met but also condescension, and even racism.

The respected author of a three-volume history of Brazilian Indians, Hemming credited Fawcett with surveying skills, but not much else, given that "the only expedition he organized was a five-week disaster."

UNSOLVED
OR
CASE
CLOSED?

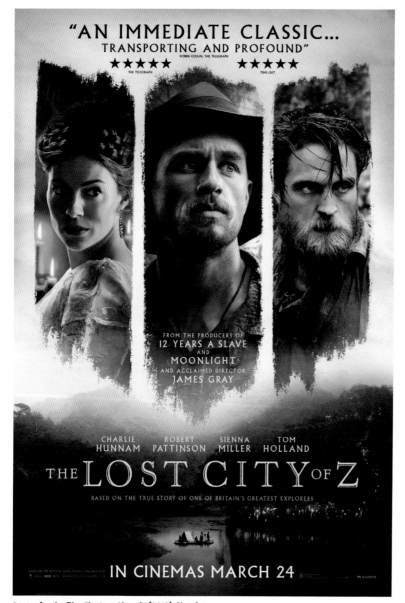

"AN IMMEDIATE CLASSIC...
TRANSPORTING AND PROFOUND"
ROBBIE COLLIN, THE TELEGRAPH

★★★★★   ★★★★★
THE TELEGRAPH   TIME OUT

FROM THE PRODUCERS OF
12 YEARS A SLAVE
AND
MOONLIGHT
AND ACCLAIMED DIRECTOR
JAMES GRAY

CHARLIE   ROBERT   SIENNA   TOM
HUNNAM   PATTINSON   MILLER   HOLLAND

THE LOST CITY OF Z

BASED ON THE TRUE STORY OF ONE OF BRITAIN'S GREATEST EXPLORERS

IN CINEMAS MARCH 24

Poster for the film *The Lost City of Z* (2016). Photofest

IS Z OUT THERE AFTER ALL?

Near the end of Grann's Fawcett-inspired adventure, he interviewed the archaeologist Michael Hecken-berger of the University of Florida, who at that point had spent more than a decade doing research in the Amazon.

Close to the spot where Fawcett believed he would find Z, Hecken-berger showed Grann evidence of a vast ancient settlement, including remnants of a defensive moat, palisade walls, and broken pottery shards.

It was just one of a network of pre-Columbian settlements he had uncovered in the Xingu region, all connected to each other by roads, bridges, and causeways.

Such discoveries have helped to overturn the traditional view that the Amazon couldn't have supported the complex civilization Fawcett envisioned.

In fact, the lush rain forest may have contained great cities similar to those of the Inca, Maya, and even medieval Europeans—perhaps even the Lost City of Z itself.

LASTING IMPACT

AS THE LAST OF A DYING BREED OF INTREPID
Victorian-era British explorers—including Richard Francis
Burton, David Livingstone, and Ernest Shackleton—
Fawcett's legend had begun growing even before he took off on
the search for Z. Sir Arthur Conan Doyle reportedly used Fawcett's Amazon adventures as inspiration for his 1912 novel *The
Lost World*, while newspapers around the world routinely covered
his explorations. Fawcett's disappearance, and the various expeditions that sought in vain to determine his fate, imbued the explorer's legendary status with an irresistible air of mystery.

The public's enduring fascination with Fawcett's quest for Z
has inspired poems, novels, radio plays, documentary and feature
films, graphic novels, children's books, and museum exhibits. He
was even said to have been one of the inspirations for Hollywood's
favorite swashbuckling explorer, Indiana Jones.

In recent years, Grann's *The Lost City of Z* has brought Fawcett
and his quest for the mystical city into the international limelight
yet again. A big-budget movie version of Grann's book came out
in 2016, ensuring the survival of Fawcett's legend nearly a century
after the explorer himself vanished. ∎

PART V

THE BERMUDA TRIANGLE

TRIANGLE

FLIGHT 19 AND THE USS *CYCLOPS*

14A Sun-Sentinel, Sunday, December 3, 1995

SUNDAY FOCUS

Event to honor 50th anniversary of disappearance of Flight 19

By KEN KAYE
Staff Writer

A large bell will be rung 14 times on Tuesday — once for each crew member of Flight 19.

Then a military officer will use a beatswain's pipe, an instrument used to make announcements on Navy ships, to say, "Flight 19 ar-

riving . . . Flight 19 departing."

That is how Flight 19 will be remembered and honored on the 50th anniversary of the legendary Lost Patrol's disappearance. The five torpedo bombers took off from Fort Lauderdale on Dec. 5, 1945, and never returned.

The Naval Air Station Fort Lauderdale Historical Associa-

tion will hold the ceremony at 2 p.m. at Navy Park, which is adjacent to the control tower on the west side of Fort Lauderdale-Hollywood International Airport. The ceremony is intended to honor the public.

The nonprofit group is dedicated to preserving the military history attached to the Fort Lauder-

dale Naval Air Station, today known as Fort Lauderdale-Hollywood International Airport.

The ceremony is intended to honor all American soldiers who died at war, said Allan McElhiney, president of the historical association.

"All paid the price for freedom of this country," said McElhiney.

As part of Tuesday's ceremony, the Fort Lauderdale High School marching band will perform and Navy planes will be on display, including an F/A-18 Hornet and a TBM Avenger, the same type of

plane in the Flight 19 squadron.

McElhiney said about 50 people were based at the Fort Lauderdale Naval Air Station during the war will attend.

One who will not attend is former President George Bush, who learned to fly torpedo bombers in Fort Lauderdale, but said he had other obligations that day.

LOST PATROL

After 50 years, patrol's fate still a mystery

FROM PAGE 1A

But 50 years later, such vagaries remain the legacy of Flight 19. As one of the great aviation mysteries of all time, it continues to taunt the imagination and spark speculation as to how and why the planes disappeared.

"There's an awful lot of folklore surrounding this flight," said Larry Kusche, a pilot and author of two books on Flight 19. "But it's one of those cases where a couple little things led to a major incident."

It was Flight 19, also remembered as the Lost Patrol, that popularized the myth of the Bermuda Triangle — the area between Fort Lauderdale, Bermuda and Puerto Rico — where dozens of boats and aircraft have disappeared mysteriously.

The most exotic and glamorized theory is that the five Navy planes were abducted by space aliens when they flew into an extraterrestrial pathway to Earth. Steven Spielberg touched on that angle in his 1977 movie *Close Encounters of the Third Kind*.

Others believe the strong gravitational pull of the moon in the Caribbean muddled the pilots' minds and disabled their compasses.

One of the more bizarre scenarios is that Taylor, the flight leader, was rescued by a Bahamian fishing boat and was the only crewman to survive, but refused to come forward for fear of court-martial.

All of that is a bunch of bunk, say historians, military buffs and people who knew, or were related to, the pilots of Flight 19.

They say what has been lost in the Flight 19 mystery is this simple fact: 27 young men died in the service of their country — not because they were victims of an alien abduction.

"Everybody wants to make it mystical," said Evans, 69, who participated in the search for Flight 19 and today is a Fort Lauderdale architect. "But that sort of cheapens their memory. These guys shouldn't have died."

What really went wrong with Flight 19?

The Navy initially blamed Taylor for losing his bearings, becoming "hopelessly confused," and not taking into account strong winds pushing the squadron east of its intended course.

From his radio transmissions, it appears Taylor thought he was over the Keys. He then led the torpedo bombers on a zig-zagging course north and east, thinking that would take him to Miami.

In reality, he was taking the planes farther from the east coast of Florida and out over deeper water.

Some think it strange that Taylor, 28, a combat veteran with 2,500 hours of flying time, could have been so wrong.

As a result, various stories swirl around his state of mind that day . . .

Fateful flight

On Dec. 5, 1945, five torpedo bombers took off from Fort Lauderdale on a routine training mission. They were never seen again. The mysterious disappearance of Flight 19, known as the Lost Patrol, popularized to the myth of the Bermuda Triangle.

KEN KAYE/Staff research
BILL McDONALD/Graphics Editor

THE MISSION

▶ Fly on a heading of 091 degrees for 56 miles.
▶ Practice low-level bombing at Hen and Chickens Shoals, a bombing range.
▶ Continue on the heading for 67 miles.
▶ Fly northwest on a heading of 346 degrees for 73 miles.
▶ Return to Fort LauderdaleNaval Air Station on heading of 241 degrees.

WHAT WENT WRONG

Somewhere in vicinity of Little Abaco Island, flight commander Lt. Charles Taylor reported he was lost and his compasses were out. He was convinced he was over the Florida Keys.

THE LAST HOURS

Based on radio transmissions from Taylor, here is a possible course the planes took before vanishing:

▶ **2:10 p.m.:** Planes take off from Fort Lauderdale Naval Air Station.
▶ **3:40:** Taylor reports he is lost.
▶ **4:00:** Taylor's transmissions are fading.
▶ **4:45:** Taylor turns northeast. "Then we will fly north to make sure we are not over the Gulf of Mexico."
▶ **5:07:** Taylor instructs flight to turn east for 10 minutes.
▶ **5:16:** Taylor reports "we will fly 270 degrees west until we hit the beach or run out of gas."
▶ **5:07:** From this point, courses flown by Flight 19 are undetermined.
▶ **6:37:** Flight 19's last radio call. An unidentified crewman asks, "What course are we on?"
▶ **7:27:** A Martin Mariner seaplane, code named "Training 49," is dispatched to look for Flight 19. It crashes 13 minutes later with 23 men aboard.

THE MYSTERY

In the past 150 years, more than 40 ships and 20 airplanes, carrying nearly a thousand people, have been lost in the Bermuda Triangle.

But this strange area of mists and mystery, extending from Fort Lauderdale to Bermuda to Puerto Rico, was not labeled until Flight 19 disappeared in December 1945.

Then, even skeptics began to think something more than coincidence was at work in this region. And, strangely, many of the incidents occurred near Christmastime.

According to Larry Kusche, author and expert on the Bermuda Triangle, here are some of the other strange occurrences:

■ **JANUARY 1921:** The *Carroll A. Deering*, a large sailboat, was found hard aground on Diamond Shoals in the Bahamas with all sails set. There was no crew on board, only two cats. A full meal was in the stove.

■ **OCTOBER 1944:** The *Rubicon*, a ghost ship, drifted near the coast of Florida with only a dog on board. The crew was missing. The ship was in excellent condition.

■ **JANUARY 1948:** The pilot of a British South American Airways airliner, approaching Bermuda, ...

"I don't think [the Flight 19 crewmen] were heroes, I think they were victims. I'd much rather people remember these men as the brightest and the best."
— Kathryn Cowan, relative of one of the crewmen who flew planes like those depicted in the mural

Staff photo/JOE RAEDLE

"All paid the price for freedom of this country. One of the reasons I do this is because I feel very fortunate to have survived the war."
— Allan McElhiney, at left, president of the Naval Air Station Fort Lauderdale Historical Association and a Navy machinist mate during World War II

The five TBM Avengers of Flight 19.
Wikimedia Commons

IN OTHER NEWS

Also in December 1945:

In the first Army–Navy football game to be televised, Army defeated Navy, 32–13, before a crowd of 100,000, including President Harry S. Truman.

The US Senate approved the United States' participation in the new United Nations organization.

General George S. Patton broke his neck in an auto accident near Mannheim, Germany, killing him.

Some twenty-eight nations signed an agreement creating the World Bank.

FLIGHT 19 1945

WHEN THE FIVE US NAVY TBM AVENGER TORPEDO BOMBERS, KNOWN COLLECTIVELY as Flight 19, took off from Fort Lauderdale in December 1945, they were supposed to complete a routine training exercise. Fly to a spot over the Bahamas, practice dropping their bombs, and fly back—something the pilots had all done many times before.

Instead, the planes would lose their way somewhere over the Atlantic Ocean and vanish seemingly into thin air, along with all fourteen men aboard. With the weather worsening, units of the US Navy, Army and Coast Guard launched one of the largest air and sea searches in history, with hundreds of planes and ships combing more than 200,000 miles of the Atlantic Ocean. More than any other single event, the mysterious disappearance of Flight 19 would fuel the legend of the Bermuda Triangle, that notorious stretch of ocean between Miami, Puerto Rico, and Bermuda where hundreds of planes and ships have purportedly vanished.

The men of Flight 19. Naval Air Station Fort Lauderdale Museum

Flight 19 – The Lost Squadron

December 5, 1945, a Squadron of 5 TBM Avengers aircraft with 14 men from the Naval Air Station Fort Lauderdale vanished in the Bermuda Triangle. A massive search and rescue ensued. 13 other men aboard a PBM Mariner from the rescue mission also disappeared. No trace was ever found. Flight 19 remains one of the great aviation mysteries.

THE SQUADRON

TBM AVENGERS

FT – 28
FT – 81
FT – 3
FT – 36
FT – 117

December 5, 1945

Naval
Air Station
Fort Lauderdale

THE MEN OF FLIGHT 19

FT-28 (lead plane)
Flight leader: NASL Instructor Lt. Charles Taylor, USNR
Crew: Gunner George Francis Devlin, USNR; Radioman: Walter Reed Parpart Jr., USNR

FT-36
Pilot: Capt. Edward Joseph Powers, USMC
Crew: Gunner Sgt. Howell Orrin Thompson, USMCR; Radioman: Sgt. George Richard Paonessa, USMCR

FT-81
Pilot: 2nd Lt. Forrest James Gerber, USMCR
Crew (only one): Pfc. William Lightfoot, USMCR

FT-3
Pilot: Ensign Joseph Tipton Bossi, USNR
Crew: Gunner Herman Arthur Thelander, S1c, USNR; Radioman: Burt E. Baluk, S1c, USNR

FT-117
Pilot: Capt. George William Stivers, USMC
Crew: Gunner Sgt. Robert Francis Gallivan, USMCR; Radioman: Pvt. Robert Peter Gruebel, USMCR

WHAT DID WE KNOW?

THOUGH FLIGHT 19 IS OFTEN CALLED THE "LOST Patrol," it wasn't really a patrol but a training flight, completing what was supposed to be a routine navigational exercise and mock bombing run. All of the pilots except for Flight 19's commander, Lt. Charles Taylor, were trainees, with approximately three hundred hours of flying time under their belts.

At 2:10 p.m. Eastern Standard Time on December 5, 1945, Flight 19's five TBM Avenger bombers set out from Fort Lauderdale Naval Air Station (now the site of an international airport). The weather was warm (around 67 degrees Fahrenheit), with a gusting southwest trade wind and billowing clouds. According to the flight plan, they were supposed to fly due east for some one hundred and twenty-three miles, doing practice bombing runs on the Hens and Chickens Shoals in the Bahamas along the way. They were then set to fly north for seventy-three miles before heading back over a one hundred twenty-mile route to the naval base. In all, the exercise was supposed to take about three hours.

Lt. Robert F. Cox, NASFL Senior Flight Instructor, shown in the center photo, was on air communicating with Flight 19 until the signal got weaker. To his left is Flight 19 crewman Bert Edward Baluk; on his right is Flight 19 crewman Bob Harmon, aka George Devlin. *Naval Air Station Fort Lauderdale Museum*

THE EVIDENCE

FLIGHT 19 HAD COMPLETED ITS ASSIGNED EXERCISE and was on its way back when, about two hours after take-off, squadron commander Lt. Charles Taylor radioed to one of the other pilots that he was uncertain of his position, and the compasses on his and several of the squad's other aircraft were malfunctioning. Over the next several hours, the five bombers headed further eastward over the Atlantic Ocean. Meanwhile, the weather was getting worse. A mass of turbulent air coming from a storm over Georgia spread east, causing squalls on the ocean's surface, 40 mph winds at 1,000 feet, and 75 mph (hurricane-strength) winds at 8,000 feet.

Two more hours of confused messages between Flight 19 and the naval air station in Fort Lauderdale followed. Their communication was adversely affected by interferences from broadcasting stations in Cuba, static, and atmospheric conditions. At 6:20 p.m. came a final distorted radio call from Taylor, in which he prepared his men to ditch their aircraft simultaneously, due to lack of fuel. Their last location was reported as approximately 130 miles east of New Smyrna, with about twenty minutes' worth of fuel remaining. In reality, the five TBM Avengers of Flight 19 might have been more than two hundred miles out to sea at that point.

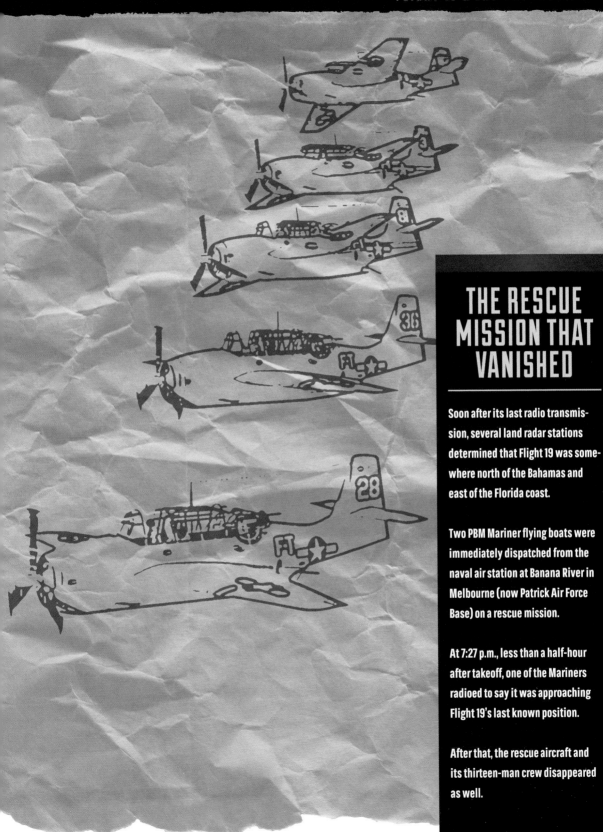

THE RESCUE MISSION THAT VANISHED

Soon after its last radio transmission, several land radar stations determined that Flight 19 was somewhere north of the Bahamas and east of the Florida coast.

Two PBM Mariner flying boats were immediately dispatched from the naval air station at Banana River in Melbourne (now Patrick Air Force Base) on a rescue mission.

At 7:27 p.m., less than a half-hour after takeoff, one of the Mariners radioed to say it was approaching Flight 19's last known position.

After that, the rescue aircraft and its thirteen-man crew disappeared as well.

HUNDREDS OF SHIPS AND AIRCRAFT FROM UNITS of the US Navy, Army, and Coast Guard joined the search for Flight 19 and the PBM Mariner rescue craft. Under the direction of US Coast Guard headquarters of the Seventh Naval District in Miami, they combed more than 200,000 miles of the Atlantic Ocean and the Gulf of Mexico. The navy alone sent nearly 250 of its planes into the air. At that point, it was the biggest rescue effort ever conducted during peacetime. Meanwhile, back on land, search parties explored remote areas of inland Florida on the off chance the planes might have crashed there unnoticed.

A tanker cruising off the coast of Florida reported a visible explosion seen at 7:50 p.m. on December 5, including flames leaping some one hundred feet into the air. While passing through a big pool of oil in the area of the explosion, the tanker circled the site using searchlights to look for survivors, but found none.

Five days of searching uncovered a number of older wrecks, but failed to turn up any of the bodies of the fourteen men aboard Flight 19, or any debris from the five Avengers. The PBM Mariner rescue aircraft, and all thirteen men aboard, were lost as well.

A PBM Mariner similar to the one that disappeared in the search for Flight 19. Library of Congress

DEVELOPING STORY

FALSE ALARM

In 1991, while looking for sunken treasure off the coast of South Florida, a team led by the British undersea explorer Graham S. Hawkes stumbled on five planes sitting upright and mostly undamaged some 550 to 750 feet beneath the ocean surface.

On the tail of one of the planes, they spotted the number "28" (the same number as the lead plane of Flight 19).

But the other tail numbers on the planes the team found did not match, and the model type suggested that most of the planes predated those lost in December 1945.

As the naval air base at Fort Lauderdale used the area nearby for low-altitude torpedo drops, the planes are thought to have crashed separately while making these runs.

"FLYING GAS TANKS"

Based on the report from the tanker off the coast of Fort Lauderdale, the PBM Mariner rescue craft that vanished while searching for Flight 19 is believed to have exploded, crashed into the sea, and sunk.

Some who flew the Mariners had actually nicknamed them "flying gas tanks," as a lit match or even the slightest spark could cause an explosion.

The navy grounded all Mariners after that one disappeared.

TOP THEORIES

1 **Out of fuel, the planes were forced to land in the Atlantic, and sank.**

Most historians and military experts believe that with the Avengers running out of fuel, the Flight 19 pilots were forced to land at night, in a heavy sea. The aircraft likely broke apart on impact; even if any crew members had survived, cold temperatures and strong winds meant their bodies, and the plane debris, would have quickly sunk beneath the waves.

2 **The planes crashed on land.**

In 2014, aviation sleuths Jon Myhre and Andy Marocco claimed the wreck of a torpedo bomber discovered in the Florida Everglades in 1989 was the lead TBM Avenger from Flight 19. They argued that an aircraft carrier off the coast of Daytona Beach picked up a radar signal from four to six unidentified planes over North Florida about 7:00 p.m. on December 5, 1945. After turning southeast, the planes dropped off the radar, likely crashing within miles of where the torpedo bomber was found. Myhre, a former air traffic controller who's been researching Flight 19's disappearance for decades, also believes a wrecked warplane with two bodies inside found near Sebastian, Florida, in the mid-1960s is linked to Flight 19, but despite a Freedom of Information request in 2013, the navy hasn't yet identified the bodies.

3 **The planes fell victim to the "Devil's Triangle."**

Flight 19's disappearance has become inextricably linked with the legend of the Bermuda Triangle, an expanse of some 40,000 miles of the Atlantic Ocean located roughly between Miami, Bermuda, and Puerto Rico. According to one theory about the Bermuda Triangle, the region contains a mysterious geomagnetic anomaly that distorts compass readings and causes navigational problems for ships and planes. ■

HISTORY'S OTHER VANISHED PLANES

1937

In perhaps history's most famous aviation mystery, Amelia Earhart's twin-engine Electra vanished over the Pacific Ocean during the famous aviator's around-the-world flight attempt. The wreckage has never been recovered.

1944

During World War II, the plane carrying big-band leader Glenn Miller from Paris to London is thought to have crashed in the English Channel. It was never found, and the cause of the crash is unknown.

Band leader Glenn Miller. Wikimedia Commons

1948 and 1949

Two British South American Airways planes, the *Star Tiger* and *Star Ariel*, vanished completely within a year of each other, while en route to Bermuda and Jamaica, respectively. No passengers or debris from either flight have been found

1962

During early stages of the Vietnam War, a propeller plane chartered by the US Army known as Flying Tiger Flight 739 failed to arrive in the Philippines from Guam; planes and ships searched the Pacific for the wreckage, but it was never found.

2014

On a routine red-eye flight from Kuala Lumpur to Beijing, with 239 people aboard, Malaysia Airlines Flight 370 disappeared somewhere over the Indian Ocean; an extensive search cost millions of dollars but turned up nothing.

UNSOLVED OR CASE CLOSED?

AN EXTENSIVE INVESTIGATION BY THE US NAVY Board of Inquiry observed that while Flight 19's leader, Lt. Charles Taylor, had mistakenly thought he was flying over the Florida Keys, some of his subordinate officers knew the planes were actually over the Bahamas. In its final report, the navy blamed the loss of Flight 19 on pilot error. But after Taylor's family protested, officials conducted several reviews, and in 1947, the Board for Correction of Naval Records exonerated Taylor of "responsibility for loss of lives and naval aircraft."

The investigation ultimately concluded that Taylor was not at fault, as both the compasses on his aircraft had stopped working. (To make matters worse, none of the aircraft had a clock, and transcripts of in-flight communications show Taylor wasn't wearing a watch.) As for the ultimate fate of the planes, the board failed to come to any significant conclusion, finding that the squadron's loss was due to "causes or reasons unknown."

LASTING IMPACT

THE DISAPPEARANCE OF FLIGHT 19 IN 1945 CEMENTED the growing legend of the Bermuda Triangle, aka "The Devil's Triangle" or the "Graveyard of the Atlantic." Though no one keeps official statistics (the US Board on Geographic Names does not even recognize the Bermuda Triangle as an official name), numerous ships and planes are said to have vanished there since the mid-nineteenth century, leading many people to believe some kind of mysterious force is operating within the region.

Journalist Vincent H. Gaddis first gave the oceanic region its name in 1964 with a cover story in *Argosy* magazine about the disappearance of Flight 19, called "The Deadly Bermuda Triangle." A decade later, Charles Berlitz (whose family created the well-known language-learning courses) popularized the legend with a book of his own, in which he claimed the lost city of Atlantis was somehow connected to the Bermuda Triangle. Since then, the myth has expanded over thousands of books, movies, TV shows, and websites.

The region does have some unusual features, including strong currents, deep underwater trenches, treacherous reefs and shoals, and frequent tropical storms and hurricanes. It's also heavily traveled, so it's logical that more ships and planes would have disappeared there than in other areas. Still, despite a thorough debunking in recent years, the myth of the Bermuda Triangle endures, fueled in part by the lingering mystery of Flight 19. ■

MORE THEORIES ABOUT THE BERMUDA TRIANGLE

Over the decades, people have come up with all sorts of explanations for why ships and planes seem to disappear there. Here are a few of the more outlandish ones:

Sea monsters or giant squid,

Extraterrestrial/alien abduction,

A "third dimension" created by unknown beings, and

Ocean "flatulence"—pockets of methane gas beneath the surface of the ocean that cause ships and planes to sink.

The blockbuster 1977 sci-fi film *Close Encounters of the Third Kind* imagined that Flight 19 had been abducted by aliens and later safely returned to earth. Photofest

LIBERTY BONDS OR GERMAN TAXES!

The New York Times.

"All the News That's Fit to Print."

THE WEATHER

NEW YORK, MONDAY, APRIL 15, 1918.—TWENTY-TWO PAGES.

TWO CENTS

VOL. LXVII...NO. 21,958.

BATTLE IN NORTH GOES ON FIERCELY; BRITISH LINES HOLD;
AMERICANS REPULSE SUNDAY MORNING ATTACK, KILLING 64;
U. S. NAVAL COLLIER CYCLOPS MISSING; MAY BE RAIDER VICTIM

THE CASE OF THE USS CYCLOPS, 1918

I N EARLY 1918, THE 19,360-TON COLLIER USS *CYCLOPS* was returning to the United States from Brazil when it disappeared somewhere in the Caribbean Sea, along with all 309 officers, crew, and passengers aboard. Despite an extensive search, the shipwreck was never found, and no one has been able to uncover exactly what happened. To this date, it is the largest non-combat-related loss of life in US naval history.

The *Cyclops*'s complete disappearance has led it to be linked to the legend of the Bermuda Triangle, that notorious expanse of the Atlantic Ocean located roughly between Miami, San Juan, Puerto Rico, and Bermuda that has supposedly claimed dozens of ships and planes since the mid-nineteenth century. Other theories have run the gamut from onboard mutiny to attack by a giant sea monster, but most of these remained purely in the realm of speculation. Nearly a century after it vanished, the loss of the USS *Cyclops* stands as one of the most puzzling maritime mysteries in history.

FAST FACTS

The USS *Cyclops*, a fuel ship with a displacement of 19,360 tons, was built by William Cramp & Sons in Philadelphia for a price of $822,500.

According to a fact sheet issued by the US Navy's Office of Information, the *Cyclops* launched on May 7, 1910, and was commissioned that November.

During the Great War, the ship carried coal and other cargo to support US naval operations in that conflict.

Measuring some 542 feet long, it had a cargo capacity of some 12,500 tons; some called it the "floating coal mine."

In January 1918, *Cyclops* left its service with the Atlantic Fleet at Hampton Roads, Virginia, and was assigned to the Naval Overseas Transportation Service, where it would begin the transportation of bulk cargo between the United States and Brazil.

The USS *Cyclops* under construction in 1910.
Library of Congress

Geroge Worley, captain of the ill-fated USS *Cyclops*

WHAT DID WE KNOW?

ARRYING SOME 9,960 TONS OF COAL, THE SHIP sailed to Bahia, Brazil, and discharged its cargo, intended for British ships in the South Atlantic. In mid-February, after being reloaded with 10,800 long tons (11,000 t) of manganese ore, the *Cyclops* sailed from Rio de Janeiro, en route to Baltimore, Maryland.

On March 3, the ship deviated from its planned route and stopped in Barbados, in the British West Indies (located some 1,800 nautical miles from Baltimore) for coal and provisions. The following day, the *Cyclops* was on its way again. On March 23, ten days after the ship was supposed to arrive in Baltimore, naval vessels were dispatched to begin a search.

Radio queries went out across the Atlantic, and all commercial vessels were asked to keep a lookout for wreckage or floating debris. But after more than three months of searching turned up nothing, the navy officially marked the *Cyclops* as "lost," and all on board were presumed dead. These included 21 naval officers and 285 enlisted men, 2 marines, and the US consul general of Brazil, Alfred L. M. Gottschalk, who was returning to New York from his post in Rio.

TOP THEORIES

1 The *Cyclops* was attacked by a U-boat or captured by Germany.

From the beginning, the loss of the *Cyclops* appeared suspicious, as the captain had never sent out a distress signal, and no storms had been reported. As the United States was at war at the time, rumors immediately surfaced that it had been the victim of a German U-boat attack. But according to the navy, there were no enemy submarines in the area then—and information obtained from Germany after the war established definitively that no U-boat or mine could have sunk the *Cyclops*.

2 The *Cyclops* fell victim to mutiny at sea.

In a confidential State Department memo written during the investigation, C. Ludlow Livingston, then serving as US consul in Barbados, gave his observations from the *Cyclops*'s stop there. According to Livingston, the ship's captain was "apparently disliked by other officers," perhaps because they suspected him of having German sympathies. En route from Brazil to Barbados, there had been "rumored disturbances" aboard the ship, including "men confined and one executed." As quoted in a *Popular Science* article about the case in 1929, Livingston's memo concluded: "While not having any definite grounds I fear fate worse than sinking . . . possibly based on instinctive dislike felt towards master."

3 The *Cyclops* was attacked by a giant squid.

In perhaps the most fantastical solution to the *Cyclops* riddle, the magazine *Literary Digest* speculated that a giant squid or octopus ensnared the hapless ship with its massive tentacles and hauled it to the bottom of the ocean. Unsurprisingly, not much was done to investigate this theory.

4 The *Cyclops* was lost in the Bermuda Triangle.

Along with the five TBM Avenger planes that made up Flight 19 (1945), the USS *Cyclops* has become one of the most popular stories fueling the legend of the Bermuda Triangle, or "Devil's Triangle." Since the mid-twentieth century, many people have been captivated by the idea that the region of the Atlantic between Miami, Puerto Rico, and Bermuda exerts some kind of supernatural force on ships and planes.

UNSOLVED OR CASE CLOSED

ALTHOUGH WE MAY NEVER KNOW FOR SURE what happened to the USS *Cyclops*, it seems likely that it was something far more prosaic than mutiny, attack, or supernatural interference. In Rio, Captain Worley had reported damage to the ship's starboard engine, which reduced its speed to no more than 10 knots. There's also evidence to suggest that the *Cyclops* had suffered structural damage due to a fire in the coal hold several years earlier. Finally, the ship was believed to be loaded at, or even beyond, its capacity, and was carrying an unfamiliar cargo.

As Marvin Barrash explained to the *Baltimore Sun*, "It was the first time she had carried manganese, which is . . . much denser than coal." Barrash, a longtime employee of the Department of Defense, authored a seven-hundred-plus-page book about the case; his great-uncle, US Navy seaman Lawrence Merkel, was a fireman second class on the ship. "If it's not properly stowed," Barrash continued, "it has a tendency for shifting if the ship began to roll, and *Cyclops* had a history of severe rolling." Faced with rough weather, the shifting cargo could have caused water to enter the hull and reduced the ship's buoyancy—with fatal results. ∎

LASTING IMPACT

The disappearance of the USS *Cyclops* dealt a major blow to the US Navy, as it was the first loss involving a formidable US-built, steel-hulled ship carrying bulk cargo.

Over the ensuing decades, however, the navy would see a number of other cargo-carrying ships go down, including two of the *Cyclops*'s sister ships, the *Nereus* and the *Proteus*, which vanished in 1941.

As Capt. Lawrence B. Brennan, US Navy (Ret.) wrote in a 2013 article for the Naval Historical Foundation about the *Cyclops*, between 1967 and 1996 more than four hundred bulk carriers were lost from all causes.

For this reason, Brennan argued, an investigation of its loss is still relevant today, and "should be undertaken to increase safety of life at sea."

PART VI

THE WRITERS

AMBROSE BIERCE AND THE CASE OF SOLOMON NORTHUP

MEXICAN WAR ENDS CAREER
Of Ambrose Bierce
Picturesque Literary Figure

He Went to the Front and Has Never Been Heard From Since—A Remarkable and Interesting Character Who Was Anything but Conventional.

By Bailey Millard

TELLS OF BIERCE DYING IN BATTLE IN MEXICO

Ex-Comrade Says Author Was Left Wounded in Retreat of Villa's Foreign Legion.

SAN FRANCISCO, April 25 (AP).—The Examiner today published an alleged eye-witness account of the death of Ambrose Bierce, the American author, whose disappearance in Mexico in 1914 gave rise to many stories as to how he came to die.

The story was told by S. Patrick Reardon, a San Francisco salesman and former soldier of fortune, who described himself as a member of the foreign contingent of Pancho Villa's rebel forces in Mexico in 1914. Bierce, a friend and adviser of Villa, was in the contingent, Reardon said.

Reardon said the contingent was en route from Juarez to Laguna and had stopped at Mocho. About 2 o'clock in the morning, Reardon said, Mexican Federals attacked the town, catching the contingent in the open.

The head of the rebel squad, Joe O'Reilly, ordered his followers to crawl to shelter, Reardon continued, but Bierce was too old (he was 72 then) to wriggle across the terrain and arose. A moment later a Federal bullet tore through his side.

EL PASO H

EL PASO, TEXAS, SATURDAY EVENING, APR

BIERCE FOUND AIDING ALLIE

Author, Believed Dead in Mexico, Is With the British Staff.

New York, April 2.—Friends of Ambrose Bierce, author, journalist and soldier, who feared he had been killed in Mexico last November, were surprised and relieved to learn that his daughter in Washington, D.C. has received a letter from him revealing that he is serving the allies in France. It was said Bierce was a member of the British staff.

The supposition that he was dead, concerning his mysterious disappearance and his unusual military career had been published.

Traced to Chihuahua City.

Bierce, who had served as a line through the civil war, left last spring when the Vera expedition started for Vera... was understood to such points in this country... invasion might reach... at last, at the request of one... in California, the state began an inquiry, as to his directing consular agents and military officials in Mex... huahua City, when he was im... when a battle was im...

Keeps Silence.

Ill., April 3.—Mrs. Helen ... maj. Ambrose Bierce, journalist, declined ... received from ... which it is under ... ments since he ... last December ... army in France.

The Bulletin.

VOL. 129, 65TH YEAR.   TWENTY-FOUR PAGES.   SAN FRANCISCO, WEDNESDAY, MARCH 24, 1920.

THE STORY OF THE CLOCKS
FOURTEEN HOURS AHEAD.

NOTED S. F. AUTHOR'S FATE DISCLOSED BY VILLA
MYSTERIOUS DEATH OF AMBROSE BIERCE CLEARED
Satirist, Who Sought to Die in Battle, Is Slain by Villistas

$700,000 DEAL IN ST. FRANCIS HOTEL STOCK

FELL BEFORE FIRING SQUAD
Ambrose Bierce, who met his death in Mexico in 1915. The portrait on the left is from a photograph taken about 1890. The one on the right is from a photograph taken in 1897, when he was at the height of his celebrity.

S. F. SUGAR CO. TO SELL AT OLD PRICE

Operation May Save Sight of $1250 Canine

THE HEADLINES

J.H.E. Partington portrait of Ambrose Bierce
Library of Congress

AMBROSE BIERCE 1913

IN 1913, AT THE AGE OF SEVENTY-ONE, AMBROSE BIERCE saddled up his horse and rode across the Texas border into Mexico. As he told friends and family, he wanted to experience the revolutionary conflict there firsthand. Within a few months, Bierce had vanished, leaving a cryptic postcard as the only clue to his fate.

As a younger man, Bierce had distinguished himself with his Civil War service. His prolific writing career spanned journalism and fiction, but he was especially known for such dark short stories as "An Occurrence at Owl Creek Bridge." By the time he headed into Mexico, Bierce had grown bitter, was drinking heavily, and considered himself washed up as a writer.

It seemed clear that Bierce had met his end somewhere in Mexico, but nobody could agree on where, when, or how. Some said he died on the battlefield, fighting with the troops of the famed bandit-turned-rebel-leader Pancho Villa. Others said Villa himself had ordered Bierce's execution. But after the search for Bierce stalled during World War I, whatever real leads might have existed grew cold, even as the legend of his fate continued to grow.

IN OTHER NEWS

In January 1914:

The first steamboat passed through the Panama Canal.

Henry Ford introduced an assembly line to produce the Model T.

The stock brokerage firm of Merrill Lynch was founded.

The city of Beverly Hills, California, was incorporated.

CHRONOLOGY

June 24, 1842	Ambrose Gwinnett Bierce was born in Meigs County, Ohio.
1859	He attended Kentucky Military Institute, but left without a degree.
1861	Bierce enlisted in the 9th Indiana Infantry of the Union Army and served in many major battles, including Shiloh and Chickamauga.
1866	He settled in San Francisco, California.
1871	Bierce married Mollie Day, daughter of a wealthy miner; they would have two sons, Day and Leigh, and a daughter, Helen.
1870s	He spent some time living and writing in England.
1875	He returned to San Francisco with his family, and became editor of the *Argonaut*.
1886	Bierce was approached by William Randolph Hearst to write for the *San Francisco Examiner*.
1888	He separated from his wife.
1889	His older son, Day, died after shooting his unfaithful girlfriend, her lover, and himself.
1891	Bierce published his most famous story collection, *Tales of Soldiers and Civilians*.
1899	He moved to Washington, DC, to continue writing for Hearst's *Examiner*, as well as *Cosmopolitan*.
1901	His second son, Leigh, died of pneumonia; Bierce had him cremated and kept the ashes in a cigar box on his desk.
1905	Bierce's former wife, Mollie, died (they had divorced a year earlier).
1909	Bierce ended his career with Hearst.

WHAT DID WE KNOW?

BIERCE ATTENDED KENTUCKY MILITARY INSTITUTE, but didn't graduate; his lack of higher education would later cause him great embarrassment. He was among the first Union soldiers to enlist when the Civil War broke out, and his wartime experience shaped the rest of his life. Bierce served in major battles at Shiloh, Chickamauga, Lookout Mountain, and Missionary Ridge; took a bullet to the head at Kennesaw Mountain; and followed Gen. William T. Sherman on his famous "March to the Sea."

After the war, Bierce made his way west. In San Francisco, he launched his journalism career at papers like the *San Francisco News-Letter*, the *California Advertiser*, and the *Argonaut*. He later landed a spot with William Randolph Hearst's publishing empire, which included the *New York Journal* and the *San Francisco Examiner*. Outside of journalism, Bierce made his literary reputation with a series of realistic short stories written from 1888 to 1891 based on his Civil War service. His other most famous work, a satirical lexicon of words and phrases called *The Devil's Dictionary* (1911), originally began as a newspaper column.

In the fall of 1912, Bierce finished selecting and arranging the twelve volumes of his forthcoming *Collected Works*. He had already buried both of his sons and his former wife, whom (despite numerous affairs with other women) he claimed was the only woman he ever loved.

Bierce circa 1866. Library of Congress

THE EVIDENCE

THE MEXICAN REVOLUTION

The long and bloody conflict, which began in 1910, would ultimately end a thirty-year dictatorship and establish Mexico as a constitutional republic.

By early 1913, rebel forces led by Venustiano Carranza, Emiliano Zapata, and Francisco "Pancho" Villa were facing off against the federal troops (Federales) loyal to President Victoriano Huerta.

The rebel alliance later dissolved due to rivalry between its leaders.

Although a constitution drafted in 1917 included many reforms the rebels had fought for, periodic violence continued until the 1930s, when the reforms were finally implemented.

IN CONVERSATIONS AND LETTERS AROUND THIS TIME, Bierce spoke in fatalistic terms about going to Mexico, then in the throes of revolution, and perhaps South America. He told multiple people that given the violence in Mexico, he might very well not return—and that was fine with him. "My work is finished and so am I," Bierce wrote to one friend. Before he left, he fought with his publisher and his brother, among others, in a way that suggests he was closing his accounts.

On October 2, 1913, Bierce left his home in Washington, DC, to travel south, through Civil War battlefields in Tennessee, Georgia, and Mississippi, then on to New Orleans and Texas. From El Paso, he crossed the border into Juárez, recently liberated by the onetime bandit Pancho Villa, now the leader of a revolutionary army.

According to his correspondence, most notably with his secretary, Carrie Christiansen, Bierce somehow got credentials from Villa to accompany his troops—despite the fact that he was seventy-one, severely asthmatic, spoke no Spanish, and hadn't been on a horse for some thirty years. In a final postcard mailed from Chihuahua City in late December 1913, Bierce wrote to Christiansen that he was headed out with Villa's army to Ojinaga, a city then under siege. Here the recorded story ends, and the legend begins.

Pancho Villa (in uniform to the right) with some of his fellow revolutionaries. Library of Congress

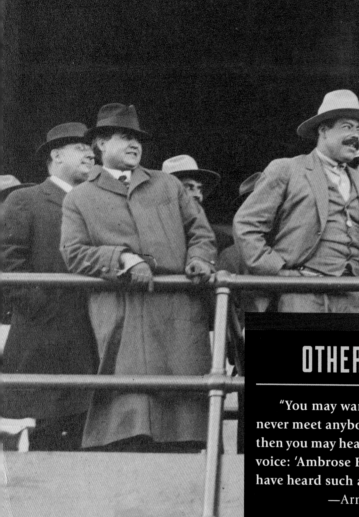

Pancho Villa and General Hugh Scott at a racetrack in Ciudad Juárez in January 1914. Scott commanded the 2nd Cavalry Brigade in the American Southwest and frequently interceded in cross-border matters, including the disappearance of Ambrose Bierce. Library of Congress

OTHER WRITERS ON BIERCE

"You may wander for years through literary circles and never meet anybody who has heard of Ambrose Bierce, and then you may hear some erudite student whisper in an awed voice: 'Ambrose Bierce is the greatest living prose writer.' I have heard such an opinion expressed."

—Arnold Bennett, in the *London New Age* (1909)

"What delighted him [Bierce] most in this life was the spectacle of human cowardice and folly. He put man, intellectually, somewhere between the sheep and the horned cattle, and as a hero somewhere below the rats. . . . So far in this life, . . . I have encountered no more thorough-going cynic than Bierce was."

—H. L. Mencken in *Prejudices: Sixth Series* (1927)

"Virtually all of Bierce's tales are tales of horror; and whilst many of them treat only of the physical and psychological horrors within Nature, a substantial proportion admit the malignly supernatural and form a leading element in America's fund of weird literature."

—H. P. Lovecraft, "Supernatural Horror in Literature" (1927)

DEVELOPING STORY

FOR WEEKS, THEN MONTHS, AFTER THAT FINAL LETTER, no word came from Bierce. His daughter, Helen, and secretary, Carrie Christiansen, began contacting government officials for help locating him. Gen. Hugh Scott, US Army chief of staff, wrote to one of Villa's associates, Felix Sommerfeld, who asked around in Chihuahua and learned only that Bierce had left there sometime in January (which, if true, contradicts the idea that he left with Villa's troops for Ojinaga in late December).

Later investigations by US Army personnel and others turned up even less information. While notices were printed in Mexican newspapers, and circulars and questionnaires distributed among all British and American consular agents in the region, no one ever came forward with any solid leads.

TOP THEORIES

1 Bierce was killed in battle at Ojinaga.

The most popular theory of Bierce's fate argues that after he was killed in the Battle of Ojinaga on January 11, 1914, his body was burned along with the other victims to curb a typhoid epidemic in the region. At least two people (an American mercenary and a US Customs agent) said they heard reports that an "old gringo" was shot at Ojinaga. One of Villa's men reportedly identified a photo of Bierce, saying he saw him there before the battle, but not after.

2 Bierce was wounded at Ojinaga, but died after crossing the US border.

According to this version of events, a young Federale wheeled a wounded gringo (presumably Bierce) over the border in a cart, thinking that an American companion would help him once he got to the United States. By the time the two men were transported to Marfa, Texas, for processing, the old American was nearly comatose, and had no papers or identification. He died soon after that, and was buried in an unmarked grave in Marfa.

3 Bierce was executed on Pancho Villa's orders.

There are several variations on the theory that Villa had Bierce murdered after the author angered him in some way. According to one, when Bierce declared he was going over to a rival camp, Villa smiled before ordering Bierce's execution at the hands of his personal gunman, Rodolfo Fierro.

4 Bierce was killed near the town of Icamole.

In an article published in the *San Francisco Bulletin* in 1920, journalist James H. Wilkins claimed that a Mexican firing squad executed Bierce in mid-1915. According to this theory, Bierce and a Mexican peasant had been transporting a machine gun and ammunition via mule train to Carranza's troops when they were taken prisoner and executed on the orders of one of Villa's subcommanders, Gen. Tomas Urbina.

Federal artillery in action during the six-day siege of the border town of Ojinaga in January 1914. The prevailing view is that Bierce was killed or wounded during the battle, though his body was never found. Library of Congress

FRINGE THEORIES

According to a cenotaph for Bierce in Sierra Mojada, a sleepy mining town in the Chihuahua Desert, the Federales executed him there on suspicion of being a spy.

Some believed that Bierce didn't die in Mexico, but succeeded in traveling further south into South America, as he said he would.

Others argued that he returned to the United States, where he died alone and anonymous, perhaps in an insane asylum.

Grand Canyon of the Colorado by Thomas Moran (1912). "The mists of the Colorado serve as [Bierce's] shroud," according to his publisher and biographer, Walter Neale. Library of Congress

DESPITE ALL OF THE COLORFUL THEORIES ABOUT Bierce's death in Mexico, no credible proof exists to suggest that any of them ever happened.

He may never even have gone to Mexico at all, despite what he said to his friends and family. In his 1929 biography of Bierce, Walter Neale suggested that the author might have used the Mexico talk as a smokescreen to conceal his true intention: to commit suicide. According to Neale, Bierce had talked of ending his own life for years. He believed Bierce had chosen to kill himself alongside one of the world's greatest natural monuments, the Grand Canyon, where his body would fall into the abyss and never be found.

In the end, the only thing that seems clear is that we'll probably never know the true story of Ambrose Bierce's demise—which is, of course, just the way he would have wanted it.

HIS PUBLISHER'S THEORY

Near the end of his 1929 biography, *Life of Ambrose Bierce*, Bierce's friend and publisher, Walter Neale, addressed the lingering mystery surrounding his fate.

"For many years before Bierce disappeared," Neale wrote, "he had told his friends privately, and some of his acquaintances publicly, that he intended to die by his own hand before he should be so advanced in years as to be in danger of senility."

According to Neale, within twelve months of his disappearance a young friend of Bierce's had purchased a German revolver as a present for the author, "which the latter thereupon said he would use when the time should come for him to blow out his brains."

Bierce had also recently taken a trip through Yellowstone National Park, and explored some of the "Cañon of the Colorado" (aka, the Grand Canyon).

In the end, Neale concluded that Bierce "died the death he sought. He has been his own undertaker; the mists of the Colorado serve as his shroud ... the walls of the Grand Cañon forever sentinel his repose."

UNSOLVED OR CASE CLOSED?

LASTING IMPACT

ALTHOUGH BIERCE'S CAREER HAD BEEN WINDING down in the years before he vanished, his disappearance spurred renewed interest in his writing, even as his fate became the stuff of literary legend.

The celebrated Mexican writer Carlos Fuentes memorably drew on Bierce's story (and that of Villa and the other rebel leaders) for his 1985 novel, *The Old Gringo*, later adapted into a movie starring Gregory Peck in the title role.

Meanwhile, Bierce's best work endures. Kurt Vonnegut once called "An Occurrence at Owl Creek Bridge" the greatest American short story, and it frequently appears in anthologies of American literature, as does "A Horseman in the Sky." As the decades passed, the shadowy mystery surrounding Bierce's death became tangled up with the darkness of his fiction, particularly his war stories, supernatural tales, and those stories that combine elements of both.

"Like the man in his famous story who was hanged on the Owl Creek Bridge," Edmund Wilson wrote of Bierce in *The New Yorker* in 1951, "he had had only, between war and war, a desperate dream of escape from an immutable doom of death." ■

THE WORLD ACCORDING TO BIERCE

Some selected definitions from *The Devil's Dictionary*:

ABSURDITY
Noun. A statement or belief manifestly inconsistent with one's own opinion.

BORE
Noun. A person who talks when you wish him to listen.

DIPLOMACY
Noun. The patriotic art of lying for one's country.

EDUCATION
Noun. That which discloses to the wise and disguises from the foolish their lack of understanding.

FAMOUS
Adjective. Conspicuously miserable.

FRIENDLESS
Adjective. Having no favors to bestow. Destitute of fortune. Addicted to utterance of truth and common sense.

PRAY
Verb. To ask that the laws of the universe be annulled in behalf of a single petitioner confessedly unworthy.

TELEPHONE
Noun. An invention of the devil which abrogates some of the advantages of making a disagreeable person keep his distance.

YEAR
Noun. A period of three hundred and sixty-five disappointments.

(From Ambrose Bierce, *The Devil's Dictionary, Tales, & Memoirs*. S. T. Joshi, editor, Library of America, 2011.)

Gregory Peck as Ambrose Bierce in *The Old Gringo* (1989). Photofest

THE CASE OF SOLOMON NORTHUP, 1857

FAST FACTS

Solomon Northup was born in July 1807 or 1808 in Minerva, New York.

He married Anne Hampton in 1829, and they had three children.

In 1834, the family moved to Saratoga Springs, where Northup worked at the United States Hotel, among other jobs.

Kidnapped in 1841, Northup spent twelve years as a slave in Louisiana, mostly on the plantation of Edwin Epps.

Samuel Bass, a Canadian carpenter doing work on the Epps plantation, helped Northup get word to friends and family in 1852.

New York's governor empowered Henry Northup, a family friend (the grandson of the man who had manumitted Solomon's father), to travel south and reclaim Solomon's freedom in early 1853.

IN 1841, TWO WHITE MEN APPROACHED SOLOMON Northup in Northup's hometown of Saratoga Springs, New York, offering him work as a fiddler in a traveling circus. Northup, a free African American, went with the two men to Washington, DC, where they drugged him, beat him severely, and sold him into slavery. He would labor as a slave in Louisiana for the next twelve years, until a chance visit to the plantation by an abolitionist carpenter led to his dramatic rescue in 1853.

Northup soon became a full-fledged celebrity, publishing a memoir of his experience entitled *Twelve Years a Slave*, and lecturing to rapt audiences throughout the northern United States. But in 1857, just four years after escaping from bondage, he dropped out of sight, and the circumstances of his later life, death, and burial remain a mystery.

Solomon Northup, depicted here in an engraving from his autobiography, was the son of a freed slave who was kidnapped and held as a slave for twelve years.

TOP THEORIES

1 Northup was murdered.
Some people have suggested that Northup's kidnappers (who had been free on bail since early 1855) killed him so he couldn't testify. But the historical evidence indicates that Northup was still alive when the charges were dropped.

2 Northup had financial problems.
What seems indisputable is that Northup's finances were failing as his celebrity waned.

Northup's book sold well enough for him to buy a house in Glens Falls with Anne, but by 1854 the bank had foreclosed on the property.

3 Northup was helping with the Underground Railroad.
There is strong evidence that Northup dropped out of public life in order to devote himself to helping fugitive slaves escape. His personal experience and reputation (including contact with major figures in the abolition movement) would have given him the opportunity and motivation to participate in the Underground Railroad.

4 Northup was kidnapped again.
Some newspaper articles in 1858 claimed that Northup "has been again decoyed south, and is again a slave." But the evidence placing him in Vermont in the early 1860s makes it reasonably certain this was not the case.

LASTING IMPACT

Solomon Northup's *Twelve Years a Slave* remains one of the most important slave narratives in US history.

Out of print before the end of the nineteenth century, it was reprinted in 1968 in an annotated version that backed up many of Northup's claims with evidence.

In 1984, the photographer and filmmaker Gordon Parks made a TV documentary, *Solomon Northup's Odyssey*, about his story.

Saratoga Springs began celebrating an annual "Solomon Northup Day: A Celebration of Freedom" in 2002.

The film version of Northup's book, *12 Years a Slave*, directed by Steve McQueen, won the Oscar for Best Picture in 2013.

Photofest

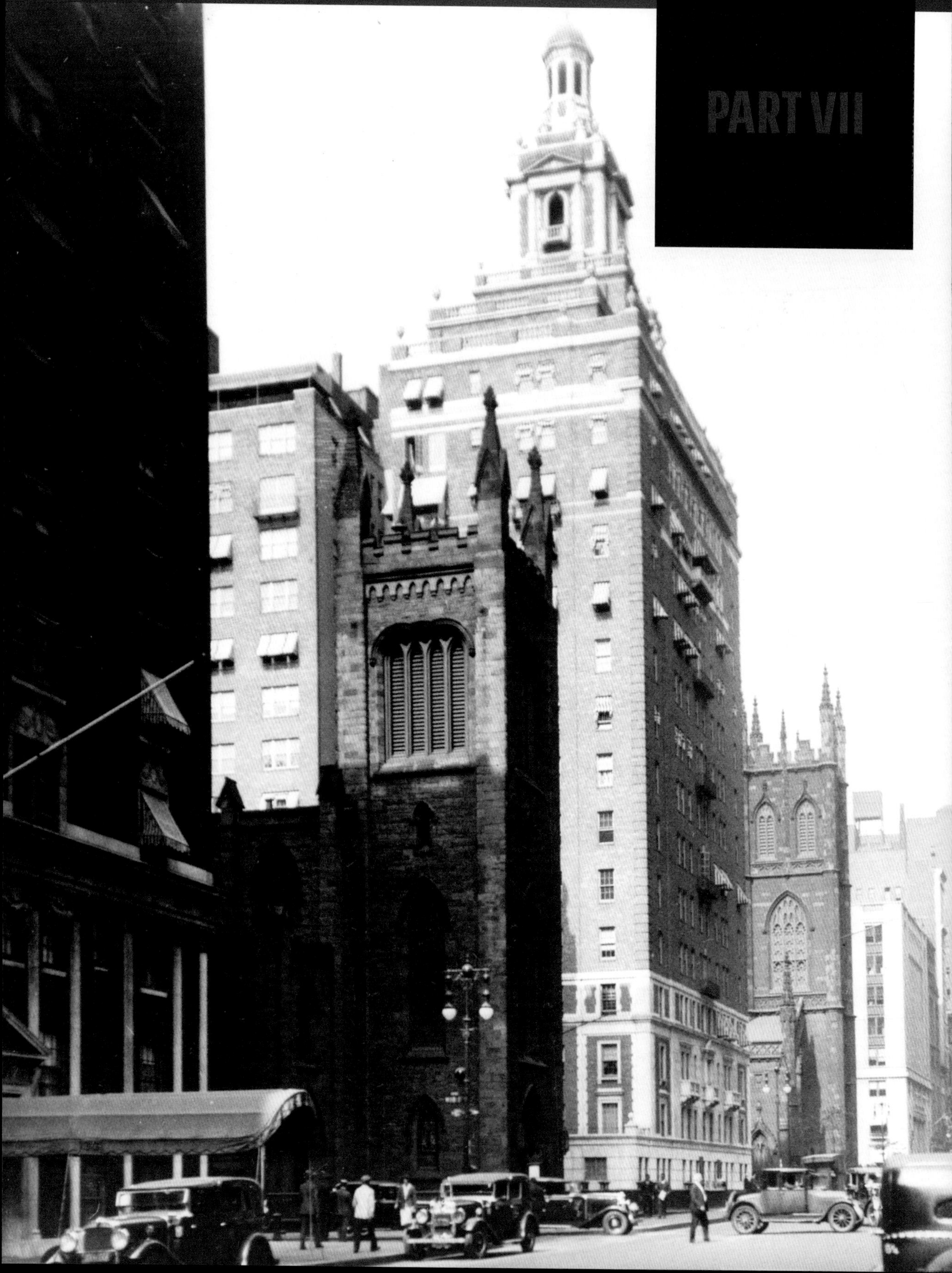

PART VII

ROGUES AND REBELS LOUIS LE PRINCE, JUDGE JOSEPH FORCE CRATER, FRANK MORRIS, JOHN AND CLARENCE ANGLIN, D. B. COOPER, AND OSCAR "ZETA" ACOSTA

THE HEADLINES

Louis Le Prince. Wikipedia Commons

LOUIS LE PRINCE 1890

THE HISTORY OF MOTION PICTURES IS NOTORIOUSLY complicated, with various inventors (including France's Lumière brothers and the "Wizard" himself, Thomas Edison) claiming credit for the earliest film technology. For all but the most devoted of movie buffs, the name Louis Augustin Le Prince may not even register. But Le Prince began designing a motion picture camera as early as 1885 (before both Edison and the Lumières), and shot what some believe was the first movie in Leeds, England, in the fall of 1888. Le Prince might have been more famous than all the rest—if he hadn't vanished just before he was due to project his films publicly for the first time.

After visiting relatives in Dijon, France, Le Prince is believed to have boarded a train from Dijon to Paris on September 16, 1890. He was never seen or heard from again, despite a search that spanned morgues and hospitals across France, his abandoned workshop in Leeds, and steamships arriving on US shores from Europe. In Le Prince's absence, his wife, Lizzie, and son, Adolphe, would spend the rest of their lives fighting to win recognition for his contributions to the origins of cinema.

IN OTHER NEWS

In the fall and winter of 1890:

The US government established Sequoia National Park and Yosemite National Park.

The Mormon Church officially outlawed polygamy.

The first Army–Navy football game took place at West Point; Navy beat Army, 24–0.

The so-called Wounded Knee Massacre took place after the US 7th Cavalry Regiment tried to disarm a Lakota Sioux camp near Wounded Knee, South Dakota. In the ensuing violence, at least 150 Sioux and 25 US troops were killed.

CHRONOLOGY

1841	Louis Aimé Augustin Le Prince was born in Metz, France.
Early 1860s	He attended university in Germany, studying physics and chemistry.
1866	Le Prince moved to Leeds, England, and began working at Whitley Partners brass foundry.
1869	He married Elizabeth (Lizzie) Whitley.
1870–71	He served in the Franco-Prussian War.
1870s	He and his wife had five children: Marie, Adolphe, Aimée, Joseph, and Fernand.
1876–77	Le Prince founded Leeds Applied School of Art with Lizzie.
1882	He emigrated with his family to New York.
1885	Le Prince began his first experiments with moving pictures.
1886	He applied for a US patent for a multi-lens movie camera.
1887	Le Prince returned to Leeds, where he quickly moved to file for patents in Britain, France, Austria, Belgium, and Italy.
1888	His US patent granted, Le Prince built a single-lens movie camera.
1889	He experimented with a single-lens projector, and acquired celluloid.
March 1890	Le Prince successfully demonstrated one of his projectors in front of officials at the Paris Opera House.

WHAT DID WE KNOW?

The Morris-Jumel Mansion in Washington Heights, New York City, where Lizzie Le Prince had hoped her husband's films would make their American debut. Library of Congress

AS A CHILD IN FRANCE, LOUIS AUGUSTIN LE PRINCE was inspired by visits to the office of a family friend, the physicist and photography pioneer Louis Daguerre (of daguerreotype fame). Le Prince later followed his university classmate John Whitley to Leeds, England, where he joined the family brass foundry and married John's sister, Elizabeth.

In 1882, the Le Princes moved to New York. Inspired by Eadweard Muybridge, as well as a group of French artists producing large circular panoramas of famous scenes, Louis began experimenting with moving images. Using a workshop at the School of the Deaf in Washington Heights, where Lizzie worked, he began designing a sixteen-lens movie camera.

When his first patent came through in early 1888, Le Prince was back in Leeds, working on a single-lens camera. He filmed several scenes—including a family gathering in mid-October 1888 and traffic on the Leeds Bridge—but struggled to find a material strong enough to withstand repeated projections. In 1889, he began working with the newly invented flexible plastic known as celluloid.

Back in New York, Lizzie prepared the Morris-Jumel Mansion, George Washington's onetime Revolutionary War headquarters, for the planned debut of her husband's films. In late summer 1890, before returning to the States, Le Prince traveled to France, including a weekend trip to Dijon to visit his brother, Albert.

IMMIGRATION SERVICE
Form 1500 A.

SALOON, CABIN, AND STEERAGE ALIENS MUST BE COMPLETELY MANIFESTED.
THIS SHEET IS FOR SECOND-CABIN PASSENGERS.

LIST OR MANIFEST OF ALIEN PASSENGERS FOR THE U. S. IMMIGRATION OFFICER AT

Required by the regulations of the Secretary of the Treasury of the United States, under Act of Congress approved March 3, 1903, to be delivered to the U. S. Officer of any vessel having such passengers on board upon arrival at a port in the United States.

9787   S. S. "Zeutonic"   sailing from   Liverpool   14th June, 1903   Arriving at Port of   NEW YORK

No. on List.	NAME IN FULL.	Age. Yrs. Mos.	Sex.	Married or Single	Calling or Occupation.	Able to— Read. Write.	Nationality. (Country of last permanent residence.)	Race or People.	Last Residence. (Province, City, or Town.)	Final Destination. (State, City, or Town.)	Whether having a ticket to such final destination.	By whom was passage paid?	Whether in possession of $50, and if less, how much?	Whether ever before in the United States; and if so, when and where?	Whether going to join a relative what relative or friend, and his name
1	Bishop Charles T.	29		M	Machinist	U.S.	England	English	London	New York NY	Yes	Self	$60	No	Central Ave
2	Anderson William	31		M	Golf Professional		do	do	do	Washington Co	No			1896-99 New York 1901	Carnoed Golf
3	Reynolds George	36		M	Bricklayer		do	do	Birmingham	New York	No		$5	do 1901	Union 700 E Street Brother
4	Marks Ephraim	49		M	Merchant		Russia	Hebrew	Manchester	do NY	Yes			No	Brother son Ward Street Mills
5	do Rebecca	19	2	S	Dau		Russia	do	do	do			No		2
6	Shapiro Abraham	37		S	Merchant		Russia	do	do	Brooklyn			$250	Yes	Friend S. Tillman
7	Teichberg Moses	50		M	Dealer		Austria	do	London	NY			$75		son Harry Teichberg 6 Clinton Street
8	Grierson Maxwell	38 363/858		M	Manager Manufacturer		England	English	London	NY Co	No		$100	1896 New York	J. Hatchett
9	Strong Herbert	35		M	Golfer		do	do	Alderley Edge	Hampstead do	Yes		$100		
10	Barnett Mrs D.	45		M	Wife		U.S. Citizen		Cambridge	Buffalo	No		$400	No	Friend Mrs Jackson St
11	Whitehead Mrs John	70		M	Widow		England	do	Buffalo	Buffalo NY	No			U.P. Co	Buffalo
12	Lafond Claude	28		M	Cook		France	French	London	New York	Yes			1902 New York	Oscar Little 126 W. 26th
13	Charrier Joseph	19		M	Cook		do	do	do	do					do
14	Morrow Marcelle	19		M	Cook		do	do	do	do	No		$40		do
15	do														

14
13

R. S. Brown
June 27.

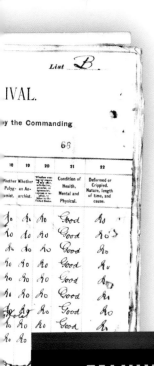

List B.

IVAL.

y the Commanding

66

18	19	20	21	22
Whether Polyg- amist.	Whether an An- archist.	Whether can legally en-ter...	Condition of Health, Mental and Physical.	Deformed or Crippled. Nature, length of time, and cause.
No	No	No	Good	No
No	No	No	Good	No'S
No	No	No	Good	No
No	No	No	Good	No
No	No	No	Good	No
No	No	No	Good	No
No	No	No	Good	No
No	No	No	Good	No
No	No			

In New York, Lizzie Le Prince scoured steamship passenger manifests like this one in hopes of finding her husband. While she did come across a "L. Leprince" on one manifest, the trail turned cold thereafter. Wikimedia Commons

FAMILY BUSINESS

Louis Le Prince's visit to Dijon wasn't just a vacation: His mother had died in 1887, and her will was not yet settled.

Some have suggested that the two brothers argued over this issue before Louis left.

According to this theory, Louis claimed he was owed money, while Albert thought his brother had already received his fair share.

By the time he boarded the Paris-bound train, however, Louis was in good spirits—at least according to Albert, who was the only one to see him off.

O N MONDAY, SEPTEMBER 16, 1890, ALBERT LE PRINCE saw his brother off at the Dijon train station. Nearly 6-foot-4, Louis stood out on the platform, and was in good spirits as he boarded. But he would never arrive in Paris.

In November, when her husband didn't show up in New York as scheduled, Lizzie asked friends to make inquiries in Leeds. They found his workshop undisturbed—and empty. After police in Britain and France were notified, they searched morgues and mental hospitals throughout both countries and railroad stations all along the Dijon–Paris route. They found no sign of Le Prince, his luggage, or any of his personal effects.

In New York, Lizzie combed the passenger lists of all incoming steamers. In mid-November, the name "L. Leprince" appeared in the steerage list on the just-docked SS *Gascoigne*. But he wasn't registered at the barge office, as he should have been upon entering the country (Le Prince had been granted US citizenship in 1888), and repeated searches of the ship turned up no trace of him.

Lizzie went to the police, who told her that according to state law she had to accuse her husband of a crime in order for them to pursue the missing persons case. As she steadfastly refused to do this, they would give her no help.

DEVELOPING STORY

EDISON AND FILM

In 1877, Edison invented the phonograph, which soon became a fixture in homes around the world.

To add a visual element to the experience, Edison tasked one of his lab assistants, William Dickson, with building a motion picture camera in 1888.

The result was the Kinetograph, the first version of which Edison patented in August 1891 (nearly a year after Le Prince disappeared).

He then had Dickson design the Kinetoscope, a kind of peep-show device for individual viewing.

The first Kinetoscope parlor opened in New York in 1894, and the device was an instant success, inspiring rival inventors.

In April 1896, a few months after the Lumières held their first successful projection, Edison brought film projection to the United States with the Vitascope.

The state-of-the-art device, introduced as "Edison's Latest Marvel," had actually been developed by another inventor, Thomas Armat, before Edison acquired it.

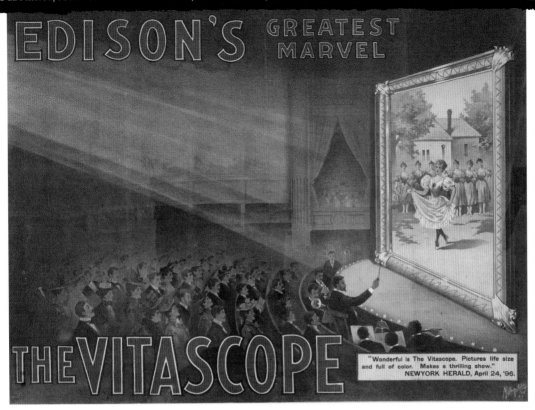

EDISON'S GREATEST MARVEL

THE VITASCOPE

"Wonderful is The Vitascope. Pictures life size and full of color. Makes a thrilling show." NEW YORK HERALD, April 24, '96.

Thomas Edison took credit for "inventing" cinematography with his Vitascope, legally challenging others like Le Prince who were the true pioneers of the motion picture industry. *Library of Congress*

LIZZIE AND HER CHILDREN HOPED FERVENTLY THAT Le Prince was still alive, but the lack of a body or any other evidence of his fate seriously hampered their options when it came to protecting his film innovations. According to patent law, no one (not even a spouse) could lay claim to a missing person's patent or invention for seven years, unless the missing person returned or was proven deceased.

During the seven-year period after Le Prince vanished, both the Lumière brothers in Paris (December 1895) and Edison in New York (April 1896) managed to hold successful film projections. The success of Edison's Vitascope projector and the Lumières' *cinématographe* (a combination camera and projector) launched a veritable craze on both sides of the Atlantic, as everyone scrambled to outdo each other in the brand-new moviemaking business.

After Dickson joined some of Edison's competitors in founding the rival American Mutoscope Company (AMC), Edison filed suit against them in May 1898. As a result of the ensuing legal battle, Le Prince's family (and his reputation) would be dragged into Edison's decade-long effort to prove he was "the original, first, and sole inventor or discoverer" of cinematography. ∎

TOP THEORIES

1 Le Prince was dispatched by his competitors in the filmmaking race.

After Le Prince vanished, Lizzie and the rest of his family immediately suspected foul play. Their suspicions increased as they saw others—particularly Edison—take credit for what they saw as Le Prince's inventions. Edison had a somewhat shady reputation when it came to dealing with his rivals in invention, but could one of his henchmen have actually "removed" Le Prince from the filmmaking race? This theory doesn't hold up under closer inspection, as no evidence has been found to suggest Edison, or any of the other competitors, had anything to do with Le Prince's disappearance.

2 Facing bankruptcy, Le Prince committed suicide.

In 1930, one of Albert Le Prince's grandsons told the French film historian Georges Potonniée that Louis had been on the verge of bankruptcy when he visited his brother in Dijon. According to Potonniée's notes (as quoted by Christopher Rawlence in *The Missing Reel*, his book about Le Prince), "his brother was convinced that the inventor committed suicide having taken all the necessary steps not to be found." Rawlence found that by September 1890, Joseph Whitley's company was going bankrupt, and Le Prince had debts of more than $80,000, incurred in his all-consuming quest to perfect his inventions. It doesn't seem too far-fetched to imagine that Le Prince would choose suicide rather than face financial ruin for himself and his family. On the other hand, critics of the suicide theory point out that friends and family said Le Prince had no suicidal tendencies. And would a man on the verge of unveiling his long-awaited life's work, as Le Prince was, really choose to take his own life?

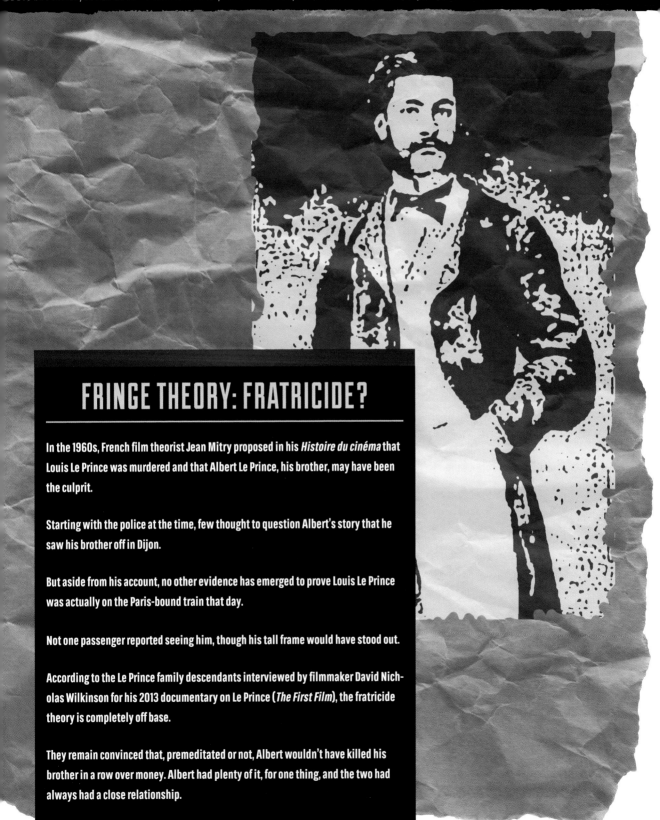

FRINGE THEORY: FRATRICIDE?

In the 1960s, French film theorist Jean Mitry proposed in his *Histoire du cinéma* that Louis Le Prince was murdered and that Albert Le Prince, his brother, may have been the culprit.

Starting with the police at the time, few thought to question Albert's story that he saw his brother off in Dijon.

But aside from his account, no other evidence has emerged to prove Louis Le Prince was actually on the Paris-bound train that day.

Not one passenger reported seeing him, though his tall frame would have stood out.

According to the Le Prince family descendants interviewed by filmmaker David Nicholas Wilkinson for his 2013 documentary on Le Prince (*The First Film*), the fratricide theory is completely off base.

They remain convinced that, premeditated or not, Albert wouldn't have killed his brother in a row over money. Albert had plenty of it, for one thing, and the two had always had a close relationship.

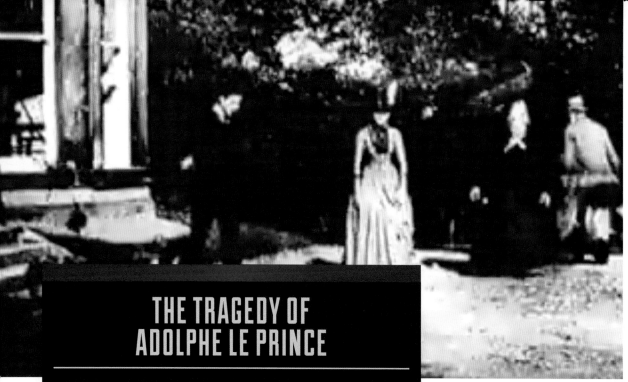

THE TRAGEDY OF ADOLPHE LE PRINCE

1888 Louis Le Prince's Roundhay Garden Scene. Wikipedia Commons

In late 1898, Adolphe Le Prince testified in defense of American Mutoscope, the company that Edison had sued for stealing his work.

Adolphe had witnessed his father's first experiments in New York at the age of twelve and worked alongside him in Leeds from 1887–89.

While a student at Columbia University, he took a year's leave of absence to gather evidence of Louis's achievements in preparation for his testimony.

But the Mutoscope legal team didn't let Adolphe exhibit his father's single-lens camera in court, and Edison's lawyers expressed doubt that it even existed.

In 1901, the court ruled in Edison's favor, effectively dismissing the validity of Le Prince's work (and that of various others).

The decision would be reversed on appeal the following year, but Adolphe didn't live to see this reversal.

In July 1901, he was found dead with his duck-hunting gun next to him near the family's summer cottage on Fire Island.

UNSOLVED OR CASE CLOSED?

WITH NO BODY, NO CRIME SCENE, NO WITNESSES, AND A TWO-MONTH DELAY in reporting Louis Le Prince missing, the case of his disappearance grew cold soon after it began. In 1897, after seven years had passed, Le Prince was officially presumed to be dead. His wife and family didn't give up hope, however, even as they waged their ill-fated battle to win credit for his moviemaking inventions.

As the *Edison v. American Mutoscope* legal battle played out, the family's hopes of fulfilling Le Prince's ambitions faded. Then in July 1901, young Adolphe Le Prince, Louis and Lizzie's son, was found dead. Like his father's disappearance, Adolphe's death remained a mystery: Was it an accident? Suicide? Or—as his mother suspected—another murder?

In 2003, a researcher going through the Paris police archives turned up an intriguing photograph from 1890. It shows the face of a drowned man who, with his grayish whiskers, strongly resembled Louis Le Prince. Despite the resemblance, there's no way to know if it was actually him; the body was buried in a pauper's grave in November 1890, soon after the photograph was taken.

LOUIS LE PRINCE

Louis Aimé August Le Prince came to Leeds in 1866 where he experimented in cinematography. In 1888 he patented a one-lens camera with which he filmed Leeds Bridge from this British Waterways building. These were probably the world's first successful moving pictures.

LASTING IMPACT

The blue plaque on Leeds Bridge in the U.K. commemorating Le Prince. Wikimedia Commons

HISTORY'S FIRST FILM?

By October 1888, Le Prince was ready to test the capability of his single-lens camera.

He used it to film his in-laws, John and Sarah Whitley, his son Adolphe, and a family friend, Annie Hartley, walking around his father-in-law's garden at Oakwood Grange, Roundhay, Leeds.

According to Adolphe Le Prince, the film was shot on October 14, 1888; it certainly couldn't have been filmed much later than that, because Sarah Whitley died just ten days later, on October 24.

With a duration of around two seconds, the *Roundhay Garden Scene*, as it is known, is believed to be the oldest surviving film in existence.

FOR MORE THAN 125 YEARS, THE FACT THAT LOUIS Le Prince disappeared under mysterious circumstances has overshadowed his life's work—not least because he vanished before he had a chance to show it to the world. But in the city of Leeds, located in West Yorkshire, England, the Frenchman is celebrated as a local hero and the true father of the motion picture industry. Le Prince's former workshop, at 160 Woodhouse Lane, later became the local headquarters of the British Broadcasting Corporation (BBC). In October 1988, on the one hundredth anniversary of the films he shot on Leeds Bridge and in Roundhay Garden, a blue plaque went up at the site, commemorating Le Prince's work.

Even beyond Leeds and West Yorkshire, Le Prince has received belated recognition in recent years for successfully making films in late 1888, some seven years before the more widely known achievements of the Lumière brothers and Thomas Edison. In 2015, *The First Film*, a feature-length documentary about Le Prince's life and inventions, premiered at the Edinburgh Film Festival. Subtitled "The Greatest Mystery in Cinema History," the documentary follows a three-decade-long quest by the actor and filmmaker David Nicholas Wilkinson to prove that Le Prince produced the world's first films in Leeds in 1888. In September 2016, the film had its US premiere at a fitting location—the Morris-Jumel Mansion in New York City, where Lizzie Le Prince had been preparing to present the first screening of her husband's films exactly 126 years earlier. ∎

RANSOM OF $20,000 ASKED FOR CRATER

Note to Judge's Wife D... Money in Small Bill... His Safe Return.

FRIENDS VIEW IT AS F...

...olice Start Hunt for ...—Grand Jury Hears S... ...rist's Disappearance.

...rs after District Attorney ...resented the evidence ...sses yesterday to the ...ury investigating the ... of Supreme Court ...Force Crater. the ...intensive search for ...n anonymous letter ...s. Crater informing ...band was alive and ...0 ransom for his

...brought to New ...Clarke, brother-... ...ater, from the ...e at Belgrade

SEARCH FOR CRATER SWINGS TO HAVANA

"Tip" in Anonymous Letter Tells Police Missing Judge Was Seen in Cuba Aug. 15.

ALSO REPORTED IN OHIO

Believed to Have Stopped at Former Home of Sister-in-Law—Inquiry in Maine at a Standstill.

All clues to the disappearance of Supreme Court Justice Joseph F. Crater failed again yesterday, the forty-eighth day since his disappearance. The police continued a futile search for Mrs. Connie Marcus, said to be a friend of the missing jurist, and the District Attorney's office prepared to resume today the county grand jury's investigation of the Crater mystery, which was adjourned yesterday for the Jewish holiday.

In Maine, where County Attorney Frank E. Southard started a Kennebec County inquiry at the request of District Attorney Crain, no progress was reported yesterday because of the continued illness of Mrs. Stella Crater, wife of the judge, at her Summer home at Belgrade Lakes and to the absence in Chicago of Mr. Southard. Captain Joseph F. Young Jr., Deputy Chief of the Main State Highway Police, who was unable to question Mrs. Crater Monday because of her nervous condition, did not renew his attempt to see her yesterday. Until the Kennebec County grand jury meets next Tuesday few developments are expected there.

In New York the police continued their watch for Mrs. Marcus, who was expected back in town after a visit to an unknown destination. Police Commissioner Mulrooney sa... that his men were still watching th... Hotel Mayflower, where, it was r... ported, Mrs. Marcus had an apar... ment until last Thursday.

Left Her Job Suddenly.

At the dress shop of Maurice M... del, Inc., 28 West Fifty-seve... Street, where Mrs. Marcus had b... employed as a saleswoman for ... eral years, Mr. Mendel said that ... left his employ suddenly on S... 13 without any explanation. The ... lice were told that Judge Crater ... been acquainted with Mrs. Ma...

Reports that one or more of ... checks drawn by Justice Crater ...

JERSEY GIRL INSISTS SHE SAW CRATER AUG. 8

Phillipsburg Pharmacist Also Tells Grand Jury Jurist's Cousin Asked Her to Change Story.

Miss Helen Murray, pharmacist, of Phillipsburg, N. J., who says she saw Joseph F. Crater, missing Supreme Court Justice, in her brother's drug store in Phillipsburg on Aug. 8, two days after the jurist's disappearance before stuck to her story yesterday. She also told the jurors that "a cousin of Crater's," presumably W. Everett Crater, who lives in Easton, Pa., just across the Delaware River from Phillipsburg, had called on her after she had told newspapers of the Crater visit and had asked her to change her story.

It was W. Everett Crater who announced after Miss Murray told of seeing a man who said he was "Joseph F. Crater," that it was he who had visited the Phillipsburg drug store and that Miss Murray was evidently mistaken as to identity and as to date. Miss Murray "absolutely identified" yesterday a photograph of Judge Crater as the man who came into the drug store.

Mr. ...rain announced that he would atte... ...et ...verett Crater, Mis... ...ur's ...d he... ...her to John... ...wh... ...ow... the phar... ...con... ...er... ...ely.

THE HEADLINES

JUDGE JOSEPH FORCE CRATER 1930

O N A HOT NIGHT IN AUGUST 1930, JOSEPH FORCE Crater, a newly appointed associate justice for the New York Supreme Court, vanished from the streets of Manhattan. News of his disappearance would spark a frenzy of scandal and speculation: The missing judge was linked to accusations of corruption in the highest reaches of New York City politics, particularly Tammany Hall, the powerful Democratic Party machine of New York County.

Crater, known to many as "Good Time Joe," had at least one longtime mistress, and a well-established fondness for showgirls and nightclubs with underworld connections. As president of a local Tammany club, he was also a person of interest in the ongoing investigation of George Ewald, who allegedly bought a judgeship with a phony "loan" of $10,000 to Martin Healy, the district leader of Crater's club.

In the years to come, the so-called "missingest man in New York" entered the ranks of legend. The New York Police Department would spend nearly fifty years, on and off, investigating Crater's fate, making his the longest-running unsolved missing persons case in the department's history.

IN OTHER NEWS

Betty Boop made her debut in the animated cartoon "Dizzy Dishes," by Max Fleischer.

Pilot Frank Hawks set a new transcontinental (west-east) flying record of twelve hours, twenty-five minutes, and three seconds, beating Charles Lindbergh's earlier record by more than three hours.

President Herbert Hoover gave a press conference offering relief plans for those affected by a series of devastating droughts.

Gandhi sent a letter (from jail) to Lord Irwin, viceroy of India, containing the terms for cessation of his civil disobedience campaign.

In New York City, Mayor Al Smith laid the cornerstone for the Empire State Building.

BACKGROUND ON TAMMANY HALL

The Society of Tammany was founded in 1789 as an organization dedicated to defending America's democratic ideals.

Over two centuries, it endured as New York City's top political machine, with its leadership often mirroring the local Democratic Party establishment.

By the late nineteenth century, however, Tammany Hall had become synonymous with corruption, and with its most notorious "boss," William Macy Tweed.

Tammany retained its popularity, however, by showing generosity to New York's poor and immigrant population, which showed its gratitude at the ballot box.

WHAT DID WE KNOW?

JOSEPH FORCE CRATER GREW UP IN EASTON, PENNSYL-
vania, where his family had a successful produce business. After earning his law degree at Columbia, he rose in the ranks of
young New York lawyers, clerking for Judge Robert Wagner of the
New York Supreme Court and teaching law at Fordham and New
York University. Crater also became president of the prestigious
Cayuga Democratic Club, earning him valuable connections in
Tammany Hall. ("Clubs" were the focus of Tammany's organization at the assembly-district level, which was the closest level to
actual voters.)

Crater had married Stella Wheeler in 1917, after representing
her in her divorce from her first husband. When Crater entered
private practice in the late 1920s, the couple moved into a co-op
apartment on Fifth Avenue. Things got even better in early 1930,
when he was considered for a soon-to-be-vacant judgeship on
the New York Supreme Court. He got the job on April 8, after
then-governor Franklin D. Roosevelt responded to an appeal by
Wagner, Crater's former boss and mentor, and now a US senator.

In November, with Tammany's help, Crater expected to win
election to a full fourteen-year term on the bench. In the mean-
time, he and Stella left town just after the court session ended in
late June, heading up to their summer cabin in Belgrade Lakes,
Maine, to escape the New York heat.

Crater's home at 40 Fifth Avenue in Manhattan. Library of Congress

THE EVIDENCE

CRATER AND CORRUPTION

At first, speculation about Crater's disappearance focused mostly on his extramarital activities (including liaisons with showgirls and frequent outings to nightclubs favored by gangsters and politicians alike).

But in mid-October, more than a month after the story broke, the *Herald-Tribune* (New York's leading Republican newspaper) publicly linked the Crater investigation to the ongoing judicial corruption probes.

The paper claimed it was "generally believed" that Crater fled because he knew something about the Ewald-Healy payoff and Tammany corruption.

Republic gubernatorial candidate Charles Tuttle even suggested during his 1930 campaign that Crater had paid for the judicial post he received from Tuttle's opponent, Governor Roosevelt.

The rumor didn't stick: Already considered the front-runner for the 1932 Democratic presidential nomination, FDR would be reelected in a landslide that November.

O N AUGUST 3, 1930, AFTER A MYSTERIOUS PHONE call, Crater told Stella he needed to return to the city, but would return by August 9 (her birthday). In New York, Crater told the couple's maid to return to clean their Fifth Avenue apartment on August 7, then take the next couple of weeks off.

According to his law clerk, Joseph Mara, on August 6 Crater spent time in his office destroying some papers, and asked Mara to cash two personal checks for him, at two different banks. After Mara returned with $5,150 (equivalent to at least $65,000 in today's currency), the two men left the courthouse with several portfolios of papers and took a taxi to Crater's apartment.

Early that evening, Crater bought a ticket to the Broadway comedy *Dancing Partner* at a ticket agency and arranged for it to be held for him at the theater. Around 8:00 p.m., he entered Billy Haas's Chophouse at 332 West 45th Street, and dined with a lawyer friend, William Klein, and the showgirl Sally Lou Ritz. When they left the restaurant at 9:15, Crater still had time to catch the last act of *Dancing Partner*, but it's not clear whether or not he did. After Klein and Ritz said good-bye to the judge and got into a taxi, Crater was never seen or heard from again.

A DISCOVERY

Stella Crater, who had refused to testify in the investigation, returned to New York a week or so after it ended in January 1931.

In a bureau drawer, she discovered four manila envelopes containing more than $6,000 in cash, personal checks, Crater's will (he left everything to his wife), bankbooks, and a five-page letter listing dozens of people who owed him money.

At the end of the letter, Crater wrote: "Am very weary" (alternatively, it could be read as "I'm very sorry"), and signed off simply "Love, Joe."

Mrs. Crater's discovery provided some new leads—though none of them turned up a trace of her husband—but also raised questions, as police swore the bureau drawer had been empty when they'd searched the apartment months earlier.

O NLY AFTER CRATER FAILED TO SHOW UP TO THE opening of the courts on August 25 did his wife, colleagues, and friends appear to become seriously concerned about his well-being. At first they tried to investigate discreetly, but all bets were off after September 3, when the *New York World* broke the news of his disappearance. Only then did Crater's friend Simon Rifkind decide to file a missing persons report with the NYPD, officially opening the case.

More than ten thousand circulars with a detailed description of Crater were sent around the country, and to foreign consulates. Rewards of $7,500 were offered, with no response, and though someone sent Stella a ransom note demanding $20,000 for her husband, it was quickly dismissed as a hoax.

As Crater "sightings" poured in, the police followed them, from New York to Vermont to Canada. Tips about Crater's various alleged female companions pointed the search to Chicago one day, Atlantic City the next. Meanwhile, the purported connection between the missing judge and the ongoing Ewald-Healy corruption trial led the DA to call a grand jury investigation into Crater's disappearance by mid-September. After forty-five sessions and thousands of pages' worth of testimony, it came up empty.

DEVELOPING STORY

TOP THEORIES

1 Crater ran away with one of his mistresses.

Police hunted Crater's longtime mistress, the former model Constance Marcus, who left the city in a hurry soon after news of his disappearance broke. But this and other promising leads went nowhere. After a while some suggested the "showgirl" and "mistress" stories might be a ruse to distract the public from the bigger issue (i.e., political corruption).

2 Crater was murdered due to involvement in New York City/Tammany corruption.

Stella Crater blamed her husband's so-called friends, with their political connections and intrigue, for his disappearance and death. She wasn't the only one. The most popular theory at the time was that gangsters had hired a hit man to get rid of Crater, so he couldn't reveal what he knew about Tammany-related dirt and other political corruption in the city.

3 Crater left town voluntarily (for similar reasons).

Others thought maybe Crater had planned to disappear of his own accord—perhaps to avoid being forced to testify in the ongoing corruption probe. The personal checks Crater had written to himself (and predated August 30), as well as the personal items he left behind (his card case, watch and chain, and fountain pen), suggested that he may have intended to drop out of sight, whether for a short time or longer. But the publicity surrounding the case made it difficult to believe he could have begun a new life somewhere else, without eventually being found out.

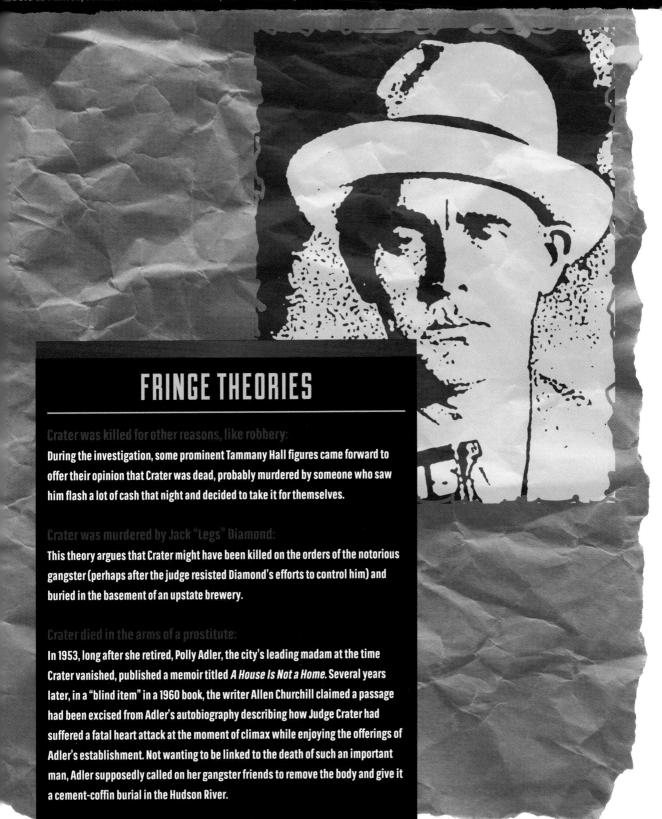

FRINGE THEORIES

Crater was killed for other reasons, like robbery:

During the investigation, some prominent Tammany Hall figures came forward to offer their opinion that Crater was dead, probably murdered by someone who saw him flash a lot of cash that night and decided to take it for themselves.

Crater was murdered by Jack "Legs" Diamond:

This theory argues that Crater might have been killed on the orders of the notorious gangster (perhaps after the judge resisted Diamond's efforts to control him) and buried in the basement of an upstate brewery.

Crater died in the arms of a prostitute:

In 1953, long after she retired, Polly Adler, the city's leading madam at the time Crater vanished, published a memoir titled *A House Is Not a Home*. Several years later, in a "blind item" in a 1960 book, the writer Allen Churchill claimed a passage had been excised from Adler's autobiography describing how Judge Crater had suffered a fatal heart attack at the moment of climax while enjoying the offerings of Adler's establishment. Not wanting to be linked to the death of such an important man, Adler supposedly called on her gangster friends to remove the body and give it a cement-coffin burial in the Hudson River.

Digging Ends in Hunt For Judge Crater

YONKERS, N.Y. (AP) — Au-thorities gave up digging yester-day for Judge Joseph Crater, who has been missing for 34 years. They found no trace of the jurist.

Under the direction of West-chester County Sheriff John E. Hoy, workers excavated a 50 by 65-foot hole, 2 1-2 feet deep, on the roadside where a Dutch clair-voyant divined that Crater had been buried.

The same clairvoyant, Gerard Croiset, had caused a Yonkers yard to be dug up five years ago. He said his extrasensory percep-tions told him that Crater was buried there.

The latest digging came about from Croiset's decision that the judge originally had been buried in the yard but was moved to this new location before the excavation.

(Continued on Page Four)

Stella Crater Kunz, Once Wed To Judge Who Vanished, Dead

The New York Times, 1955
Mrs. Stella Crater Kunz

Mrs. Stella Crater Kunz, for-mer wife of Justice Joseph Force Crater, who disappeared Aug. 6, 1930, died Sunday at the Davis Nursing Home in Mount Vernon, N.Y., where she had lived for six years. She was about 70 years old.

Mrs. Kunz, whose maiden name was Wheeler, was mar-ried in 1917 to Mr. Crater, the lawyer who obtained her di-vorce from her first husband.

When Judge Crater was last seen, getting into a taxicab out-side Billy Haas's restaurant on West 45th Street, Mrs. Crater was at their country home at Belgrade Lakes, Me., where she testified later, she last saw her husband on Aug. 3, 1930.

He left for New York that day, she said, intending to re-turn six days later. After 10 days, Mrs. Crater sent their chauffeur to the city to in-vestigate. Several of the judge's friends told the chauffeur they were sure everything was all right.

When the courts opened on Aug. 25 the judge's colleagues started a private search, but it was not until Sept. 3 that the police were notified.

Mrs. Crater refused to ap-pear before a grand jury in-vestigating the disappearance, which finally ruled:

"The evidence is insufficient to warrant any expression of opinion as to whether Crater is alive or dead, or as to whether he absented himself voluntarily, or is a sufferer from a disease in the nature of amnesia, or the victim of a crime."

Mrs. Crater said later that

judge, a Tammay Hall stalwart, occurred at the beginning of the Seabury investigations which led to the resignation of Mayor James Walker.

Mrs. Crater was evicted from the couple's apartment at 40 Fifth Avenue, and worked as a secretary. In 1939, the judge was declared legally dead, and Mrs. Crater received $20,561 in life insurance. She had married Carl Kunz, an electrical engineer, in 1938. They separated in 1950.

In 1961 Mrs. Kunz and Os-car Fraley wrote a book, "The Empty Robe," telling her story.

Mrs. Kunz leaves a sister, Mrs. H. G. Herbert of New Rochelle, N. Y.

A funeral service was he

THE EMPTY ROBE

At Stella Crater's request, a probate court declared her husband legally dead in 1939.

In the process, her lawyer advanced the theory that gangsters had mur-dered Crater in a blackmail conflict over yet another showgirl. In a book about her experience, *The Empty Robe* (1961), written with Oscar Fraley, Stella seemed to endorse her lawyer's dubious theory.

For years, Stella—who had remarried and divorced—reportedly continued to honor her second husband's memory each August 6 by ordering two cocktails in a Greenwich Village bar, drinking one of them, and leaving the other untouched.

She died in a New York nursing home in 1969.

UNSOLVED OR CASE CLOSED?

OFFICIALLY, THE CRATER CASE IS STILL OPEN, AL-though the NYPD has classified it as inactive. But in 2005, a piece of new evidence brought the missing judge back into the public eye—if only briefly. After Stella Ferrucci-Good of Bellero-se, Queens, died that April, her granddaughter found an envelope marked "Do not open until my death" among her possessions. In the note inside, Ferrucci-Good claimed that her late husband, Robert Good, had murdered Crater along with two other men—an NYPD cop named Charles Burns, and Burns's brother Frank, a cabdriver—and buried his body under a section of the Coney Island boardwalk.

Police looked into the story, but the section she mentioned—near West Eighth Street—had been excavated in the 1950s during construction of the New York Aquarium, back before the technol-ogy existed to identify potential human remains. Judge Crater's fate remains a mystery today.

LASTING IMPACT

"PULLING A CRATER"

Because of the controversy surrounding it, Crater's disappearance almost immediately entered the public consciousness in a way few missing persons cases do.

For years after he vanished, the expression "pulling a Crater" became shorthand for disappearing suddenly.

Comedians used the missing judge as fodder for their nightclub standup routines, including the popular gag "Judge Crater, call your office."

Groucho Marx had a bit where he joked he was going to "step out and look for Judge Crater," and *MAD* magazine published a cartoon showing Lassie, the trusty collie, finding Crater.

IN 1933, A MARKETING CAMPAIGN FOR THE WARNER Brothers movie *Bureau of Missing Persons* offered Judge Crater $10,000 (worth more than $130,000 today) if he would show up to the box office in person to claim the money. And even in 1980, fifty years after his disappearance, the NYPD's Missing Persons Bureau continued to receive a slew of calls each August from people claiming to have seen Crater.

Crater's disappearance shocked the system of a city and country still reeling from the stock market crash less than a year earlier, and mired in the early stages of the Depression. As Richard J. Tofel wrote in *Vanishing Point*, his 2004 book about the case, Judge Crater became a symbol of a major change in New York City politics: the decline and fall of Tammany Hall. Caught up in the ever-widening corruption scandal, Democratic mayor James Walker resigned in 1932. His successor was Fiorello La Guardia, who over three terms would successfully chip away at Tammany's power and influence—with the help of President Franklin D. Roosevelt—inflicting damage from which it would never fully recover. ∎

THE HEADLINES

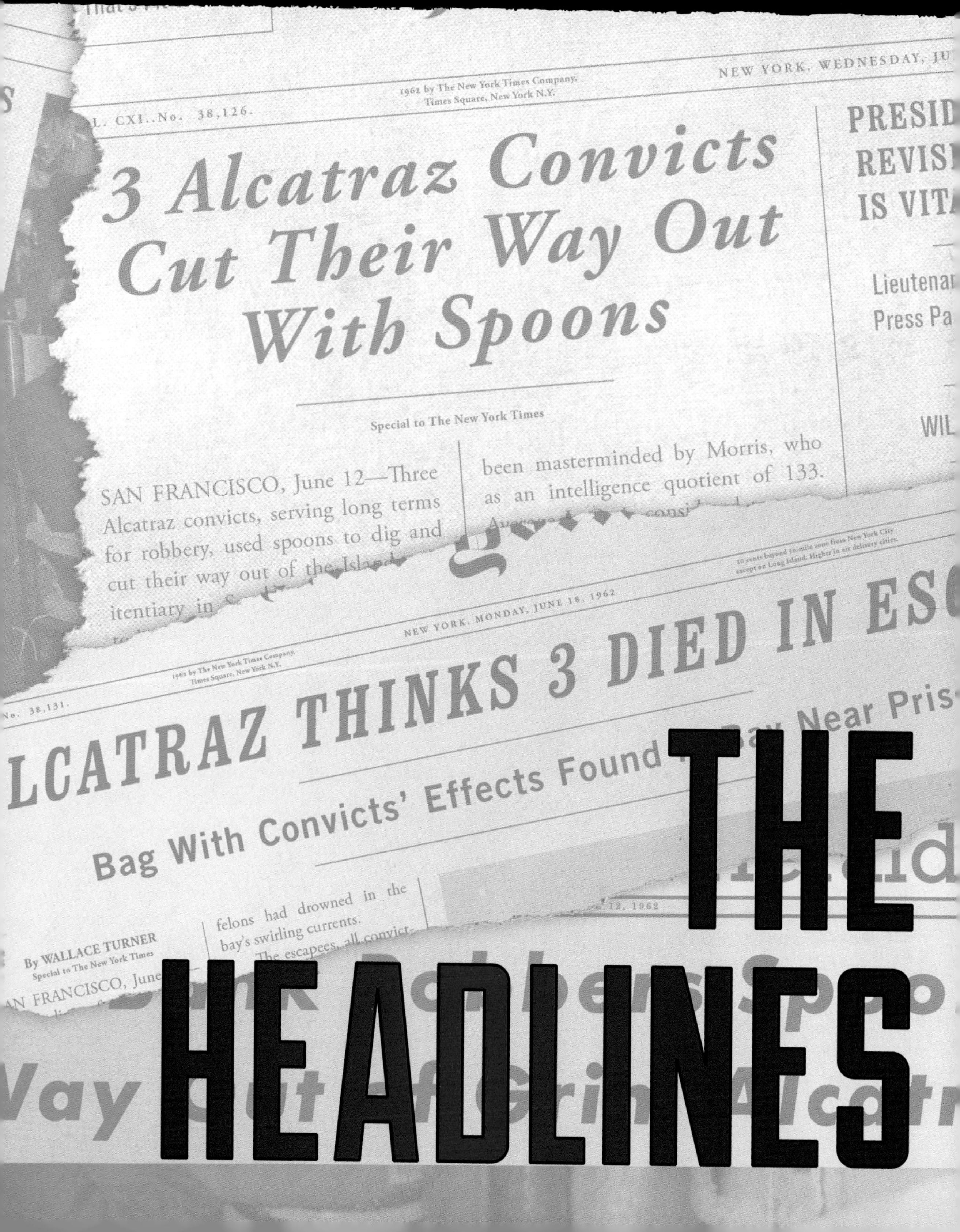

3 Alcatraz Convicts Cut Their Way Out With Spoons

Special to The New York Times

L. CXI..No. 38,126.

1962 by The New York Times Company,
Times Square, New York N.Y.

NEW YORK, WEDNESDAY, JU

SAN FRANCISCO, June 12—Three Alcatraz convicts, serving long terms for robbery, used spoons to dig and cut their way out of the Island itentiary in S

been masterminded by Morris, who as an intelligence quotient of 133.

PRESID
REVISI
IS VITA

Lieutenar
Press Pa

WIL

ALCATRAZ THINKS 3 DIED IN ESC

Bag With Convicts' Effects Found Bay Near Pris

NEW YORK, MONDAY, JUNE 18, 1962

1962 by The New York Times Company,
Times Square, New York N.Y.

No. 38,131.

10 cents beyond 50-mile zone from New York City
except on Long Island. Higher in air delivery cities.

By WALLACE TURNER
Special to The New York Times

AN FRANCISCO, June

felons had drowned in the bay's swirling currents.
The escapees, all convict

Prison guard uses flashlight to show the hole made by Alcatraz convicts to escape their cell.
FBI photo

ESCAPE FROM ALCATRAZ? 1962

FROM THE TIME IT OPENED IN 1934, THE FEDERAL prison on Alcatraz Island struck fear into the hearts of even the most hardened criminals. "The Rock," as it was known, was considered America's only escape-proof prison. Built on a twenty-two-acre island in San Francisco Bay, the prison measured 80,000 square feet of impenetrable concrete and steel, with a ratio of one guard to every three prisoners. Once they put you in the Rock, you were never getting out.

But on the night of June 11, 1962, Frank Morris and two brothers, John and Clarence Anglin, may have done just that. During months of preparation, they had used spoons and other crude tools to dig themselves out of their cells. That night, they put dummies in their beds to fool the guards and worked their way through vents, between walls, and over barbed-wire fences to the edge of the island. With makeshift paddles and a crude inflated raft stitched together from rubber raincoats, the three men set off into the bay's frigid waters. After a massive manhunt turned up no bodies, and few clues, the inmates' possible escape from the world's toughest prison fascinated the public. Had someone finally managed to break the Rock?

IN OTHER NEWS

The United Nations was forced to borrow $2 million to meet expenses for its Congo force, an emergency force in Egypt, and other routine activities.

Soviet premier Nikita Khrushchev declared that an agreement to form a coalition government in Laos could be a model solution for other problems between the West and the Soviet bloc.

Vietnam's first lady, Madame Ngo Dinh Nhu, told residents of the growing American colony in the country to abide by the regime's new puritanical regulations and desist from dancing.

BACKGROUND ON ALCATRAZ

In the early 1930s, J. Edgar Hoover and the Bureau of Prisons designed the new federal penitentiary on Alcatraz as the nation's first supermax prison.

Already a military prison during the Civil War, the building got a serious upgrade, including a new cellblock with top-grade steel and keyless locks.

Guards toting machine guns patrolled outside the cells, conducting thirteen head counts and multiple prisoner verifications each day.

Inmates were prohibited from gathering in small groups, even during meals or rest hour.

Other security measures included remote-controlled canisters of tear gas, metal detectors throughout the prison, and multiple gun towers.

By the early 1960s, much of the prison's concrete had begun to crumble due to exposure to wind, fog, and moisture.

Aerial view of Alcatraz Island and its federal penitentiary in January 1932. FBI photo

WHAT DID WE KNOW?

I N THE TWENTY-NINE YEARS OF ITS OPERATION, THE federal prison on Alcatraz Island housed nearly 1,500 inmates. Some of the nation's most notorious criminals did time there, including Al Capone, George "Machine Gun" Kelly, and James "Whitey" Bulger. Before 1962, there had been twelve escape attempts—including a violent incident in 1948 that left two guards and three inmates dead—and none of the prisoners involved were thought to have made it out alive.

Frank Morris, who arrived on the Rock in 1960, reportedly had an IQ of 133—higher than 98 percent of the population. Orphaned, sent into foster care, and convicted of his first crime at the age of thirteen, he escaped from Louisiana State Penitentiary while serving a ten-year sentence for bank robbery, but was caught in a burglary attempt and sent to Alcatraz. John and Clarence Anglin had served time in Alabama, Florida, and Georgia before they were arrested for bank robbery in 1958 and sent to the federal penitentiary in Leavenworth, Kansas, then on to Alcatraz.

In late 1961, a fellow prisoner told Morris and the Anglins that there was a secret passage to the roof accessible through a ventilator shaft running behind the cellblock walls. Fashioning a chisel from a spoon, Clarence Anglin began chipping away at the weathered concrete in his cell, and the escape plot was born.

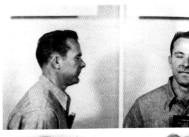

Alcatraz escapees Clarence Anglin, John Anglin, and Frank Morris. FBI photos

THE EVIDENCE

The cell of Alcatraz escapee Clarence Anglin, and the roof vent and escape route used by Clarence, his brother John, and Frank Morris. FBI photo

THE MANHUNT

The alarm sounded on the morning of June 12, 1962: Three inmates were missing from the cells.

As prison officials combed the 12-acre island, FBI agents hurried to aid in the search.

Over the next ten days, the Bureau of Prisons, FBI, US Coast Guard, California Highway Patrol, and local police officers made an extensive search of the Golden Gate, bay islands, and the shoreline of Marin County, north of Alcatraz.

Some two hundred US Army troops were deployed to aid in the search.

It was called the biggest manhunt since the kidnapping of Charles Lindbergh's baby son in 1932.

GUARDS WHO WALKED PAST THE THREE INMATES' cells at 9:30 p.m. on the night of June 11, 1962, saw them inside. But by the time the first bell rang at 7:00 a.m. the next morning, Morris and the Anglins had vanished, replaced by pillows stuffed under their bedclothes and papier-mâché heads.

Federal agents, state and local police officers, coast guard boats, and military helicopters combed Alcatraz Island, San Francisco Bay, and the surrounding countryside, in the largest manhunt since the kidnapping of the Lindbergh baby in 1932.

On Angel Island (located two miles north of Alcatraz and a mile from the Tiburon headlands of Marin County), searchers found the shredded remnants of a crude rubber raft, a makeshift oar, and a plastic bag containing personal effects belonging to the Anglins, including phone numbers and addresses of friends and relatives. Aside from those few clues, the manhunt turned up no trace of Morris or the brothers. ∎

Officials Say Erosion Helped 3 Escape Alcatraz

Walls Debilitated by Age— Manhunt Extended as 200 Army Troops Deploy

By LAWRENCE E. DAVIES
Special to The New York Times.

SAN FRANCISCO, June 13 —Three convicts who dug escape hatches with spoons through cell walls on Alcatraz Island were aided by the erosion and debilitation of the Federal penitentiary.

This was indicated today by prison officials, while an intensive search continued for Frank L. Morris, 35-year-old Louisiana bank robber; John W. Anglin, 32, and Clarence Anglin, 31, bank-robbing brothers of Florida.

A force of 200 armed guards, two state...... Angel Al- traz, in ...... the fourth ...... A ...... w...... se...... with ...... ng co...... cts at th...... anta ...... er al...... son befo...... r tr...... er to ...... catraz, ... port...... ha...... an...... e ho...... his ...... xt to that of Morris.

He did not join the others in fleeing, however. He is serving a ten-year sentence for interstate transportation of stolen automobiles.

Warden Olin G. Blackwell said there was "a remote possibility" that the three were still on the island.

The extent of the search coordinated by the Federal Bureau of Investigation, however, indicated a general view that the prisoners had sought refuge on the mainland or another island in San Francisco Bay.

Fred J. Wilkinson, assistant Federal director of prisons, who flew here from Washington, noted that Alcatraz was old, and its concrete, plumbing and bars were debilitated. He estimated it would take $5,000,000 to raise the prison to a high standard of security.

Cell of Jo...... ...... tains dum...... ...... he...... used .... a robe co...... l...... a hole at...... re...

crete in th...... nch-th...... with...... cell walls was no...... rumb...... but had suffered s...... eros...... atte...

A hole big e...... gh...... a...... mak...... to squirm thro...... b...... been o...... in the concre...... ur ce...... at ni...... with spoons from the prison...... piece of pipe that enabled them dining hall.

The work, presumably in progress for weeks or months, said. had been camouflaged by removable sections of plaster painted to conform with the wall area. Musical instruments or towels were used to help cover the operations.

A question bothering Mr. Wilkinson was how the...... "the...... make...... to bend a steel bar and get through the roof ventilator, he said.

The prisoners probably had a...... Prison officials had not ascertained how the convicts made and hid dummy heads, remarkably lifelike, which they left on their pillows to mislead guards making bed checks Monday night. The......

ANOTHER INMATE, ALLEN WEST, HAD PLANNED TO escape as well, but was left behind when it proved impossible to remove the ventilation unit in his cell. With information from West, authorities later pieced together details about the escape attempt.

Early on, the FBI, Bureau of Prisons, and other authorities concluded the men had most likely drowned in the frigid waters and swift currents of the San Francisco Bay. About a month after the escape, a Norwegian freighter reported seeing a body dressed in prison-issue denim floating in the Pacific Ocean just past the Golden Gate Bridge.

In 1963, a set of bones washed ashore at Point Reyes National Seashore, but the remains were too badly deteriorated to make an identification. Decades later, in 2010, the Anglin family allowed investigators to exhume the remains of a third brother, Alfred, who had been electrocuted in 1964 while making his own prison break in Alabama. When they compared Alfred Anglin's DNA with the bones, it was not a match, although the remains could still belong to Morris, who has no living relatives to provide DNA.

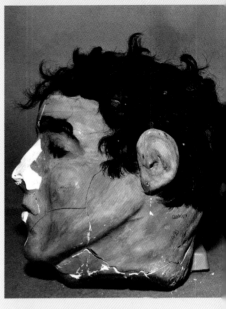

In cell 138, Frank Morris placed a papier-mâché dummy head on the pillow to fool prison guards. FBI photo

HOW THE ESCAPE WENT DOWN

Using spoons and a crude drill made from a vacuum cleaner, Morris and the Anglins made holes they could squeeze through into a small utility corridor.

In a secret workshop they created above the cellblock, they stitched together an inflatable raft made of fifty rubber raincoats and made realistic-looking papier-mâché dummy heads topped with real hair from the prison barbershop.

When the time came, they retrieved the raft and other materials and climbed through the ventilator shaft to the roof, where they had prepared an escape hatch through a fan grille.

In sight of a gun tower, they crossed the roof, scaled a 50-foot wall illuminated by a searchlight, and climbed over two barbed-wire fences, each some 12 feet high.

They reached the island's northeast shoreline, where they inflated their raft using an accordion-like instrument stolen from another inmate, and pushed off into the dense fog sometime after 10:00 p.m.

TOP THEORIES

1 The three inmates drowned during their attempt to escape.

Federal officials concluded that the escapees had drowned in San Francisco Bay's swift currents and cold water, the temperature of which hovered around 50 to 55 degrees Fahrenheit. To support this theory, officials pointed to the fact that no car robberies or other thefts were reported in the surrounding area on the night of the escape.

The biggest problem with this theory? Proof of death. Statistically, most bodies of people who drown in the San Francisco Bay float to the surface within days. In this case, not one of the bodies ever surfaced.

2 They survived, and made their way to freedom.

The Anglin brothers' sister, Marie Anglin Widner, was convinced from the start that her brothers survived. According to her, they even attended their mother's 1973 funeral—disguised as women. "I always believed they made it, and I haven't changed my mind yet," Widner said in a press conference held on the Rock on the escape's fiftieth anniversary.

In 1993, a former Alcatraz inmate told *America's Most Wanted* that he had helped to plan the escape attempt. Based on the "significant new leads" he provided, the US Marshals reopened the case.

3 They managed to escape, but were then killed.

In 2002, the US Marshals received an intriguing (anonymous) tip: The three inmates had survived the escape attempt and headed for Canada, but something went wrong; their handlers betrayed them, and they were murdered.

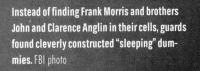

Instead of finding Frank Morris and brothers John and Clarence Anglin in their cells, guards found cleverly constructed "sleeping" dummies. FBI photo

A LONG-RUNNING MYTH AND A SCIENTIFIC EXPERIMENT

Myth: Morris and the Anglins were eaten by sharks. According to one long-standing rumor—often used to emphasize the Rock's terrifying reputation—man-eating great white sharks prowl the waters between Alcatraz and the mainland. Although San Francisco Bay does have sharks, the majority are small, bottom-feeding varieties that display few man-eating tendencies. But great whites are prevalent in the Pacific Ocean, outside the Golden Gate Bridge.

Science: In 2014, a team of Dutch scientists studying the tides in San Francisco Bay simulated dozens of possible routes the three inmates could have taken on the night of the escape. According to their findings, the men could have survived—if they had left between 11:30 p.m. and midnight, and had paddled north hard in order to make it north of the Golden Gate Bridge. But if they had left earlier, or later, the odds of survival greatly decreased.

The Alcatraz escapees' route off of the northeast side of the island. FBI photo

UNSOLVED OR CASE CLOSED?

REVELATIONS FROM THE ANGLIN FAMILY

Federal authorities long looked at members of the Anglin family with suspicion after the 1962 escape, and in return the Anglins sat on information, feeling harassed and mistreated.

But the family continued to believe John and Clarence Anglin had successfully escaped the Rock, and had even made it all the way to South America.

In the documentary *Alcatraz: Search for the Truth*, which aired on HISTORY® in 2015, Ken and David Widner, nephews of Clarence and John Anglin, turned to a retired US marshal, Art Roderick, to help support their claims.

Roderick later told the *New York Post* that the evidence provided by the Widners—which included a photo purportedly showing the Anglin brothers on a farm in Brazil in 1975—was "absolutely the best actionable lead we've had" in the long-running case.

OUT OF THE FORTY-ONE PRISONERS WHO AT-tempted to escape from Alcatraz over its years as a federal prison, Morris and the Anglins are among five inmates officially listed as "missing and presumed drowned." Although the FBI officially declared Morris and the Anglin brothers dead in 1979, and closed the case, the US Marshals subsequently took it on, and are still actively pursuing the three former Alcatraz inmates.

According to its policy, the US Marshal Service will continue to pursue Morris and the Anglin brothers until they are either arrested, positively determined to be deceased, or reach the age of ninety-nine. As US Marshal Don O'Keefe told the press at the time of the fiftieth anniversary, the continuing investigation "serves as a warning to fugitives that regardless of time, we will continue to look for you and bring you to justice."

LASTING IMPACT

A view of Alcatraz today. Library of Congress

Clint Eastwood as Frank Morris in *Escape from Alcatraz.* Photofest

THE HOLLYWOOD VERSION

Directed by Don Siegel, 1979's *Escape from Alcatraz* starred Clint Eastwood as Frank Morris, and Jack Thibeau and Fred Ward as Clarence and John Anglin. Patrick McGoohan played a hostile (unnamed) prison warden.

In the movie, Morris is thrown into the hole after a fight with another inmate; he starts planning his escape after he gets out.

At the end, the movie leaves things ambiguous, but strongly implies that the inmates' escape attempt succeeded.

Escape from Alcatraz was well received by critics and took in some $43 million at the US box office.

ON MARCH 21, 1963, MORE THAN A YEAR AFTER Morris and the Anglins made their Houdini-like escape, the federal prison on Alcatraz Island closed for good. Robert F. Kennedy, then US attorney general, determined that it had grown too expensive to continue operations at the prison, which badly needed repairs and updates. Today, the Rock and its abandoned penitentiary is a tourist attraction, maintained by the National Park Service.

Over the decades since the escape, multiple TV documentaries have covered the events of June 11, 1962. The 1963 book *Escape from Alcatraz*, by J. Campbell Bruce, investigated the 1962 escape, as well as the other escape attempts made during the years a federal prison operated on the Rock. The book inspired a movie of the same name, released in 1979 and starring Clint Eastwood as Frank Morris.

Of the fourteen Alcatraz escape attempts, officials count thirteen as failed. No matter what happened to Morris and the Anglin brothers, one thing is clear: They didn't die behind bars, but managed to make it to freedom, however short-lived it may have been. ∎

Hijacker Collects Ransom of $200,000; Parachutes From Jet and Disappears

By EARL CALDWELL
Special to The New York Times

RENO, Nov. 25—Authorities in four Western states were [search]ing a 500-mile corridor [of mo]untains and river valleys [ ] for a hijacker who [parach]uted from a jet airliner [with $]200,000 in ransom money.

[The] crime, accomplished by [a] middle-aged man in a [business] suit, was apparently [careful]ly planned. The ran[som pai]d by Northwest Air[lines] was the biggest ever sur[rendered] in a United States [case an]d it was the first [ ]ker had parachuted [ ].

[Spokesm]an for the Federal [Bureau of] Investigation said [the sear]ch for the para[chutist was be]ing concentrated [in a wilder]ness area 25 miles [of Po]rtland, Ore., but [the FBI] acknowledged [that the author]ities are [uncertain about the] position [ ]

HIJACKER FLEES, TAKING $200,000

Releases 38 in Seattle and Orders Flight to Mexico

By The Associated Press

RENO, Nev., Nov. 24—A man apparently armed with a bomb hijacked a Northwest Airlines jetliner tonight, collected $2[00,000] in ransom and was not f[ound a]board pl[ane] when it [la]nded here for re fueling, [the Fe]deral [Avia]tion Administra[tion sa]id.

The h[ijacker] was [not] even found [and he] parachu[ted] b[efore the] airline[r lan]ded when th[e plane le]ft Seattle.

Offic[ials said the] ha[d] parachuted from the Boeing identified by 727 while it was in flight or "[D.B.] Cooper," jumped out as it taxied up to the airport terminal with its cabin lights out.

The hijacker took over the Boeing 727 shortly before it was to land here on a flight from Washington, D. C. On the ground, he allowed all 36 passengers and two stewardesses to leave, and an airline employe took the four parachutes and the $200,000 to the plane. Four crew members remained aboard and the three-engine jet was refueled.

Airline officials said the stairwell must be retracted for take[off] [lan]ding but would be

[flig]ht [ ]boa[rd] [ ]ing to [ ]had [brie]fing [ ]cylin[der] [ ]v[isible] [ ]g [ ]ew members, unless his demands were met.

The man, wearing dark

glasses but otherwise undistinguished from the rest of the passengers, demanded that when the plane landed in Seattle there be $200,000 in ransom and four parachutes.

"He was quite relaxed, sitting in the back seat on the starboard [right] side," said Robert B. Gregory of Sumner[ ] [Wa]sh[ington, a pass]enger[ ] [He] was [in the ai]sle [ ] man, [ ] no[t]he[ ] [ ]other[s]a[nd]a [ ]ca was up[ ] [ ]I saw [ ]dess [or a]an[other] [ ]pped," [ ]calle[d]Ric[ ]mons, [ ]ru[n]con[ ]bilitatio[n]rogr[am]n S[ ] "She [was] calmed [and] [gulped. I guess she learned] [ ]what was happening then."

Capt. Wil[liam Scott] [the pi]lot, [rad]ioe[d]pr[oper] [ ]p[ ]ahead [t]o Seattle. [The] a[ ]r[ ]enger said [he]not deman[ded] [specific] infor[m]ation [and de]cli[ned]y whe[n] [ ]s we[re]arked in any [ ]ine [ ]ers had [te]s[ ]to asser[t]l[ ] [s]tage [ ]ach[ ]a [or]dinary use in commercial air travel, proved an-

Continued on Page 73, Column 4

[ ] at Reno airport

Tina Mucklow, stewardess, appeared tired
United Press International

FBI artists's rendering of D.B. Cooper. FBI photo

D. B. COOPER 1971

ON THE DAY BEFORE THANKSGIVING IN 1971, THE man in the dark suit used cash to buy a one-way ticket on Northwest Orient Airlines Flight 305 from Portland, Oregon, to Seattle, Washington. He sat in the last row of the plane, ordered a bourbon and soda, and smoked a cigarette. Once the flight had taken off, he calmly informed one of the flight attendants that he had a bomb in his briefcase. He requested $200,000 and four parachutes, or he would blow up the plane, its crew, the thirty-five other passengers, and himself.

When the plane landed in Seattle, the man released the other passengers but held back the pilot and some of the crew. Once he received the money and parachutes, the plane took off again, at his request, flying at a low altitude toward Mexico City. Somewhere between Seattle and Reno, Nevada, the hijacker jumped from the plane into a driving thunderstorm and subzero temperatures. He was never seen again. Known to most people as D. B. Cooper, he remains the enigmatic culprit behind the only unsolved skyjacking in US history.

IN OTHER NEWS

November 25–December 3, 1971:

British Labour Party leader Harold Wilson proposed that Britain should work toward a withdrawal from Northern Ireland.

The unmanned Soviet space probe *Mars 2* became the first spacecraft to crash-land on Mars.

The United Arab Emirates declared its independence from Great Britain.

India invaded West Pakistan, beginning the Indo-Pakistani War of 1971.

Copy of D.B. Cooper's plane ticket. FBI photo

QUOTES ABOUT D. B. COOPER

"There's nothing unusual about him. He is middle-aged and was wearing dark glasses."

—Richard Simmons of Seattle, another passenger on Flight 305, quoted in the *New York Times*

"He was not nervous. He seemed nice, other than he wanted certain things to be done."

—Flight attendant Tina Mucklow in an interview after the skyjacking

"Parachuting out of a plane in flight like that, you know, he's John Dillinger with an airplane."

—Former FBI assistant director Tom Fuentes, quoted in the HISTORY®'s *D. B. Cooper: Case Closed*

"[A] rodent, a dirty rotten crook, a sleazy rotten criminal who jeopardized the lives of more than 40 people."

—Ralph Himmelsbach, the FBI agent who tracked Cooper the longest

WHAT DID WE KNOW?

O N NOVEMBER 24, 1971, THIRTY-SIX passengers board-ed Northwest Orient Airlines Flight 305, a Boeing 727-100 bound from Portland, Oregon, to Seattle. One of them was a man calling himself Dan Cooper. Once the plane was airborne, Cooper took a note from his pocket and handed it to Florence Schaffner, a flight attendant. "I have a bomb. Sit by me," the note read. A glimpse inside the man's attaché case revealed a tangle of wires and red sticks resembling an explosive device.

Cooper instructed the pilot to proceed to Seattle and pick up $200,000 in cash by 5:00 p.m., along with four parachutes. Captain William Scott radioed Seattle-Tacoma International Airport officials, who contacted Northwest Orient. The airline authorized the $200,000 payment—the equivalent of some $1.2 million today. When the plane landed at Sea-Tac and Cooper got the parachutes and money, he let the passengers off but ordered the pilot and several crew members to stay. With the plane refueled, he told Scott to set a course for Mexico City, at an altitude of only 10,000 feet and a speed of under 200 mph. At that altitude and speed, Scott told him, the jet could travel only 1,000 miles, to around Reno, Nevada, before having to refuel again.

ARCHIVES　1971

Parachuting Hijacker Sought in Wooded Area

SPECIAL TO THE NEW YORK TIMES　NOV. 28, 1971

THE EVIDENCE

THE INVESTIGATORS

The FBI called their investigation into the events of November 24, 1971, NORJAK, for Northwest Hijacking.

As leads came pouring in, the FBI pursued some 1,200 of them, to no avail.

In order to keep track of the money given to Cooper, the FBI had microfilmed the 10,000 $20 bills before giving them to him.

NORJAK investigators distributed 100,000 copies of a pamphlet to banks listing the serial numbers of the bills.

Over the first five years of the investigation, the FBI looked into more than eight hundred suspects, quickly ruling out all but a few dozen.

AFTER TAKEOFF FROM SEA-TAC, COOPER TOLD THE remaining flight attendant, Tina Mucklow, to go into the cockpit with the rest of the crew. Around 8:00 p.m., the crew saw a red light indicating the aft stairs were being lowered. "Is everything okay back there?" Scott called over the intercom.

"Everything is okay," Cooper answered. Those were the last words the pilot and crew heard from him. A few minutes later, Scott noted a slight dip in the jet's nose and then the tail. When the plane landed in Reno at 10:15 p.m., they waited for several minutes and called over the intercom again. Receiving no response, they opened the cockpit door to find the passenger cabin empty, and the aft stairs lowered.

FBI agents swarmed the plane, recovering one of the parachutes, eight cigarette butts, a black tie and tie tack with a mother-of-pearl detail, and sixty-six fingerprints that did not match any of the crew members or other passengers. The weather was so bad that investigators had to wait until the next day to pursue the hijacker himself. When they did, they found nothing. The man calling himself Dan Cooper, his overcoat, his black suitcase, the cash, and the other parachute had vanished into thin air.

A Boeing 727 showing its unique rear stairway that provided D.B. Cooper's getaway from Northwest Orient Airlines flight 305. Photo by Icholakov

The crumbling $20 bills that were discovered in the Columbia River in 1980. FBI photo

D. B. OR DAN?

When a reporter asked FBI agents whether they had any suspects in the hijacking, the agent said "D. Cooper." The reporter misheard it as "D. B. Cooper," published the name, and it stuck.

The mistake actually helped the FBI, as any leads that came in about "D. B. Cooper" could be ignored, while leads that mentioned "Dan Cooper" were taken seriously.

In 2008, international press coverage of a new discovery—an old white military parachute, found within Cooper's drop zone—led the FBI to a new and potentially important clue: "Dan Cooper" was the name of a French comic book series about a Canadian airman that was popular in 1971. One issue, published near the date of the hijacking, even showed Cooper parachuting from a plane.

The comic book was never published in English, so if the hijacker was aware of it, it's likely he spent time overseas.

INVESTIGATORS CONCLUDED THAT COOPER had likely parachuted into a wooded area east of Woodland, Washington, but when they searched there they could find no trace of Cooper, the chute, or the money.

Artists combined eyewitness accounts from passengers and crew to make a composite sketch of Cooper: white man in his forties, 5-foot-10 to 6 feet tall, 170 to 180 pounds, short brown hair, brown eyes. Although the FBI first thought Cooper was an experienced jumper, perhaps a paratrooper, they soon ruled this out: Someone experienced would never have jumped in such dangerous conditions, and would have noticed that the reserve parachute he was given was for training, and had been sewn shut.

The most significant break in the case came in early 1980, when a young boy found $5,800 in crumbling $20 bills in the Columbia River, some 40 miles upstream from the Woodland area. A check of the serial numbers showed that the bills were part of the ransom given to Cooper. The discovery seemed to confirm that Cooper had landed in the Woodland area, but an extensive search of the river, including scuba divers and sonar, yielded nothing.

DEVELOPING STORY

TOP THEORIES

1 Cooper didn't survive the jump.

At 10,000 feet, the air temperature would have been minus-7 degrees Fahrenheit, and the terrain below included woods, rocks, and the Columbia River. Cooper also wasn't dressed for winter, and couldn't have had help waiting on the ground, as he jumped into a random location with zero ground visibility.

2 Cooper was actually Richard Floyd McCoy.

After committing a similar hijacking several months after Cooper's, McCoy broke out of jail in 1974 and was killed in a shoot-out by agents. Though he was too young, not a physical match, and had an alibi, he remained a favorite suspect for some in the Bureau.

3 Nope—he was actually Kenneth Christiansen.

A Minnesotan named Lyle Christiansen has claimed that his late brother, who had worked as a mechanic and flight purser for Northwest Orient, was Cooper. Despite some parallels—Kenny Christiansen loved bourbon, and bought a house shortly after the hijacking—he didn't match Cooper's description, and had been a paratrooper (which the FBI didn't think the hijacker was).

4 Maybe he was Lynn Doyle Cooper.

In 2011, an Oklahoma woman told authorities she believed her late uncle was the hijacker. A Korean War vet from the Pacific Northwest, L. D. Cooper would have been familiar with the area where the hijacker jumped. The DNA didn't match, but this reportedly didn't officially rule him out as a suspect.

One of the unused parachutes that Cooper left behind on the plane. FBI photo

"I AM DAN COOPER"

Various people have claimed to be history's most famous skyjacker. Here are a few of them.

Duane Weber: On his deathbed in 1995, this Floridian claimed to be the elusive skyjacker. Weber's wife later revealed he was an ex-con who had served time in the Seattle-Tacoma area (so would have been familiar with the vicinity where Cooper jumped). But the FBI eliminated Weber as a suspect because his DNA didn't match the tie left on the plane.

Barbara/Bobby Dayton: Former pilots Pat and Ron Forman say their friend Barbara Dayton—a World War II vet, born Robert Dayton—confessed to hijacking Flight 305. After receiving the first sex-change operation performed in the state of Washington, in 1969, Dayton purportedly reverted to her male persona to pull off the crime. The FBI never commented publicly on Dayton, who died in 2002.

William Gossett: A former ROTC instructor and military law professor at Weber State University in Ogden, who died in 2003, Gossett told his sons and a few friends that he was the elusive Cooper. Other than the statements Gossett made, however, the FBI could find no evidence linking him to the crime.

UNSOLVED OR CASE CLOSED?

ANOTHER POTENTIAL SUSPECT

In 2016, HISTORY® aired the two-part special, *D. B. Cooper: Case Closed?*, which followed the efforts of a team of investigators to solve history's most famous skyjacking.

Led by investigative journalists Tom Colbert and Jim Forbes, the team built a case (based on circumstantial evidence) that Robert Rackstraw, whom the FBI initially identified as a suspect back in 1979, was in fact Dan Cooper.

A Vietnam vet who served as an army helicopter pilot and had paratrooper experience, Rackstraw was never charged for the skyjacking, but spent a year in Folsom State Prison after being convicted of check fraud.

Rackstraw declined to give his own version of events on the show, but when reached by a *People* magazine reporter after it aired, he strongly denied the investigators' claims.

Seattle Special Agent Larry Carr, who took over the D.B. Cooper case in 2007. FBI photo

I N 1976, WITH THE CASE STILL UNSOLVED, the US government charged Cooper with piracy in absentia. Most people took the discovery of some of the money in the Columbia River in 1980 as evidence of Cooper's demise; some believe he survived, but ditched the money due to concerns about being traced through the serial numbers; still others think he just dropped some of the cash on the way down, then escaped with the rest. In any case, the remaining money has never been found.

In July 2016, the FBI announced that after following all credible leads for forty-five years, it would no longer be actively pursuing the NORJAK investigation, but would be redirecting resources spent on the case to "focus on other investigative priorities." Geoffrey Gray, author of the 2011 book *Skyjack: The Hunt for D. B. Cooper*, subsequently released hundreds of FBI documents on the case on *True Ink*, the online magazine he founded. "We're trying to solve one of the greatest unsolved mysteries of our time," Gray wrote, "and we need your help."

LASTING IMPACT

BEFORE THE 1970S, PLANE HIJACKINGS WERE RELA-
tively rare. By the middle of the decade, however, at least
150 planes had been "skyjacked," with Cooper's crime only
the most famous example of a new trend that would change aviation history. More stringent security regulations were put into
place in the United States and around the world. After the late
'70s, Cooper's attaché case would most likely never have made it
onto the plane, as international aviation authorities had begun
making passengers pass through metal detectors and submit their
hand luggage to be X-rayed before boarding.

In addition to the practical impact his crime (and others like
it) had on air travel, Cooper has lived on in the popular imagination as one of America's most famous outlaws, joining the ranks
of Billy the Kid and Bonnie and Clyde, among others. He didn't
harm any of the passengers or crew on the plane, after all, and
showed the breathtaking audacity to jump out of an airplane (into
a thunderstorm, no less). In Ariel, a town in Washington State
near where Cooper is believed to have landed, residents hold an
annual festival in his honor, offering the ultimate testament to
his enduring folk-hero appeal: D. B. Cooper look-alike contests. ■

WHO SAYS
YOU CAN'T TAKE IT
WITH YOU?

THE PURSUIT OF

D.B. COOPER

POLYGRAM PICTURES Presents in association with PETER GUBER and JON PETERS A MICHAEL TAYLOR - DANIEL WIGUTOW Production
ROBERT DUVALL • TREAT WILLIAMS • KATHRYN HARROLD "THE PURSUIT OF D. B. COOPER" Also Starring ED FLANDERS
Music Score by JAMES HORNER • "SHINE" Written and Sung by WAYLON JENNINGS Director of Photography HARRY STRADLING, A.S.C.
Executive Producers WILLIAM TENNANT and DONALD KRANZE Based on the book "FREE FALL" by J.D. REED
Screenplay by JEFFREY ALAN FISKIN Produced by DANIEL WIGUTOW and MICHAEL TAYLOR Directed by ROGER SPOTTISWOODE
Soundtrack Album on Polydor Marketed by PolyGram Records   READ THE DELL BOOK

PG PARENTAL GUIDANCE SUGGESTED
SOME MATERIAL MAY NOT BE SUITABLE FOR CHILDREN

PolyGram Pictures   A UNIVERSAL RELEASE

D. B. COOPER IN POPULAR CULTURE: A PARTIAL LIST

Movies: *The Pursuit of D. B. Cooper* (1981); *Without a Paddle* (2004)

Novels: *Rainbow's End* (1975) by James M. Cain; *D. B.: A Novel* (2004) by Elwood Reid

Songs: "The Ballad of D. B. Cooper" (2006) by Chuck Brodsky

Comics: Appearances in *The Far Side* and *Dilbert*

TV documentaries: *Unsolved Mysteries* (1988); HISTORY®'s *D. B. Cooper: Case Closed?* (2016)

Movie poster for *The Pursuit of D.B. Cooper* (1981). Photofest

THE CASE OF OSCAR "ZETA" ACOSTA 1974

FANS OF HUNTER S. THOMPSON'S *FEAR AND LOATHING in Las Vegas* will remember Dr. Gonzo, the outrageous attorney who accompanies his client Raoul Duke (Thompson's alter ego) on a surreal, drug-fueled rampage through Sin City. Though Thompson refers to Gonzo in the book as a "300-pound Samoan," and gives few identifying details, the real-life Dr. Gonzo was actually Oscar "Zeta" Acosta, a brash attorney involved in high-profile civil rights cases in Los Angeles in the late 1960s. He was also a leading Chicano activist, a celebrated novelist, and a fascinating figure in his own right.

By 1974, three years after the trip to Vegas that inspired Thompson's book, Acosta had given up the law, launched his own writing career, and entered a full-throttle pursuit of his outsize appetite for food, drugs, and reckless behavior. That May, after a cryptic telephone conversation with his son, he vanished off the coast of Mazatlán, Mexico. The mystery surrounding Acosta's fate—and the debate over his contributions to Thompson's most famous work—endures today.

Oscar Acosta. Wickipedia Commons

FAREWELL TO "DR. GONZO"

"One of God's own prototypes. A high-powered mutant of some kind never even considered for mass production. Too weird to live, and too rare to die."

—Hunter S. Thompson on Oscar Acosta, from "The Banshee Screams for Buffalo Meat" (*Rolling Stone*, December 1977)

WHAT DO WE KNOW?

I N THE 1960S, ACOSTA MOVED TO LOS ANGELES. IT WAS a particularly explosive period in the Chicano protest movement, and he worked as a defense attorney in several high-profile cases, including the indictment of thirteen activists for planning a walkout protesting inequality in the schools, and a case involving the Roman Catholic Church's involvement in Chicano politics. He would also defend several "Brown Berets" charged with felonies after the disruption of a speech by then-governor Ronald Reagan at the Biltmore Hotel in 1969.

Tensions heightened in 1970, after the well-known *LA Times* columnist (and vocal police critic) Ruben Salazar was killed by a Los Angeles County sheriff's deputy following a Vietnam War protest rally. That same year, Acosta ran for sheriff of LA County as a candidate of the Raza Unida Party; even with a tiny budget, he came in second, winning more than 100,000 votes.

The trip that would earn Acosta literary immortality occurred during this tumultuous period. Having met Thompson (who was living in Colorado at the time) through friends in the mid-1960s, Acosta approached him to write a story about Salazar's murder and the subsequent cover-up. While researching this piece, the pair went on their famous road trip as Raoul Duke and Dr. Gonzo. The two-part narrative of the trip appeared in Rolling Stone, and was later published as Fear and Loathing in Las Vegas.

FAST FACTS

Oscar "Zeta" Acosta was born in El Paso, Texas, on April 8, 1935.

He was raised in California's San Joaquin Valley, near Modesto.

He enlisted in the US Air Force at age seventeen and did a tour in Latin America, where he converted to Protestantism, and became a Baptist missionary in a leper colony in Panama (he would later renounce Christianity).

Honorably discharged after four years of service, Acosta entered Modesto Junior College and later attended San Francisco State University, where he started writing.

Acosta got his law degree at night, from San Francisco Law School, and passed the state bar in 1966.

He worked at the East Oakland Aid Society, an antipoverty organization. He married twice and had a son, Marco, born in 1959

CIRCUMSTANCES OF DISAPPEARANCE

IN JUST TWO YEARS, ACOSTA PUBLISHED TWO AUTOBI-
ographical novels—*Autobiography of a Brown Buffalo* (1972)
and *The Revolt of the Cockroach People* (1973)—that became
important texts in the Chicano civil rights movement. The latter book, which included an incident based on Salazar's killing, concluded on a largely hopeless note, with many Chicanos
choosing to assimilate into white culture rather than achieving
unity within their community.

In May 1974, while traveling in Mazatlán, Mexico, Acosta
vanished. In his last known telephone call, Acosta told his son
that he was "about to board a boat full of white snow." Marco
Acosta later told the *New York Daily News* that he believed the
reference—which he assumed was to drugs—was the key to his
father's disappearance.

UNSOLVED OR CASE CLOSED

No one has discovered what truly
happened to Oscar Acosta. Although
his friends, family, and most outside
observers at the time believed he
died in Mexico, rumors initially
circulated that he was still alive. As
no solid evidence ever surfaced, all
theories about his disappearance
and death remain pure speculation.

Benicio del Toro as Oscar Acosta (right) drives
Hunter S. Thompson (Johnny Depp) in this
scene from the film adaptation of *Fear and
Loathing in Las Vegas* (1998). Photofest

TOP THEORIES

1 Acosta was a victim of drug-related murder.

Acosta's son, Marco, believed that his father was most likely killed during an argument over drugs, and his body dumped somewhere where it could never be found. Mexico's Sinaloa province, where Mazatlán is located, is notorious for its drugs and violence.

2 According to Hunter S. Thompson, Acosta's disappearance could have been drug-related, or a politically motivated assassination.

In a long obituary for Acosta, called "The Banshee Screams for Buffalo Meat," published in *Rolling Stone* in 1977, Thompson speculated that his friend's disappearance could definitely have been drug-related. He claimed Acosta was both addicted to amphetamines and fond of LSD. Alternatively, Thompson wrote, his death could have been some kind of politically motivated assassination, perhaps aimed at silencing his friend's voice on behalf of the Chicano movement.

3 Acosta may have suffered a drug overdose or a breakdown.

Some have speculated that Acosta may have overdosed on drugs while in Mexico, or that he may have suffered some kind of nervous breakdown. ∎

LASTING IMPACT

In *Fear and Loathing in Las Vegas*, Hunter S. Thompson took the established style of "New Journalism"—where a writer goes along for the ride with his subjects—and turbocharged it. While Thompson has admitted being inspired by his larger-than-life friend to take his journalism style to that next level, some have gone further, suggesting that Acosta (the real "Dr. Gonzo," after all) did as much to invent so-called "Gonzo Journalism" as Thompson did.

Such claims suggest that Thompson was inspired by, or outright lifted passages from, Acosta's letters, and/or relied heavily on taped conversations with him. Acosta's sister, Annie, told *GonzoToday* that she has evidence proving her brother was actually the coauthor of Thompson's famous book.

Acosta himself, in a rather inscrutable letter to *Playboy*'s Forum section in October 1973, wrote: "Your [article] on Mr. Hunter S. Thompson as the creator of Gonzo Journalism, which you say he both created and named … Well, sir, I beg to take issue with you. And with anyone else who says that."

For the 1998 movie version of *Fear and Loathing in Las Vegas*, Benicio Del Toro gained some fourty-five pounds to play Gonzo/Acosta opposite Johnny Depp as Duke/Thompson. "I recognized in Oscar [someone] who would push things one more notch toward the limit," Thompson told the *LA Times* around the time the movie came out. "You never knew with Oscar what was going to happen next."

BIBLIOGRAPHY

AMELIA EARHART

Adler, Jerry. "Will the Search for Amelia Ever End?" *Smithsonian*. January 2015. http://www.smithsonianmag.com/history/will-search-for-amelia-earhart-ever-end-180953646/

Alapo, Lola. "Researcher to review evidence of Amelia Earhart theory." Phys.org. January 11, 2017. https://phys.org/news/2017-01-evidence-amelia-earhart-theory.html

"Amelia Earhart Biographical Sketch." Purdue Libraries Amelia Earhart Collection. Purdue University. http://collections.lib.purdue.edu/aearhart/biography.php

"An Answering Wave: Why the Navy Didn't Find Amelia." *Naval Institute Proceedings*. February 1993. https://tighar.org/Projects/Earhart/Archives/Documents/Answering_Wave.html

Campbell, Mike. *Amelia Earhart: The Truth at Last*. Mechanicsburg, PA: Sunbury Press, 2013.

Fleming, Candace. *Amelia Lost: The Life and Disappearance of Amelia Earhart*. New York: Schwartz & Wade Books, 2011.

Hanes, Elizabeth. "What Happened to Amelia?" History.com. July 2, 2012. http://www.history.com/news/what-happened-to-amelia-9-tantalizing-theories-about-the-earhart-disappearance

Rothman, Lily. "Why the Official Search for Amelia Earhart Was Abandoned." *Time*. June 2, 2015 (updated February 14, 2017). http://time.com/3904826/amelia-earhart-search-history/

Wootson, Cleve R. Jr. "Amelia Earhart didn't die in a plane crash, investigator says." *Chicago Tribune*. September 15, 2016. http://www.chicagotribune.com/news/nationworld/ct-amelia-earhart-plane-crash-20160915-story.html

Young, Stephanie. "Itasca and the Search for Amelia Earhart." *Coast Guard Compass*. July 2, 2012. http://coastguard.dodlive.mil/2012/07/itasca-the-search-for-amelia-earhart/

THE *MARY CELESTE*

Blumberg, Jess. "Abandoned Ship: The *Mary Celeste*." *Smithsonian*. November 2007. http://www.smithsonianmag.com/history/abandoned-ship-the-mary-celeste-174488104/?no-ist

Chase, Sean. "The mystery of Nova Scotia's infamous *Mary Celeste*." *Daily Observer* (three-article series). July 15, 22, and 29, 2015. http://www.thedailyobserver.ca/2015/07/15/the-mystery-of-nova-scotias-in-famous-mary-celeste http://www.thedailyobserver.ca/2015/07/22/she-was-steering-very-wild-and-evidently-in-distresshttp://www.thedailyobserver.ca/2015/07/29/this-case-of-the-mary-celeste-is-startling

Hicks, Brian. *Ghost Ship: The Mysterious Story of the* Mary Celeste *and Her Missing Crew* (New York: Ballantine Books, 2004)

Nash, Jay Robert. *Among the Missing: An Anecdotal History of Missing Persons from 1800 to the Present* (New York: Simon & Schuster, 1978)

Thompson, Jonathan. "Dating of wreck's timbers puts wind in sails of the 'Mary Celeste' mystery." *Independent*. January 23, 2005. http://www.independent.co.uk/news/uk/this-britain/dating-of-wrecks-timbers-puts-wind-in-sails-of-the-mary-celeste-mystery-487927.html

JIMMY HOFFA

Abadinsky, Howard. *Organized Crime* (Tenth Edition). Belmont, CA: Wadsworth, Cengage Learning, 2013.

Anderson, Curt. "Longtime friend doubts Hoffa will ever be found." *Ocala Star Banner* (Associated Press). May 30, 2006. http://www.ocala.com/news/20060530/longtime-friend-doubts-hoffa-will-ever-be-found

Epstein, Edward Jay. *The Annals of Unsolved Crime*. Brooklyn: Melville House, 2012.

"Events in the disappearance of Jimmy Hoffa." *San Diego Union Tribune* (Associated Press). June 19, 2013. http://www.sandiegouniontribune.com/sdut-events-in-the-disappearance-of-jimmy-hoffa-2013jun19-story.html

Filkins, Dexter. "Anthony J. Giacalone, 82, Man Tied to Hoffa Mystery." *New York Times*. February 26, 2001. http://www.nytimes.com/2001/02/26/us/anthony-j-giacalone-82-man-tied-to-hoffa-mystery.html

Lengel, Allan. "Mob Expert: Feds and Historians Got It Wrong About the Jimmy Hoffa Murder." *Deadline Detroit*. July 15, 2016. http://www.deadlinedetroit.com/articles/15372/mob_expert_feds_and_historians_got_it_wrong_about_the_jimmy_hoffa_murder#.WGp47pJSJyU

Maranzani, Barbara. "9 Places Jimmy Hoffa Probably Isn't Buried." History.com. June 20, 2013. http://www.history.com/news/history-lists/9-places-jimmy-hoffa-probably-isnt-buried

Marshall, Jessica Bloustein. "Why Are We Still Looking For Jimmy Hoffa?" *Mental Floss*. http://mentalfloss.com/article/51291/why-are-we-still-looking-jimmy-hoffa

Moldea, Dan E. "The Disappearance of Jimmy Hoffa: Forty Years Later." *Gang Land News*. July 30, 2015. http://www.moldea.com/Hoffa-40.html

Philbin, Tom. *The Killer Book of Cold Cases*. Naperville, IL: Sourcebooks, Inc., 2012.

Sloan, Arthur. *Hoffa*. Cambridge, MA: MIT Press, 1991.

"Who was Jimmy Hoffa?" *USA Today*. June 18, 2013. http://www.usatoday.com/story/news/nation/2013/06/18/who-was-jimmy-hoffa/2434633/

Wisely, John. "40 Years Later, Jimmy Hoffa Mystery Endures." *Detroit Free Press*. July 30, 2015. http://www.freep.com/story/news/local/michigan/oakland/2015/07/29/hoffa-disappearance-anniversary-teamsters/30862419/

THE ROANOKE COLONY

Emery, Theo. "The Roanoke Island Colony: Lost and Found?" *New York Times*. August 10, 2015. https://www.nytimes com/2015/08/11/science/the-roanoke-colonists-lost-and-found.html?_r=0

Horn, James. *A Kingdom Strange: The Brief and Tragic History of the Lost Colony of Roanoke*. Philadelphia: Basic Books, 2010.

Klingelhofer, Eric. "What happened to the lost colony of Roanoke Island?" *BBC History Magazine*. August 3, 2016. http://www.historyextra.com/article/feature/what-happened-lost-colony-roanoke-island

Lawler, Andrew. "We Finally Have Clues to How the Lost Colony Vanished." *National Geographic*. August 7, 2015. http://news.nationalgeographic.com/2015/08/150807-lost-colony-roanoke-hatteras-ouierbanks-archaeology/

Miller, Lee. *Roanoke: Solving the Mystery of the Lost Colony*. New York: Arcade Publishing, 2011.

Walbert, David. "The Search for the Lost Colony." LEARN NC: North Carolina: A Digital History. UNC School of Education. 2008. http://www.learnnc.org/lp/editions/nchist-twoworlds/1835

Wolfe, Brendan. "The Roanoke Colonies." Encyclopedia Virginia. Virginia Foundation for the Humanities. June 13, 2014. http://www.encyclopediavirginia.org/Roanoke_Colonies_The

THEODOSIA BURR ALSTON

Arnold, Chloe. "8 Facts About Theodosia Burr Alston." *Mental Floss*. http://mentalfloss.com/article/81741/8-facts-about-theodosia-burr-alston

Côté, Richard N. *Theodosia Burr: Portrait of a Prodigy*. Mount Pleasant, SC: Corinthian Books, 2003.

Heit, Judi. "Wreckers and the 'Legend of Nag's Head.'" *North Carolina Shipwrecks*. June 4, 2012. http://northcarolinashipwrecks.blogspot.com/2012/04/wreckers-legend-of-nags-head.html

Michie, James L. "Theodosia! Some Facts Relating to the Last Days of Theodora Burr Alston and the Patriot." *Carologue*, Summer 1998, pp. 16–20.

Pidgin, Charles Felton. *Theodosia: The First Gentlewoman of Her Time*. Boston: C. M. Clark, 1907.

DOROTHY ARNOLD

Abbott, Karen. "'Mrs. Sherlock Holmes' Takes on the NYPD." Smithsonian.com. August 23, 2011. http://www.smithsonianmag.com/history/mrs-sherlock-holmes-takes-on-the-nypd-60624549/

Blakinger, Keri. "The unsolved mystery of the NYC heiress who vanished from Fifth Avenue in 1910, never to be seen again." *New York Daily News*. August 4, 2016. http://www.nydailynews.com/news/national/unsolved-mystery-sexy-nyc-heiress-vanished-1910-article-1.2738134

Churchill, Allen. "The Girl Who Never Came Back." *American Heritage*. Volume 11, issue 5, August 1960. http://www.americanheritage.com/content/girl-who-never-came-back

"The Disappearance of Dorothy Arnold, One of New York's Strangest Mysteries." *The Bowery Boys: New York City History* (article and podcast). May 27, 2016. http://www.boweryboyshistory.com/category/mysterious-stories

Nash, Jay Robert. *Among the Missing: An Anecdotal History of Missing Persons from 1800 to*

the Present. New York: Simon & Schuster, 1978.

Whalen, Bernard, and Jon Whalen. *The NYPD's First Fifty Years: Politicians, Police Commissioners, and Patrolmen*. Lincoln, NE: Potomac Books, 2014.

JIM THOMPSON

Alioto, Daisy. "The Architect Who Changed the Thai Silk Industry and Then Disappeared." *Time*. May 9, 2016. http://time.com/4319751/jim-thompson-history/

Cohen, Celia. "A Murder Mystery for GOP Chairman Terry Strine." *Delaware Grapevine*. May 24, 2004. http://www.delawaregrapevine.com/5-04%20strine%20house.asp

Gray, Denis D. "CIA past of Bangkok's American 'Silk King' emerges." Associated Press. January 18, 2012. https://www.yahoo.com/news/cia-past-bangkoks-american-silk-king-emerges-111521473.html

Kent, Jonathan. "Mystery of missing Thai Silk King." BBC News. March 25, 2007. http://news.bbc.co.uk/2/hi/asia-pacific/6484761.stm

Kurlantzick, Joshua. *The Ideal Man: The Tragedy of Jim Thompson and the American Way of War*. Hoboken, NJ: John Wiley & Sons, Inc., 2011.

Mhaoileoin, Niamh Ni. "The Case of the Missing Thai Silk King." OZY. March 21, 2014. http://www.ozy.com/flashback/

the-case-of-the-missing-thai-silk-king/6641

Wallace, Lary. "Silk Thread: The Strange Mystery of Jim Thompson." *The Paris Review*. April 15, 2013. https://www.theparisreview.org/blog/2013/04/15/silk-thread-the-strange-mystery-of-jim-thompson/

Warren, William. *Jim Thompson: The Unsolved Mystery*. Singapore: Archipelago Press, 1998.

SEAN FLYNN

Brady, Brendan. "Claims of Sean Flynn Remains in Cambodia Spark Feud in U.S." *Time*. May 2, 2010. http://content.time.com/time/world/article/0,8599,1983766,00.html

Buncombe, Andrew. "How Errol Flynn's son was lost in Cambodia." *The Independent*. March 30, 2010. http://www.independent.co.uk/news/world/asia/how-errol-flynns-son-was-lost-in-cambodia-ndash-all-but-a-pile-of-bones-1931662.html

Crossley, Lucy. "Did this camera once belong to Errol Flynn's missing war photographer son? Battered Nikon bought on eBay has same initials as Sean Flynn who disappeared in Cambodia." DailyMail.com. November 24, 2014. http://www.dailymail.co.uk/news/article-2847395/Did-camera-belong-Errol-Flynn-s-war-photographer-son-Battered-Nikon-bought-eBay-initials-Sean-Flynn-disappeared-Cambodia.html

Gillet, Kit. "The Search for Sean

Flynn." *Wall Street Journal.* February 21, 2014. https://blogs.wsj.com/scene/2014/02/21/the-search-for-sean-flynn/

Price, Lydia. "Inside the Mysterious Disappearance of Errol Flynn's Son." *People.* May 11, 2015. http://www.people.com/article/inside-erroll-flynn-son-mysterious-disappearance

"Searchers: Remains of Errol Flynn's son found." Associated Press. March 29, 2010. http://www.nbcnews.com/id/36078623/ns/world_news-asia_pacific/t/searchers-remains-errol-flynns-son-found/

Young, Perry Deane. "Commentary: Remembering two of the missing from a long-ago war." McClatchy Newspapers (DC Bureau). April 6, 2010. http://www.mcclatchydc.com/news/nation-world/national/article24579034.html

SIR JOHN FRANKLIN

"John Franklin's final North-West Passage expedition 1845" and "Franklin expedition relics." Royal Museums Greenwich. http://www.rmg.co.uk/discover/explore/exploration-endeavour/sir-john-franklin http://www.rmg.co.uk/discover/museum-collections/relics-sir-john-franklins-polar-expedition

Beattie, Owen, and John Geiger. *Frozen in Time: The Fate of the Franklin Expedition.* Vancouver: Greystone Books, 2014. Cookman, Scott. *Iceblink: The Tragic Fate of Sir John Franklin's Lost Polar Expedition.* New York: John Wiley & Sons, 2000.

"Franklin expedition ship found in Arctic ID'd as HMS Erebus." CBC News. October 1, 2014. http://www.cbc.ca/news/politics/franklin-expedition-ship-found-in-arctic-id-d-as-hms-erebus-1.2784268

"Franklin Search." Historica Canada (The Canadian Encyclopedia). http://www.thecanadianencyclopedia.ca/en/article/franklin-search/

McKie, Robin. "Why our explanation of the 1845 polar tragedy should be put on ice." *The Guardian.* January 25, 2014. https://www.theguardian.com/science/2014/jan/26/lead-poisoning-polar-sir-john-franklin

"Researchers acquit tins in mysterious failed Franklin expedition." Phys.org. April 9, 2013. https://phys.org/news/2013-04-acquit-tins-mysterious-franklin.html

"Study debunks lead poisoning theory in Franklin mystery." CBC News. April 8, 2013. http://www.cbc.ca/news/canada/north/study-debunks-lead-poisoning-theory-in-franklin-mystery-1.1396399

Watson, Paul. *Ice Ghosts: The Epic Hunt for the Lost Franklin Expedition.* New York: W.W. Norton & Company, 2017.

Watson, Paul. "Ship found in Arctic 168 years after doomed Northwest Passage attempt." *The Guardian.* September 12, 2016. https://www.theguardian.com/world/2016/sep/12/hms-terror-wreck-found-arctic-nearly-170-years-northwest-passage-attempt

Young, Lauren. "Lady Jane Franklin: The Woman Who Fueled 19th-Century Polar Exploration." *Atlas Obscura.* February 23, 2017. http://www.atlasobscura.com/articles/cool-lady-jane-franklin-polar-exploration

PERCY FAWCETT

Andrews, Evan. "The Enduring Mystery Behind Percy Fawcett's Disappearance." History.com. May 29, 2015. http://www.history.com/news/explorer-percy-fawcett-disappears-in-the-amazon

Grann, David. *The Lost City of Z: A Tale of Deadly Obsession in the Amazon.* New York: Doubleday, 2005.

Fawcett, Percy. *Exploration Fawcett: Journey to the Lost City of Z.* New York: The Overlook Press, 2010.

Hemming, John. "The Lost City of Z is a very long way from a true story—and I should know." *The Spectator.* April 1, 2017. https://www.spectator.co.uk/2017/04/the-lost-city-of-z-is-a-very-long-way-from-a-true-story-and-i-should-know/#

Hill, Brian. "The Lost City of Z and the Mysterious Disappearance of Percy Fawcett." *Ancient*

Origins. June 20, 2015. http://www.ancient-origins.net/unexplained-phenomena/lost-city-z-and-mysterious-disappearance-percy-fawcett-003265

FLIGHT 19

"Bermuda Triangle Fact Sheet." Department of the Navy—Naval Historical Center. http://www.dod.mil/pubs/foi/Reading_Room/UFO/195.pdf

Golden, Tim. "Mystery of Bermuda Triangle Remains One." *New York Times*. June 5, 1991. http://www.nytimes.com/1991/06/05/us/mystery-of-bermuda-triangle-remains-one.html

Kaye, Ken. "Flight 19: Has mystery of Lost Patrol been solved?" *Sun Sentinel*. April 7, 2014. http://articles.sun-sentinel.com/2014-04-07/news/fl-flight-19-sleuths-20140406_1_flight-19-lost-patrol-jon-myhre

Mayell, Hillary. "Bermuda Triangle: Behind the Intrigue." *National Geographic*. Updated December 15, 2003. http://news.nationalgeographic.com/news/2002/12/1205_021205_bermudatriangle.html

McDonell, Michael. "Lost Patrol." *Naval Aviation News*. June 1973, pp. 8–16. https://www.history.navy.mil/research/library/online-reading-room/title-list-alphabetically/l/lost-patrol.html

"The Mystery of Flight 19." Naval Air Station Fort Lauderdale Museum website. http://www.nasflmuseum.com/flight-19.html

Rosenberg, Howard L. "Exorcising the Devil's Triangle." *Sealift*. Number 6, June 1974, pp. 11–15. https://www.history.navy.mil/research/library/online-reading-room/title-list-alphabetically/e/exorcizing-the-devils-triangle.html

Weisberger, Mindy. "Is the Bermuda Triangle Really Dangerous?" *LiveScience*. March 21, 2016. http://www.livescience.com/32240-is-the-bermuda-triangle-really-dangerous.html

USS *CYCLOPS*

Allen, Bob. "Mysterious Disappearance of USS *Cyclops*: Naval Vessel That Vanished in 1918." *Owings Mills Times*. November 11, 2010. https://www.sott.net/article/217763-Mysterious-Disappearance-of-USS-Cyclops-Naval-Vessel-That-Vanished-in-1918

"Bermuda Triangle Fact Sheet." Department of the Navy—Naval Historical Center. http://www.dod.mil/pubs/foi/Reading_Room/UFO/195.pdf

Brennan, Lawrence B. "The Unanswered Loss of USS *Cyclops*—March 1918." Naval Historical Foundation website. June 13, 2013. http://www.navyhistory.org/2013/06/unanswered-loss-uss-cyclops-march-1918/

Latson, Jennifer. "Famous Bermuda Triangle Disappearance May Have Been Botched Mutiny." *Time*. March 4, 2015. http://time.com/3720512/bermuda-triangle-history/

Rasmussen, Frederick N. "Disappearance of USS *Cyclops* remains one of the sea's most enduring mysteries." *Baltimore Sun*. October 1, 2010. http://articles.baltimoresun.com/2010-10-01/news/bs-md-backstory-shipwreck-20101001_1_barbados-guests-voyage

Reck, Alfred P. "Strangest American Sea Mystery is Solved At Last." *Popular Science*. June 1929, pp. 15–17 and 137. https://books.google.com/books?id=XSgDAAAAMBAJ&pg=PAPA157#v=snippet&q=cyclops&f=false

Rosenberg, Howard L. "Exorcising the Devil's Triangle." *Sealift*. Number 6, June 1974, pp. 11–15. https://www.history.navy.mil/research/library/online-reading-room/title-list-alphabetically/e/exorcizing-the-devils-triangle.html

AMBROSE BIERCE

"Ambrose Bierce." The Poetry Foundation website. https://www.poetryfoundation.org/poems-and-poets/poets/detail/ambrose-bierce

Bierce, Ambrose. *The Devil's Dictionary, tales, & memoirs*. New York: Library of America, 2011.

Gander, Forrest. "Very Trustworthy Witnesses." *The Paris*

Review. October 17, 2014. http://www.theparisreview.org/ blog/2014/10/17/very-trust- worthy-witnesses/

Morris, Roy Jr. *Ambrose Bierce: Alone in Bad Company.* New York: Crown Publishers, Inc, 1995.

Nash, Jay Robert. *Among the Missing: An Anecdotal History of Missing Persons from 1800 to the Present.* New York: Simon & Schuster, 1978.

Neale, Walter. *Life of Ambrose Bierce.* New York: Walter Neale, Publisher, 1929.

Rafferty, Terrence. "Ambrose Bierce: The Man and His Demons." *New York Times Book Review.* October 28, 2011.

Swaim, Don. "Mystery of Ambrose Bierce." The Ambrose Bierce Site (DonSwaim.com). http://www.donswaim.com/ bierce-disappearance.html

Wilson, Edmund. "Ambrose Bierce on the Owl Creek Bridge." *The New Yorker,* December 8, 1951. http://www.nytimes. com/2011/10/30/books/review/ ambrose-bierce-the-man-and- his-demons.html

SOLOMON NORTHUP

Fiske, David, Clifford W. Brown, and Rachel Seligman. *Solomon Northup: The Complete Story of the Author of* Twelve Years a Slave. Santa Barbara, CA: Praeger, 2013.

Klein, Christopher. Solomon Northup After His '12 Years a Slave.' History.com. October 28, 2013. http://www.history.com/ news/solomon-northup-after- his-12-years-a-slave

Northup, Solomon. *Twelve Years a Slave.* New York: Penguin Books, 2013.

Robichaux, Mark. "What Really Became of Solomon Northup After His '12 Years a Slave.'" *Wall Street Journal.* October 23, 2013. http://blogs.wsj.com/speakeasy/ 2013/10/23/what-really-became- of-solomon-northup-after-his- 12-years-a-slave/

Stromberg, Joseph. "The *New York Times*' 1853 Coverage of Solomon Northup, the Hero of '12 Years a Slave.'" Smithsonian. com. March 3, 2014. http:// www.smithsonianmag.com/ history/new-york-times-1853- coverage-solomon-northup- hero-12-years-slave-180949944/

LOUIS LE PRINCE

Casey, Kieron. "The Mystery of Louis Le Prince, the Father of Cinematography." Science and Media Museum blog. August 29, 2013. http://blog.national- mediamuseum.org.uk/louis-le- prince-created-the-first-ever- moving-pictures/

Howells, Richard. "A movie murder mystery." *Times Higher Education.* July 23, 1999. https:// www.timeshighereducation. com/features/a-movie- murder-mystery/147314.article#

"Louis Le Prince, Father of the Cinema." *The Yorkshire Reporter.* http://www.yorkshirereporter. co.uk/zyxc/louis-le-prince- father-of-the-cinema/

Martea, Ion. "Roundhay Garden Scene (1888)." *Essential Films.* January 15, 2017. http://essential- films.squarespace.com/article/ roundhay-garden-scene-1888. htmlhttp://guerilla-group.com/ tff/

Myrent, Glenn. "100 Years Ago, the Father of Movies Disap- peared." *New York Times.* Sep- tember 16, 1990. http://www. nytimes.com/1990/09/16/ movies/100-years-ago-the- father-of-movies-disappeared. html

Rawlence, Christopher. *The Miss- ing Reel. The Untold Story of the Lost Inventor of Moving Pictures.* London: Collins, 1990.

Wilkinson, David. *The First Film.* Documentary feature. Produced/ directed by David Nicholas Wilkinson, screenplay by David Nicholas Wilkinson and Irfan Shah. Released 2015. Guerilla Films.

Youngs, Ian. "Louis Le Prince, who shot the world's first film in Leeds." BBC News. June 23, 2015. http://www.bbc.com/ news/entertainment- arts-33198686

JUDGE JOSEPH FORCE CRATER

Feuer, Alan. "Judge is Still Missing, But Novel Tracks Him Down." *New York Times.* August 4, 2010. http://www.nytimes. com/2010/08/05/nyregion/ 05crater.html

Garrett, Robert. "Good Night Judge Crater, Wherever You Are." *New York Magazine*. August 11, 1980, pp. 11–12.

"Judge Crater Disappearance Possibly Solved." Fox News. August 19, 2005. http://www.foxnews.com/story/2005/08/19/judge-crater-disappearance-possibly-solved.html

Nash, Jay Robert. *Among the Missing: An Anecdotal History of Missing Persons from 1800 to the Present*. New York: Simon & Schuster, 1978.

Philbin, Tom. *The Killer Book of Cold Cases*. Naperville, IL: Sourcebooks, Inc., 2012.

Rashbaum, William K. "Judge Crater Abruptly Appears, at Least in Public Consciousness." *New York Times*. August 20, 2005. http://www.nytimes.com/2005/08/20/nyregion/judge-crater-abruptly-appears-at-least-in-public-consciousness.html

Rogers, Stuart. "Justice Joseph Force Crater disappears in 1930." *NY Daily News*. August 5, 2015 (originally published September 4, 1930). http://www.nydailynews.com/new-york/justice-joseph-f-crater-disappears-1930-article-1.2307718

Sternberg, Billy. "The Roosevelt: An Even More Intimate History." *Observer*. September 16, 2014. http://observer.com/2014/09/a-mysterious-disappearance-and-suspicious-death-a-curious-story-surrounds-fdr/

Tofel, Richard J. *Vanishing Point: The Disappearance of Judge Crater, and the New York He Left Behind*. Chicago: Ivan R. Dee, 2004.

Wulfhorst, Ellen. "Judge Crater's Fate a Mystery for 50 Years." *Los Angeles Times*. http://articles.latimes.com/1995-08-13/news/mn-34675_1_judge-crater

FRANK MORRIS, JOHN ANGLIN, AND CLARENCE ANGLIN

Alcatraz: Search for the Truth. Written by Brad Bernstein, David Karabinas, and Chip Rives. Aired on HISTORY® in October 2015. Texas Crew Productions.

"A Byte out of History: Escape from Alcatraz." Federal Bureau of Investigation website. June 8, 2007. https://web.archive.org/web/20080709032857/http://www.fbi.gov/page2/june07/alcatraz060807.htm

Cohen, Ronnie. "U.S. marshals still hunt Alcatraz escape artists. 50 years later." Reuters. July 11, 2012. http://www.reuters.com/article/us-usa-alcatraz-idUSBRE85B01E20120612

Donnelly, Tim. "The proof that 3 men survived their escape from Alcatraz." *New York Post*. October 10, 2015. http://nypost.com/2015/10/10/relatives-have-proof-alcatraz-escapees-are-still-alive/

Gannon, Megan. "Prisoners of 'Ingenious' 1962 Alcatraz Escape Could Have Survived." *LiveScience*. December 15, 2014.

http://www.livescience.com/49134-alcatraz-escaped-prisoners-could-have-survived.html

"The Great Escape from Alcatraz." Alcatraz History website. http://www.alcatrazhistory.com/alcesc1.htm

Higbee, Arthur. "American Topics: Alcatraz Escapees May Still Be Alive." *New York Times*. November 13, 1993. http://www.nytimes.com/1993/11/13/news/13iht-topics_29.html

Leithead, Alistair. "Alcatraz escape still surprises, 50 years on." BBC News. June 12, 2012. http://www.bbc.com/news/world-us-canada-18404134

McCoy, Terrence. "The Alcatraz escapees could have survived—and this interactive model proves it." *Washington Post*. December 15, 2014. https://www.washingtonpost.com/news/morning-mix/wp/2014/12/15/the-alcatraz-escapees-could-have-survived-and-this-interactive-model-proves-it/?utm_term=.ae536fd64b0d

McFadden, Robert D. "Tale of Inmates Who Vanished From Alcatraz Maintains Intrigue 50 Years Later." *New York Times*. June 9, 2012. www.nytimes.com/2012/06/10/us/anniversary-of-a-mystery-at-alcatraz.html

Sullivan, Laura. "50 Years Later, Mystery of Alcatraz Still Endures." NPR. June 12, 2012. http://www.npr.org/2012/06/12/154766199/50-years-later-mystery-of-alcatraz-escape-endures

D. B. COOPER

Clark, Nicola. "Why Airline Hijackings Became Relatively Rare." *New York Times.* March 29, 2016. https://www.nytimes.com/2016/03/30/world/middleeast/airline-hijacking-history.html

D. B. Cooper: Case Closed. Directed by Ted Skillman. Aired on HISTORY® in July 2016. LMNO Cable Group.

"D. B. Cooper Hijacking." Federal Bureau of Investigation. Last updated July 12, 2016. https://www.fbi.gov/history/famous-cases/db-cooper-hijacking

Dodd, Johnny. "Man Identified in HISTORY® show as Notorious Skyjacker D. B. Cooper Denies Accusation." *People.* July 12, 2016. http://people.com/crime/db-cooper-robert-rackstraw-accused-in-history-channel-show-denies-accusation/

Gray, Geoffrey. *Skyjack: The Hunt for D. B. Cooper.* New York: Crown Publishers, 2011.

Hauser, Christine. "Where is D. B. Cooper? F.B.I. Ends 45-Year Hunt." *New York Times.* July 13, 2016. https://www.nytimes.com/2016/07/14/us/where-is-db-cooper-fbi-ends-45-year-hunt.html

Perry, Douglas. "45 years after his disappearance, D. B. Cooper mystery continues to spin out new conclusions." *The Oregonian/*

OregonLive. November 21, 2016. http://www.oregonlive.com/trending/2016/11/45_years_after_his_disappearan.html

Philbin, Tom. *The Killer Book of Cold Cases.* Naperville, IL: Sourcebooks, Inc., 2012.

Seven, Richard. "D. B. Cooper—Perfect Crime or Perfect Folly?" *Seattle Times.* November 17, 1996. http://community.seattletimes.nwsource.com/archive/?date=19961117&slug=2360262

Shapira, Ian. "Online magazine to open up FBI files on the 'D. B. Cooper' skyjacking case." *Washington Post.* November 24, 2016. https://www.washingtonpost.com/local/online-magazine-to-open-up-fbi-files-on-the-db-cooper-skyjacking-case/2016/11/23/f7f98d56-b1b3-11e6-8616-52b15787add0_story.html

OSCAR "ZETA" ACOSTA

Barrios, Gregg. "When Zeta met Hunter." *San Antonio Current.* July 30, 2008. https://www.sacurrent.com/sanantonio/when-zeta-met-hunter/Content?oid=2283835

"Biographical Sketch—Guide to the Oscar Zeta Acosta Papers." Online Archive of California. http://www.oac.cdlib.org/findaid/ark:/13030/tf187004xn/admin/#ref7

Blakinger, Keri. "On what would have been his 81st birthday, the real-life son of Dr. Gonzo from 'Fear and Loathing' remembers his dad." *New York Daily News.* March 8, 2016. http://www.

nydailynews.com/news/national/story-real-dr-gonzo-fear-loathing-article-1.2557283

Denevi, Timothy. "Hunter S. Thompson and Oscar Acosta in the Desert: A 45-Year Retrospective." *American Short Fiction.* May 9, 2016. http://americanshortfiction.org/2016/05/09/hunter-thompson-oscar-acosta-desert-45-year-retrospective/

Doss, Yvette C. "The Lost Legend of the Real Dr. Gonzo." *Los Angeles Times.* June 5, 1998. http://articles.latimes.com/1998/jun/05/entertainment/ca-56718

Pratt, David. "The Zeta Affair: Did Oscar Co-write Fear and Loathing?" *Gonzo Today.* August 21, 2015. http://gonzotoday.com/2015/08/21/the-zeta-affair-did-oscar-co-write-fear-loathing-3/

Thompson, Hunter S. "The Banshee Screams for Buffalo Meat." *Rolling Stone.* December 15, 1977. http://www.rollingstone.com/culture/news/the-banshee-screams-for-buffalo-meat-19771215

Wood, Jamie Martinez. "Oscar Zeta Acosta." *Latino Writers and Journalists.* New York: Facts on File, Inc., 2007.

ABOUT THE AUTHOR

SARAH PRUITT HAS BEEN A FREQUENT CONTRIBUTOR to History.com, the website for the HISTORY®, for more than ten years, including the "History in the Headlines," "Ask History," "History Lists," and "This Day in History" features. She has a BA in history and a certificate in American Studies from Princeton University, and a master's degree in Spanish language and literature from Middlebury College. She lives in New Hampshire. ■

ACKNOWLEDGEMENTS

THANKS TO KEITH WALLMAN FOR BRINGING THIS project to me, and shepherding it through much of the writing, editing, and production process. I'm also grateful to Rick Rinehart for guiding the book the rest of the way, and to everyone else at Globe Pequot/Lyons Press, including Stephanie Scott, Sally Rinehart, Melissa Hayes, Jessica Kastner, and Caroline McManus.

Many thanks as well to Kathleen Williams, Carrie Knoblock, Laura Schumm, Barbara Maranzani, Christine Tancinco, Christopher Klein, and the other colleagues I've worked with at A+E Networks and HISTORY® over the years.

Most of all, I owe thanks to Bert and Amelia, for being the most excellent sources of distraction I could imagine.

HISTORY® would like to thank Paul Cabana, Kim Gilmore, Margeaux McAvoy, and Monique Williams for their roles in seeing this book through to production. ■